Sherlock and
Transmedia Fandom

Sherlock and Transmedia Fandom

Essays on the BBC Series

Edited by LOUISA ELLEN STEIN *and*
KRISTINA BUSSE

McFarland & Company, Inc., Publishers
Jefferson, North Carolina, and London

ALSO OF INTEREST

Teen Television: Essays on Programming and Fandom.
Edited by Sharon Marie Ross and Louisa Ellen Stein (McFarland, 2008).

Fan Fiction and Fan Communities in the Age of the Internet: New Essays.
Edited by Karen Hellekson and Kristina Busse (McFarland, 2006).

LIBRARY OF CONGRESS CATALOGUING-IN-PUBLICATION DATA

Sherlock and transmedia fandom : essays on the BBC series /
edited by Louisa Ellen Stein and Kristina Busse.
    p.   cm.
Includes bibliographical references and index.

ISBN 978-0-7864-6818-8

softcover : acid free paper ∞

1. Sherlock (Television program : 2010–)   2. Detective and
mystery television programs — Great Britain — History and
criticism.   3. Television viewers — Attitudes.   I. Stein, Louisa
Ellen.   II. Busse, Kristina, 1967–
PN1992.77.S475S54 2012
791.45'72 — dc23   2012008361

BRITISH LIBRARY CATALOGUING DATA ARE AVAILABLE

On the cover: Benedict Cumberbatch as Sherlock Holmes

Manufactured in the United States of America

McFarland & Company, Inc., Publishers
  Box 611, Jefferson, North Carolina 28640
  www.mcfarlandpub.com

*Dedicated to all Sherlock Holmes
fans — past, present, and future.*

Table of Contents

Part Three: Adaptations and Intertextuality

Part Four: Interpreting *Sherlock*

Part Five: Postmodern Sherlock

Acknowledgments

This collection would not exist without the support of a host of people including family, friends, and colleagues. Thank you to our families, Ben and Penelope, Ryan, Gabriel, and Matthias, for their support and patience with our ever-growing preoccupation with all things transmedia Sherlock. We also want to thank Kathleen Fitzpatrick, Avi Santos, and all the folks at MediaCommons for their help and the use of their infrastructure for the peer-to-peer review. Thank you to our external peer reviewers, Jason Mittell and Suzanne Scott, for bringing your outside eye and considerable insight to the project. Thank you to Alexis Lothian, Melanie E.S. Kohnen, and Jennifer Hock for brainstorming, draft-reading, and encouragement. We're also grateful to all of the collection's contributing authors, who went far beyond the normal commitment of writing one's own essay, as they agreed to participate in the peer-to-peer online review process, and spent significant time commenting on each other's essays and thus contributing to the vision of the collection as a whole. This collection is what it is because of the dedication, passion, and insight each one of you brought to the project.

And finally, thank you to *Sherlock* and Sherlock Holmes fandom, in all its manifestations, to Sir Arthur Conan Doyle for gifting us with Sherlock Holmes and John Watson in the first place, and to Steven Moffat and Mark Gattis, Mark Freeman and Benedict Cumberbatch, for animating these beloved characters anew.

Abbreviations

The following texts are cited throughout the collection and will therefore be abbreviated. The code in brackets designates the abbreviations used. Online references are cited in text where possible. All other references can be found in the Works Cited.

[I, II]	Conan Doyle, Sir Arthur. 2005. *The New Annotated Sherlock Holmes*, Vol. 1 & 2, ed. Leslie Klinger. New York: Norton.
[III]	Conan Doyle, Sir Arthur. 2006. *The New Annotated Sherlock Holmes*, Vol. 3, ed. Leslie Klinger. New York: Norton.
[ASiP]	*A Study in Pink.* 2010. *Sherlock,* disc 1. BBC. DVD.
[ASiP Commentary]	Vertue, Sue, Mark Gatiss, and Stephen Moffat. 2010. *A Study in Pink* Commentary. *Sherlock,* disc 1. BBC. DVD.
[TBB]	*The Blind Banker.* 2010. *Sherlock,* disc 1. BBC. DVD.
[TGG]	*The Great Game.* 2010. *Sherlock,* disc 2. BBC. DVD.
[TGG Commentary]	Mark Gatiss, Benedict Cumberbatch, and Martin Freeman. 2010. *The Great Game* Commentary. *Sherlock,* disc 2. BBC. DVD.
[Unlocking]	*Unlocking Sherlock: The Making of.* 2010. *Sherlock,* disc 2. BBC. DVD.

Prologue: Why Sherlock? Narrator Investment in the BBC Series

Lyndsay Faye

All novels are sequels; influence is bliss. — Michael Chabon, *Maps and Legends*

I am often asked by concerned longstanding Sherlockian scholars (perhaps due to the fact that I turned thirty last year) whether I think there is any hope for the near-extinct species identifying themselves as Sherlock Holmes enthusiasts, and — if there is hope — what steps might be taken to brighten it. My response, following stark surprise, is that there are millions of young Sherlock Holmes aficionados living all over the world; they simply self-identify as *fans* and correspond largely via Internet media, invisible to the faraway naked eye of the local Sherlockian club member. I even claim that the world of Sherlockiana is richer than ever, due in part to vibrant new incarnations including the highly thoughtful BBC series *Sherlock*. However, as part of a generation of younger devotees who are both involved in longstanding Sherlockian clubs and versed in the vibrant fannish world of the web (I am an invested member of both the Adventuresses of Sherlock Holmes and the Baker Street Irregulars, and a great admirer of the Internet), I find myself frequently in the awkward position of being an apologist for one group to the other. The comforting thread running through these conversations, however, is a position from which I will never waver: fandom and traditional Sherlockiana have more in common than not, and, as John LeCarré said so eloquently in his introduction to Leslie Klinger's *New Annotated Sherlock Holmes*, "no one writes of Sherlock Holmes without love" (I:xv). Whether that spark of ownership over the characters is engendered by the original canon or by more modern adaptations like the carefully wrought

1

world of Moffat and Gatiss is, I think, rather a moot point. Our regard is undeniable, our claim already staked. What we want is more stories, and we will find them — one way or another, and by various methods, each suited to our nature and our age and our tastes and our creativity. The question has never been, to my mind, will people continue to weave tales about Sherlock Holmes? Of course we will. I am much more intrigued by the query *Why do we want them so badly?*

When I came to the end of the Sherlock Holmes mysteries, at about age eleven, I decided at once that there must be more. If Conan Doyle had ungenerously decided to provide me with only sixty adventures to inhabit, well then, I would take matters into my own hands, and my remedy was one doubtless very familiar to every participant in BBC *Sherlock*'s fan culture, or indeed any fan culture, far predating the arrival of the Internet: I would write more myself. I did pen more, but never finished a single one, and find them in retrospect to have been predictably terrible. Then I discovered that other similarly preoccupied souls had gone one better than me, and actually published new "pastiches" regarding the life of the Great Detective and the Good Doctor. I purchased dozens of them, whatever I could afford, and now own scores if not literally hundreds — some good, many bad, many indifferent, devoured indiscriminately. When the production of printed matter failed to meet my appetite for my subject, I later discovered that friends more savvy were willing to tell me where the fan fiction was, and that much of it is very, very good indeed, considerably better than printed matter, and that even less well-written examples of fan fiction are far more engaging than going without a new Sherlock Holmes story for a month. Enter the 2009 Warner Bros. film titled *Sherlock Holmes,* as well as BBC's far more canonically driven *Sherlock*: there is now so much not-for-profit Sherlock Holmes fiction in existence online that literally no one could read it all, much less parse it all, and yet people lament to me — despite the overwhelming success of both the WB and BBC versions worldwide — that Sherlockians are a dying breed.

The *Chicago Sun-Times* recently went so far as to report, "Young people, for reasons mysterious, are not racing to join Sherlockian groups, and the membership ages" (Steinberg n.d.). This evaluation is partial at best and, at worst, overtly dismissive of widespread fan participation. Admittedly, Sherlock Holmes fandom is venerable and historied, and admirers have been penning adventures for Sherlock Holmes and Dr. John Watson since before Conan Doyle had finished writing the originals. Technology has now advanced to the giddy point that anyone with a vested interest in the characters can contribute their own fanworks, which shifts the classic author-reader relationship to a much more varied, collaborative, inter-textual one, though the Internet merely speeds this process rather than claiming to have invented it; zines and other media, of course, long predate web culture. But while Sherlock fans and Sherlockians often fail to interact directly, surely it would be facile to conclude that there are no fan fiction enthusiasts amongst Sherlockians, or conversely no scholars amongst Sherlock fans.

As the writer of one published Sherlock Holmes novel, several commercially published short stories, and a comic series, as well as a devourer of both pastiche and of fan fiction, I realize that it is important briefly to note some of the delineations between fan fiction and pastiche as they are understood within Sherlockian communities. Most apparently, fanworks (including but not excluded to stories, art, icons, and videos) are made for the pleasure of the creator and his or her community and never for fiscal profit, while the writers of pastiche hope to see work published commercially. Second, online fandom is a living culture as much as it is a repository for creative effort, highly focused on participatory commentary and meritocratic feedback, and thus to conflate the democracy of fandom with pecuniary pastiche marketing would be injudicious and offensive. However, it would be equally ridiculous to suggest that Sherlockian pastiche writers and scion members garner neither joy nor community feeling from their subject — they congregate just as avidly as do fans, albeit in person, and all the while largely unaware that their interactions are being mirrored by similar communities which are allowed to exist electronically. The cross-cultural popular phenomena of writing new Sherlock Holmes stories, whether for fandom or for profit, surely bear a common ancestry. The key question at issue remains *why Sherlock Holmes?* And how does the Steven Moffat and Mark Gatiss adaptation *Sherlock* inform the larger world of the character?

The highly durable nature of the canonical Sherlock Holmes, and by extension the hero of Moffat and Gatiss's *Sherlock,* cannot be denied. Currently, the *Sherlock*-based works of fiction posted to fanfiction.net — many of them multi-chapter or works in progress, and set exclusively within the world of the television series — number 4,305 (August 12, 2011). One of several Live-Journal communities devoted to *Sherlock* and its followers and fanworks, Sherlockbbc, boasts 8,320 members (August 12, 2011; www.livejournal.com). Sherlock Holmes's popularity is shockingly inarguable, even 123 years after his first appearance. While the number of fanworks devoted to a book or series cannot be considered an absolute litmus test for the dedication of the fandom, particular sets of characters clearly inspire admirers to draw within and between the lines, as "the growing repository of ideas in any given interpretive community shape fan creativity" (Stein and Busse 2009, 197), and *Sherlock* qualifies resoundingly as a thriving creative organism.

In the June 23, 1927, *Times Literary Supplement,* regarding the then-recently released *Casebook of Sherlock Holmes,* it is the character's vividly delineated, highly specific attributes that are praised as accounting for his remarkable popularity:

> We all know what Holmes is at. It helps us to realize how intricate the puzzle is that Holmes should fill his oldest and foulest pipe before sitting down to it. So, too, with his drugs; they are prescribed by that cunning physician, Sir Arthur, for their effect on the reader's imagination, not for their effect on Holmes's intellect.

And yet astonishingly, eighty-three years later, Moffat and Gatiss have created one of the most highly praised Sherlock Holmes adaptations for modern times — lauded by fans and by critics alike — while incorporating almost none of these supposedly magical specifics.

Benedict Cumberbatch's Sherlock Holmes is not a smoker; he blames the high cost of cigarettes in London for his reliance on nicotine patches and laments, "Bad news for brainwork." As of yet, we have never seen him indulge in hard drugs, although hints in "A Study in Pink" suggest that there may have been a time when he was not the clean and sober individual he now appears. Gone are the non-canonical though iconic deerstalker, the equally non-canonical cape-backed greatcoat, the high starched collar and walking stick. Fans and scholars of the original tales often speak of London as the essential third character almost ever-present beside the Doctor and the Detective, and when they say "London," they intentionally connote hansom cabs, gaslit streets, impenetrable fogs, opium dens, and vague shapes huddled in shadowed doorways. But Victoriana in its usual cobblestone trappings plays no overt part in *Sherlock*, and as for London, while the Eye looms above the viewer in the opening theme, one cannot help but wonder whether this *particular* Sherlock and John might not do just as well for themselves in New York's homeless communities or in San Francisco's Chinatown as in London's. Writes G. K. Chesterton of the original stories, "Conan Doyle triumphed and triumphed deservedly, because he ... lavished a hundred little touches of real knowledge and genuine picturesqueness on the police novelette. Above all, he surrounded his detective with a genuine atmosphere of the poetry of London" (1953, 174–5). If Sherlock Holmes's longevity is due to those very "hundred little touches" and the "genuine atmosphere" of 1895 London, however, the widespread acclaim garnered by the BBC *Sherlock* grows mystifying indeed.

This is not to say that Moffat and Gatiss fail to produce an authentic modern Holmes, or a vibrant and compelling modern London. Nor is it to suggest that their many small attentions to detail go unnoticed by fans. Sherlock pinning a letter to his mantelpiece with a jackknife is a masterful touch, for instance, as is the effortless interweaving of Conan Doyle's "The Naval Treaty" and "The Bruce-Partington Plans" in the BBC's "The Great Game."

Rather, it is to argue that no *one* element of the character can now be argued indispensible. When Benedict Cumberbatch steeples his fingers before his lips in thought, or blithely assures Mrs. Hudson that the game is on, or sits quietly monastic and aloof while Martin Freeman as his John Watson indulges in a hasty meal, fans and Sherlockians alike inevitably will notice and appreciate these canonical flourishes. No single *particular* flourish is cardinal, however, to the character as a whole.

What aspects of a character remain essential to the winning formula if no one biographical detail is indispensable? If we take as given that Sherlockian purists and the fans of BBC's *Sherlock* are called to something similar at heart, and the details — however beloved — have been proven disposable, what then remains? First, Sherlock Holmes as a popular heroic figure displays a remarkable level of tantalizing opacity. When Michael Chabon confesses in *Maps and Legends* to penning a Holmes pastiche when he was a child, he expands that confession to suggest that our desire to know more about the characters we love is what motivates us as writers, be that writing commercial material or fan fiction; humans are compelled to fill in the blank spaces upon the map, and thus one may argue that a hero about whom very *little* is known proves to be the most compelling sort of protagonist to muse over once the plot has ended and the book is closed. This notion marches in direct opposition to the concept that Holmes is loved for his Stradivarius, his shag tobacco, his seven percent solution, his silent but ready laugh — individual details, as we have seen, mean but little in and of themselves no matter how striking. The concept of heroic opacity at once explains, however, why thousands upon thousands of works of derivative fiction are devoted to Holmes. We are told a finite amount of data by Watson, what we are told is fascinating, and thus we desire to know ever more.

When my pastiche *Dust and Shadow* was published, it was suggested by a few readers that I had indulged in self-insertion in the person of a particular original character. This critique fascinated me not because I was innocent of self-insertion; on the contrary, I was deeply, wholly guilty of it. Those readers had simply failed to realize that the entirety of my very conscious and deliberate self-insertion was lodged in my first-person narrator, *John H. Watson, M.D.* Ever since first becoming acquainted with the original material I have wondered, just as countless other fans and Sherlockians have done, what it would be like to walk in Watson's shoes — to have in the person of your closest friend an unparalleled genius and the ultimate source of adventure and intrigue, to live with an arrogant fellow who nevertheless owns a dry and charming sense of humor and attracts mayhem like a homing beacon, to be the steady one ever relied upon to bring the service revolver? Simply because I am female does not mean that the notion of being John Watson doesn't hold tremendous appeal; on the contrary, and — from the sheer number of fanworks already created — it doesn't seem to me that fans of BBC's *Sherlock* would claim ignorance of this sensation. When I pick up the metaphorical pen to write in first-person Watsonian narrative, it is for the simple reason that I'd very much like to know more about Sherlock Holmes, but will never, in fact, comprehend him entirely, while still attempting to annex further territory for myself. Therein lies the magic, I would posit, both for fans and for Sherlockians, at least for those inclined to create their own transformative works.

In the worlds of pastiche and of fan fiction, the gaps in knowledge of Sherlock Holmes's character lead directly to the desire to fill in the blanks on the map, to own a greater knowledge of the detective than the detective himself would willingly allow. The Sherlock Holmes of the canon presents himself as monastic, and yet his extreme reticence to discuss any aspect of his sexual inclinations has led to speculative romances for him of every nature imaginable. BBC's Sherlock replies when asked if he has a girlfriend, "Girlfriend? No, not really my area" (ASiP). When asked if alternately he has a boyfriend, his reply grows still cagier, assuring John, "I know it's fine," implying that he does not suppose either of them homophobic while still refusing to answer John's question without furtiveness (ASiP). Vagaries and evasions of this sort are irresistible to authors who desire, alongside John Watson, to know the inner workings of Sherlock Holmes's mind, whether they argue him heterosexual, homosexual, asexual, or elsewhere under the gray-A umbrella. Likewise, Cumberbatch's Sherlock dryly insists that his brother Mycroft is his "arch-enemy," dropping tenebrous hints about who "upset" the family matriarch in a longstanding feud. Enter the fans, drawing in the margins and reading between both spoken and unspoken lines, ever desiring more narrative. As Krasner puts it, "Often we glimpse a furious anxiety to know what is lying behind the placid exterior of the narrator; his frustration is created by his combination of mental distance and physical proximity to Holmes's thoughts, and is passed on to the reader" (1997, 425). The reader in the cases of pastiche and of fan fiction then *becomes* the writer, creating more readers to interact with new texts, perpetuating the cycle *ad infinitum*.

The ever-shifting world of electronic communication and Internet technology have admittedly altered the face of Sherlockian culture, allowing enthusiasts without the desire to travel for meetings nevertheless to engage in meaningful social dialogue and creative effort revolving around their hero. A strong desire to engage directly with Holmes and Watson, however, rather than simply finishing the original canon and walking away, is a shared characteristic between erudite fandom enthusiasts and the apt attendees of scholarly Sherlockian conferences, some of whom are very possibly — who can know, after all? — the same people. It is a testament to the balance of Conan

Doyle's world, his hero's mixture of specific oddities with unknowable personal history, that Moffat and Gatiss's *Sherlock* boasted 7.3 million viewers in the United Kingdom during the airing of "The Great Game" (Millar 2010). And such avid participation is bound inevitably to continue. As Michael Chabon muses:

> The power of maps to fire the imagination is well known. And, as Joseph Conrad's Marlow observed, there is no map so seductive as the one marked, like the flag-colored schoolroom map of Africa that doomed him to his forlorn quest, by doubts and conjectures, by the romantic blank of unexplored territory [2008, 30].

The map that Conan Doyle left us, the un-careful and at times reluctantly rendered guide to Sherlock Holmes's brain-attic, leaves the precise amount of negative space necessary to fire the imagination of his readers. It will never cease to inspire, as BBC's *Sherlock* and other modern adaptations so readily prove. We are as indebted to Conan Doyle's inconsistencies, to his deliberate coyness, to his at times infuriating ostracizing of his readers, as we are to the adjectives "tall," "pale," "thin," "hawk-like," that make up our mental conception of Sherlock Holmes (III:29–30). If all novels are sequels, may the reading world encounter more such prequels — stories that skirt the most exquisite edge of the definite and the inconceivable, and thus produce fandoms that are true "sites of play and carnival, poetry and magic" (Brooker 2007, 429).

Works Cited

Brooker, Will. 2007. Everywhere and nowhere: Vancouver, fan pilgrimage and the urban imaginary. *International Journal of Cultural Studies* 10:423–44.

The casebook of Sherlock Holmes. 1927. *Times Literary Supplement* June 23. 1325: 438.

Chabon, Michael. 2008. *Maps and Legends: Reading and writing along the borderlands.* San Francisco: McSweeney's.

Chesterton, G. K. 1953. *A handful of authors: Essays on books and writers,* ed. Dorothy Collins, 168–174. Lanham, MD: Sheed and Ward.

Krasner, James. 1997. Watson falls asleep: Narrative frustration and Sherlock Holmes. *English Literature in Transition, 1880–1920* 40: 424–436.

Millar, Paul. 2010. BBC One's "Sherlock" surges to 7.3m. *Digital Spy.* August 9. www.digitalspy.co.uk.

Stein, Louisa Ellen, and Kristina Busse. 2009. Limit play: Fan authorship between source text, intertext, and context. *Popular Communication* 7.4:192–207.

Steinberg, Neil. n.d. "Probing mystery of the Sherlockians." *The Chicago Sun-Times.* www.suntimes.com.

Introduction: The Literary, Televisual and Digital Adventures of the Beloved Detective

LOUISA ELLEN STEIN *and* KRISTINA BUSSE

Reinventing Sherlock for the Digital Age

In the fanvid "Whole New Way," vidder Mr. E. Sundance brings together footage from a wide range of representations of the famous sleuth Sherlock Holmes and his loyal supporter John Watson. The video intertwines the classic illustrations of Sidney Paget from *The Strand* with images from comic books, from the 2009 film adaptation, and of course from the new BBC series *Sherlock* (2010-). In addition, the vid includes images from fan artwork, fan video, and screen captures of online fan fiction. Through the use of this broad scope of source texts, this vid at its base exemplifies the wide reach, breadth, and multiplicity of Holmes and Watson (or Sherlock and John) as cultural figures meaningful to authors and fans, and to fans turned authors. Indeed, through the intersection of these various sources, old and new, combined with the music of The Scissor Sisters, the vid "Whole New Way" proposes that the recent incarnations of Sherlock offer avenues of fan devotion and investment that may seem new because of their location within digital culture, but in fact have long histories in Sherlock Holmes fandom and in the original Conan Doyle narratives. The new BBC *Sherlock* has reactivated engagement with Sherlock Holmes within digital contexts, and yet Holmes has been with us all along, or at least since he came on the scene in 1887 in Conan Doyle's first Sherlock Holmes story, *A Study in Scarlet.*

Our collection focuses on the BBC's recent televisual reincarnation of Sherlock Holmes in the series *Sherlock*, and on its reception, but does so with great awareness of the rich history of Sherlock Holmes as a figure and as an expansive transmedia text. The essays in this volume collectively paint a picture of Sherlock Holmes as an evolving transmedia figure, at the center of myriad cultural intersections and diverse representational and fan traditions. Essays consider the literary, media, and reception histories informing *Sherlock*, the industrial and cultural contexts of *Sherlock*'s release, the text of *Sherlock* itself as adaptation and transformative work, and *Sherlock*'s critical and popular reception. This collection's investigation of *Sherlock* and its reception offers insight into not only the BBC series itself, but also into its literary source, and with it, into the cultural and international resonance of the Victorian detective and his trusted sidekick. With only one series aired so far (BBC 2010), the show succeeds in looking forward and backward at the same time: staying close to Conan Doyle's canon and its sense of history while at the same time looking forward with a 21st century sensibility and the promise of more adventures in the future. As such, studying the latest incarnation of arguably the oldest of media fandoms also allows us to look at the relationship between different fan traditions and reception cultures. Fan studies has long sidestepped investigation of the impact of Sherlock Holmes fandom on the evolution of fan communities and fan engagement; *Sherlock* promises a compelling contemporary route to bridge this gap. It is our intention that this collection contribute to both long-standing conversations about Holmes as a literary and cultural figure and to current debates in fan studies.

When the BBC premiered *Sherlock*, it re-envisioned a character who had been adapted and re-adapted in multiple media forms for over a century. One hundred and thirteen years earlier, Sir Arthur Conan Doyle introduced Sherlock Holmes in his first serial incarnation. The logical detective solving unsolvable crimes became a key archetypal figure in the mystery and detective genres, spanning media and centuries. Innumerable adaptations have since crossed media and genre lines, from television to film, from professional novels to comics, from *Dressed to Kill* (1946) and *Sherlock Holmes* (2009) to *The Great Mouse Detective* (1986) and *Without a Clue* (1988). The figures of Sherlock Holmes and John Watson have become synonymous with a range of cultural referents and meanings; key images and phrases, such as Holmes' pipe and hat, "Elementary my dear Watson" (which did not originate in Conan Doyle but emerged in later adaptations and interpretations) and "the game is afoot" (an intertextual Shakespeare reference in itself) have entered into the wider lexicon of recognizable phrases and images, inseparable from the figure of Sherlock Holmes yet carrying their own cultural weight.

The series recasts the famous detective as a millennial thinker, showcasing his youthful technological expertise as he easily navigates flows of digital information that others would find confounding. Indeed, in depicting Sherlock as a millennial technowizard, the series updates and bolsters the basic canonical vision of Holmes' internal deduction as logical yet somehow still magical. The new, millennial Sherlock still uses the standard processes of deduction made famous by Conan Doyle, but at the same time he unpacks contemporary crimes via digital tools. By visually highlighting Sherlock's digital know-how through the layering of text on image, the series draws attention to this millennial Sherlock's modernized skill set: hand in hand with his traditional deductive prowess, Sherlock demonstrates his intuitive use of operations such as the interrelated actions of search and filter, two key digital tools so embedded in our culture that they have become fundamental cultural logics. The processes of searching and filtering impact the way we as a culture understand our relationship to both information and visibility. Search and filter convey the rendering of insight through the sorting of information and the making visible of preferred or more relevant findings. Sherlock's dependence on the protocols of search and filter in his deductive processes highlights the way in which, according to Lev Manovich (2001), digital logics become cultural logics become personal logics.

Indeed, the introduction of digital logics like search and filter into Sherlock Holmes' tool set impacts what we might mean by Sherlock's "science of deduction," even as arguably these digital logics may have their roots in Holmesian deductive reasoning. In a sense, the series posits that a Sherlock of today could not embody the necessary cultural brilliance without extreme digital literacy. But, as Matt Hills and Roberta Pearson, among others in this volume, suggest, this digitization of Sherlock's cultural know-how necessitates either an epistemological shift or collapse. Sherlock's knowledge is no longer located in his "brain attic" but in the digital "cloud." Much of this new millennial Sherlock's skill is now based not in honed internal perfection, but rather in knowing how to navigate digital data quickly and instinctively in order to arrive at insight into a given mystery. Through its invocation of such logics as interface, operations, gameplay, and ludic exploration, the digital thus necessarily saturates this modernized *Sherlock*, determining the narrative landscape and constituting the larger frameworks of Sherlock's deduction.

However, as creators Steven Moffat and Mark Gattis have emphasized, this re-envisioning of Sherlock as a fully modern figure is in a key sense not a re-envisioning at all, but rather an updating of a character who was crucially modern within his original Victorian context. The original Sherlock Holmes was a modern man of his time, in touch with the popular culture of the late Victorian period, and employing if not inventing state of the art scientific methods. Likewise, the BBC's Sherlock is fully immersed in and dependent on close knowledge of his space and place, including its digital dimensions; thus his deductive logics and skills are necessarily reflective of their contemporary (digital) contexts. The digitally-informed dimensions of the BBC's adaptation of Sherlock manifest in the series' use of televisual language. The program renders Sherlock's thought processes as both audio and visual layers, with text layers serving as representations of his digital navigation. This televisual breaking down of details in video and audio are not new to television, but rather have been popularized in recent procedurals such as the CSI franchise. The series uses this technique to highlight Sherlock's knowledge of space and exploration of details through visuals of his thought processes, which serve doubly to tie the viewer to Sherlock's unique subjectivity.

The televisual dimension of *Sherlock*, where audio, text, and image in counterpoint all invite the viewer into the workings of Sherlock's mind, reveal one way in which *Sherlock* arguably deviates from previous renditions of the Holmes narrative. No longer is John Watson our sole guide through the narrative as he was in the Conan Doyle original. Watson still provides a primary point of entry, framing our official introduction to the character of Sherlock Holmes. But we, as viewers, are also tied televisually into Sherlock's experiences and have access to his thought processes. Our first encounter with Sherlock takes the form of a series of text messages authored and signed by him, displayed not only on diegetic cell phones but layered on the image as text. This textual/digital introduction paves the way for the multidimensional representation of Sherlock's viewpoint.

Where Conan Doyle framed Holmes' voice as part of Watson's writings, and film and television adaptations allowed audiences to see and hear Holmes explain to Watson his reasoning, in *Sherlock* we do not only hear his explanations but see, in the layered imagery and digital texts, his thought-processes made visual. Thus in addition to explaining Sherlock's reasoning, the show makes us privy to his use of operations (search and filter), as his navigation of search engines manifests as text layers on the screen. Through these multiple levels, he becomes an accessible (if still somewhat magical) millennial televisual protagonist. This increased emphasis on character accessibility is also manifest in the series' move from last to first name, from Watson and Holmes to John and Sherlock, perhaps a more crucial shift for the character of Holmes than for John Watson, who was already rendered accessible. Here the whole series is presented as "Sherlock," announcing the more human presentation of the character.

Transmedia Narrative/Transmedia Fan Engagement

Sherlock makes obvious narrative use of digital tools as it re-imagines the Sherlock Holmes narrative. Watson writes up Holmes' investigations in blog form rather than publishing Holmes' exploits in hard copy print as in Conan

Doyle's original. Thus, *Sherlock* updates the in-story mode of dissemination to its modern, digital context. Watson is depicted as an inexperienced blogger using a standard interface akin to blogger.com, thus making him an everyday (albeit not extraordinarily skilled) digital citizen.

In addition to John's blog, Sherlock himself maintains a web site. Rather than simply publishing the results of his knowledge as academic treatises, as in Conan Doyle's canon, Sherlock uses his web site, "The Science of Deduction," as a digital home for his consulting service, where he offers his expertise and interacts with potential clients. Thus, alongside the unfolding televisual narrative, the storyworld also suggests within it two additional narrative threads or perspectives, both (again, within the storyworld) maintained on digital spaces, one explicitly as a narrative (John's blog), another as a more disparate collection of related information and online social interactions (Sherlock's site). Indeed, at key moments in the narrative, characters communicate via Sherlock's web site, or attain important information from having read John's blog.

Given the centrality of these two fictional online spaces to the series' narrative, it is perhaps unsurprising that the BBC has developed both John's blog and Sherlock's site as transmedia narrative extensions (and have also added two peripheral in-world transmedia sites as well), so that the viewer can visit either John's blog or Sherlock's site to explore their digital traces beyond the bounds of the televisual program. However, these official transmedia extensions do not encourage (or actually even allow) fan engagement with the characters or story directly, nor do they host a forum to allow for fan engagement with other fans — indeed the web sites function as hermetically sealed transmedia extensions. The sites do offer Alternative Reality Game (ARG)-like (though limited) puzzles, but fans must turn to other interfaces such as the question/answer structure of about.com in order to team together to solve the self-contained mysteries offered in these official transmedia extensions.

However, far beyond about.com, *Sherlock* fans have congregated in a host of other online interfaces to engage with the series and with each other, building their own transmedia webs of text and image. Indeed, the online fandom for *Sherlock* has grown at break-neck speed, only after the fact encouraged in part by official frames such as the PBS-sponsored twitter event that accompanied the initial U.S. airing of the series. *Sherlock* fandom has manifested visibly in a wide range of online spaces, from livejournal.com to denofgeek.com, from twitter.com to tumblr.com, from archiveofourown.org to fanfiction.net.

In 2007, Henry Jenkins defined transmedia storytelling as "a process where integral elements of a fiction get dispersed systematically across multiple delivery channels for the purpose of creating a unified and coordinated entertainment experience (March 22, 2007; www.henryjenkins.org; see also Jenkins 2006). More recently, scholars have debated whether transmedia narratives necessarily need to be dispersed "systematically" by official authors, or whether audience engagement across platforms intended and unintended could also constitute transmedia. A looser definition of transmedia would suggest that audiences as well as official authors co-construct transmedia narratives, storyworlds, and frames for engagement, and indeed we hope that our study of the multifaceted, deeply interwoven *Sherlock* text and fandom will demonstrate the value of this more expansive definition of transmedia.

For a canon storyworld that has been hailed as transmedia in its original form, and a televisual re-envisioning that has at its core digital and transmedia logics, the most visible transmedia paratexts are limited in scope and do not invite direct audience participation, though they certainly have not precluded the breadth of audience engagement elsewhere in more organic online forms of participation. Accordingly, studying *Sherlock* within its transmedia context is compelling in part precisely because of its wide range of fan-instigated transmedia authorship, held in tension with its surprising limitation and control in terms of official transmedia extensions.

The quick and extensive growth of online *Sherlock* fan activity should come as no surprise. Most obviously, of course, the series cultivated the interest of already-dedicated Sherlock Holmes fans, including fans of the books, of the various adaptations — especially the long-running series starring Jeremy Brett, and fans of the recent *Sherlock Holmes* (2009) film, starring Robert Downey, Jr. and Jude Law. The series unites participants in the highly active traditions of Sherlock Holmes fandom with long-time fans of Holmes who have not acted on that fandom in community contexts. These diverse fans come together with those from other communities, such as science fiction, slash, and anime fandom. The series also has capitalized on its close association with the fan/cult favorite, *Doctor Who*; *Sherlock* co-creator Steven Moffat has been the lead writer and executive producer of *Doctor Who* from the relaunched fifth series onward, and *Sherlock* co-creator/actor Mark Gattis is a *Doctor Who* writer and actor. Because of this direct connection with *Doctor Who*, *Sherlock* has drawn on the highly-active *Doctor Who* fandoms. In addition, the series' focus on the close relationship between Sherlock and John and its playful address of their relationship means that it has tapped into the extensive web of slash fandoms invested in reading a romantic relationship in a series featuring two central male characters.

The literary heritage of long-time Sherlock Holmes and Conan Doyle fans situates them in an interesting space between traditionally scholarly and fannish reading practices, a position that is challenged with the influx of new *Sherlock* fans whose traditions have developed from a range of media fandoms, bringing with them their own rules and terminologies. Transformative works are called pastiches, for example, among Sherlockians/Holmesians whereas most other media-based fandoms call them fan fiction. Thus *Sherlock* fandom combines not only different fan groups and their particular interpretations but also their varied backgrounds and traditions.

This collection brings together essays that consider the literary and reception histories informing *Sherlock*, the industrial and cultural contexts of *Sherlock*'s release, the text of *Sherlock* itself as adaptation and transformative work, and *Sherlock*'s critical and popular reception. Consequently, the intended audience for the book encompasses a range of disciplines and interests: literary Victorianists, Conan Doyle scholars, and detective fiction academics may particularly be interested in the ways the character of Sherlock Holmes and the detective genre has been re-envisioned with *Sherlock*; TV and new media scholars may be interested not only in this particular televisual adaptation but also the transmedia aspects within and beyond the show; finally, fan studies scholars may be particularly interested in the focus on the coming together of various fan communities and fannish engagements.

Writing for such diverse audiences offers certain challenges: Sherlockians, media fans, literary and media scholars not only have different backgrounds and expectations but also different styles and terminologies. As Roberta Pearson (1997, 2007) describes in her overviews of classic Sherlock Holmes fandom, the terms *Sherlockian* and *Holmesian* are often used to distinguish between British and North American Conan Doyle aficionados, yet most of the contributors do not differentiate among the two. Likewise, the term *canon* has a very specific meaning within Sherlock Holmes fandom, similar to the way media fandom uses the term to describe source texts but also, as Ashley D. Polasek describes in this volume, alluding to a very specific approach to Conan Doyle's stories and the *Grand Game* of reading the stories as documenting actual historical events. In turn, many terms familiar to media fans and their scholars may seem foreign to Sherlockians: whether it is the choice of using *fan* or *aficionado*, *fan fiction* or *pastiche*, similar concepts circulate with different names depending on the specific discourse communities. Indeed, fan fiction writers have created an extensive vocabulary describing their stories, whether by genre (slash, hurt/comfort, AU [alternate universe]) or formal aspects (challenge fic, drabble, fix-it).

And yet it is important to remember that regardless of terminology and self-understanding, diverse Sherlock fans share many key impulses, investments, and practices. Fans old and new are united not only in their love for Sherlock Holmes but also in their ways of engaging with this character and his world. In an influential blog post about fandom and fan authorship, fan obsession_inc affixed the terms *affirmational* and *transformational* to describe different forms of engagement with the source text: whereas the former analyzes and interprets the source text, creating shared meaning and characterizations, the latter aggressively alters and transforms the source text, changing and manipulating it to the fans' own desires (June 1, 2009; www.dreamwidth. org). Sherlock Holmes fan communities exhibit wide ranges and creativities, both affirmational and transformational, be it within more traditional fan communities such as the Sherlock Holmes Society or the Baker Street Irregulars, or in the most recently developed communities such as livejournal's sherlockbbc and Tumblr's fuckyeahsherlock.

The *Sherlock* series provides the opportunity to explore the intersection of personal and community fan histories, as well as the convergence of different generations and modes of fandom. In this way, the transmedia fandom that has developed online offers a unique and at times disparate combination of a wide range of fannish investments, histories, and trajectories, including fan/interpretive communities historically separated by gender. It is partially because of this diversity and unique combination that we have decided to embark upon this book project, as we feel *Sherlock* offers an unusual opportunity to study the anatomy of a fandom that contains highly visible multiplicity at its center, and extends outward to a complex, multifaceted web of cultural and textual practices and fannish histories. Likewise, as a reflection of this multiplicity, the various authors contributing to this volume represent not only a diverse set of interdisciplinary scholarly interests and areas of expertise, but also a diverse set of fannish affiliations, experiences, and investments.

Sherlock and the Adventure of Peer-to-Peer Digital Review

As the scope of intersecting topics demonstrates, this collection brings together concerns of literary studies and literary traditions with explorations of new directions in televisual and transmedia authorship and reception. The synthesis of concerns, old and new, emerges directly from the duality of the series' own project and modern re-envisioning of an embedded cultural figure. Likewise, it was our intention that the creative process of this collection mirror this duality. As Matt Hills argues in this volume, our modernized Sherlock draws on networked logics of knowledge specific to digital culture. Likewise, this volume has been written with a belief in the value of networked academic and fan knowledge. We worked with MediaCommons to employ a process of closed-community, peer-to-peer feedback, to which we also invited external peer reviewers. All of the authors involved in this volume participated in an ongoing dialogic process in which they not only provided feedback to each other but also entered into conversations that informed rewrites. It was our intention that this approach would bind the different essays together by giving authors the opportunity to explore the commonalities and distinctions in their arguments. We now feel that this collection represents a coming together of individual and collective knowledge, and at the same time unites and brings into dialogue a wide range of in some cases deeply felt positions about Sherlock Holmes as a figure and storyworld, *Sherlock* as an adaptation, and the many communities and creative works that have circulated and continue to flourish around the detective in all his incarnations.

Furthermore, we especially value the union of digital and hard copy that this volume represents. It has been our intention to marry digital processes of critical dialogue with the traditional literary circulation of a finite hard copy, thus echoing the *Sherlock* series' layering of old modes of knowledge, as embodied in Sherlock Holmes' deductive methods, onto new modes of knowledge production through digital media. In so doing, we hope to model new possibilities for collective, peer-to-peer review that take advantage of the strength of community knowledge and modes of constructive critique modeled in transmedia fandom.

Chapter Overview

Various thematic threads resonate through all sections of this book. Throughout the book, essays engage with questions of paratexts, intertexts, and cross- and transmedia engagement; *Sherlock* as inheritor of long traditions of cross-media fandom; *Sherlock* fan engagement with the series' digital-savvy aesthetic and narrative; expansions of the already transmedia *Sherlock* in multimedia fan texts; and fannish intertextuality between *Sherlock* and other media texts. Rather than relegate discussion of digital media and transmedia extensions to only one section of the book, essays throughout explore questions of transmedia and digital extensions. Likewise, the tension of a Victorian source in a contemporary context generates myriad issues about individual identity and representation that carry through the collection: gender, race, and sexual identity are some of the concerns repeatedly addressed by different essays and writers. The particular Englishness of both Conan Doyle's world and Sherlock's 2010 London invoke themes of place and national identity. Essays throughout explore the series' careful construction of London as a synthesis of Victorian and contemporary aesthetics and discourses of nationality in *Sherlock* fandom and fan texts.

Fundamentally, as the title suggests, this volume merges two key preoccupations: (1) the persistent figure of Sherlock Holmes in all his myriad incarnations

and the fans who love him and (2) the transmedia web of paratexts and intertexts that bring Sherlock and his world into continued being. The first theme
encompasses the collection from front cover to the afterword, from the first
glimpse any of us had of Sherlock Holmes to our anticipation for the second
series of *Sherlock*, from the initial idea of creating this collection to writing
the index. Lyndsay Faye's prologue "Why Sherlock?" raises the question we
all continue to grapple with even as none of us can answer it in a way that
fully satisfies. As a fan of the old and the new Sherlock alike, affirmational
society member and transformational pastiche writer, Faye celebrates our love
both for the character and for fannish engagements with Conan Doyle's world.

Whereas the first theme connects all contributors (and hopefully readers)
emotionally, the second serves as a thread thematically: we understand transmedia not only in terms of the industry's transmedia extensions but also
include the text's digital and transmedia logics and the way transmedia features
heavily in audience reception and creative fan responses. In so doing, Part
One, "Transmedia and Collective Intelligence," opens up the conversation
and outlines the terrain the other essays will explore. Both authors begin with
the famous Sherlockian pursuit of the "grand game," the (mostly) tongue-in-
cheek pretense that Sherlock Holmes actually existed and Conan Doyle was
simply chronicler of his exploits.

Matt Hills looks at ways knowledge, information, and intelligence play
out (extra-)diegetically in the series in his "*Sherlock*'s Epistemological Economy
and the Value of 'Fan' Knowledge: How Producer-Fans Play the (Great) Game
of Fandom." He argues that *Sherlock*'s central appeal is the way it models an
"epistemological economy" as it presents a knowledge and inquiry-driven
world that fan discourses in turn replicate and expand. Analyzing the way
media texts and information technology function within *Sherlock*, Hills suggests that the show exemplifies a contemporary approach to knowledge where
ready access to and easy searchability of data is more important than comprehensive intelligence or superior memory. Within such an epistemological
economy, fan intelligence — especially as it relates to Conan Doyle's texts —
must both be expanded and policed. In so doing, the series' creators can
simultaneously assert their awareness of canon (which Hills calls "heretical
fidelity") and their ability to creatively move beyond that canon, thus reassert-
ing their own authorial power and separating them more clearly from (other)
Conan Doyle fans. Where Hills uses *Sherlock*'s heretical fidelity to show how
it strengthens authorial discourses, Ashley D. Polasek's "Winning 'The Grand
Game': *Sherlock* and the Fragmentation of Fan Discourse" examines the ways
such a return to (and reimagining of) Conan Doyle's canon complicates the
collective intelligence of Sherlockian's Grand Game. In the game, fans presume
a non-fictional Holmes, using historical rather than literary research to expand

knowledge. Updating (and thus aggressively dehistoricizing) Holmes and Watson results in a change in fan approaches, Polasek argues. Looking at fan fiction in both Holmes and Sherlock fandom, she suggests that the contemporary setting as well as the already transformative aspect of *Sherlock* more readily invite fans to engage in transformative play rather than the affirmational engagements of the Grand Game.

Neither The Grand Game nor BBC's *Sherlock* series could even be conceivable without Sir Arthur Conan Doyle's creations. Part Two, "Sherlock Then and Now," looks specifically at the relationship between Conan Doyle's fiction and the 2010 BBC series *Sherlock*. In so doing, the three contributors explore the ways Moffat has reimagined the characters, plots, the setting and tropes, always balancing the nostalgic harkening back to a supposedly more ideal and homogeneous England with an awareness that such nostalgia necessarily invokes oppressing Otherness in all its forms.

Much has been written about the startling scene in "The Great Game" where Sherlock expresses his ignorance of the solar system even as he obtains and uses necessary astronomical knowledge soon after. Ariana Scott-Zechlin uses this scene (and its canonical precursor in Conan Doyle's *A Study in Scarlet*) in "'But It's the Solar System!': Reconciling Science and Faith Through Astronomy" as a route to consider a broader historical tension between scientific inquiry and methodology on the one hand and faith in larger metanarratives on the other. She suggests that whereas Holmes illustrated Victorian ideals of scientific and technological progress in opposition to concepts of faith and religion, Sherlock more accurately represents our current awareness of scientific teleological certainty as all but another belief system. Fan fiction plays out this more complicated, less binary relationship between faith and science as it exemplifies and extrapolates in multiple ways the interplay between faith and science underlying the show itself. As Scott-Zechlin contrasts 19th and 21st century versions of Sherlock Holmes, she finds that it is his changing relation to arch-nemesis Moriarty that perhaps most pointedly highlights the ever more complex ideological nexus of this new Sherlock. In turn, Ellen Burton Harrington concentrates on the changing role of Moriarty in her "Terror, Nostalgia, and the Pursuit of Sherlock Holmes in *Sherlock*." Moffat's version enhances Moriarty's role, emphasizing the doubling of Holmes and Moriarty in the original series by making Moriarty author of all of the crimes Sherlock encounters in *Sherlock*. Not only has Moriarty become Sherlock's greatest fan, but he also ultimately scripts all of the crimes Sherlock solves. In so doing, Sherlock's 21st century reinvisioning of the detective/criminal relationship suggests an implicit connection between the criminal and the author, but more specifically aligns the criminal and the fan-author, as Moriarty shares the "fan" title with many Sherlock viewers (and indeed, with

Moffat and Gattis, who also proclaim themselves to be long time Sherlock fans). Like Hills in the first essay, Harrington thus suggests the show's uneasy contemporary relationship with its own transformative origins and its contested relationship with its fans over the past century.

The complex relationship between Victorian Holmes and contemporary Sherlock is likewise explored in Anne Kustritz and Melanie E. S. Kohnen's "Decoding the Industrial and Digital City: Visions of Security in Holmes' and Sherlock's London." Kustriz and Kohnen examine *Sherlock*'s representations of the city to address how the supposed changes from Holmes's 19th century to Sherlock's 21st century London (namely, as they describe, "from industrial to post-industrial, scientific to digital, and imperial to neo-colonial") are not as dramatic as one might expect or hope. In its stead, they present a Sherlock who in turn succeeds and fails in updating his previous modes of inquiry to a world that doesn't easily follow linear inferences. In so doing, the show questions not only Sherlockian methods in the present but retroactively undermines Conan Doyle's ordered universe of the past. Moreover, by presenting the city as a fully digitalized space, the series foregrounds surveillance technologies which have become central to Sherlock's inquiries. And yet the slick and modern fully digital London only exacerbates the Orientalist images that connect the 21st to the 19th century thematically and ideologically.

As one of the oldest and most diverse fandoms (and, at this point, mostly out of copyright), Sherlock Holmes has spawned thousands of official novels and short stories; films, stage, and radio play; art, board, and video games. Such works range from the dedicated to-the-letter adaptations of the Jeremy Brett version to the irreverent homage of the U.S. medical procedural *House, M.D.*; from Holmes encountering Jack the Ripper in various films and novels to becoming a hologram on the USS *Enterprise*; from early silent films to *Sherlock*'s 21st century version of the detective.

All three essays in Part Three, "Adaptations and Intertextuality," shape the specifics of a given interpretive adaptation. Elizabeth Jane Evans's "Shaping Sherlocks: Institutional Practice and the Adaptation of Character" looks at the significance of industry framing of Sherlock Holmes as authored franchise. She explores the relationship between production companies' policies and practices (in her study, Warner Bros., BBC, and Asylum) and the particular Sherlock Holmes adaptations, and argues that in the case of the BBC adaptation, Holmes becomes a product of contemporary public service broadcasting, straddling two traditions of "quality" television and encapsulating the BBC's practice of bridging the gap between heritage and modernity. Focusing on one particular intertext, CB Harvey's "Sherlock's Webs: What the Detective Remembered from the Doctor About Transmediality" investigates the specific relationship between these two central figures of British popular culture. Harvey traces the influence of Conan Doyle's Holmes on the character of Doctor Who, only to show how indebted the new *Sherlock* is to *Doctor Who*, not only in terms of characterization but also of visual aesthetics and narrative logics. Returning to the central thread of transmedia, Harvey closely analyzes *Sherlock*'s transmedia extensions and their seamless intersection with fan cultures to show how to read the new *Sherlock* series within convergence culture. Like Evans, Tom Steward illustrates how industrial and media contexts shape the adaptation of fictional characters. In his "Holmes in the Small Screen: The Television Contexts of Sherlock," he reads the show within the context of its televisual format and industrial location, considering *Sherlock* as one instance in a history of televisual adaptations of the famous sleuth. This essay examines how *Sherlock* bears the imprint of the BBC's televisual needs (BBC programming conventions, questions of time slot, intended audience, network branding, etc.) and also of its creators' specific styles as TV auteurs (as indicated in their previous texts, most importantly, their work on *Doctor Who*).

Moffat and Gattis have described London as a central character in their adaptation of Sherlock Holmes, and indeed Holmes as a cultural figure is deeply embedded in his British cultural context, just as *Sherlock* is very visibly a product of the BBC. However, at the same time, *Sherlock* was co-produced with WGBH Boston for the American Masterpiece anthology series, and thus is transnational from its inception. More broadly-speaking, Holmes is a figure who has been disseminated internationally over his history, circulating in many different national and transnational contexts, and indeed *Sherlock* has aired in Britain, the U.S., Australia, Sweden, the Netherlands, Norway, Belgium, Denmark, and Germany, not to mention its unofficial but ubiquitous circulation through peer-to-peer file sharing. With this breadth of circulation in mind, Part Four of the book, "Interpreting *Sherlock*," explores the ways in which specific viewing contexts and interpretive communities affect individual receptions. Roberta Pearson addresses the heterogeneous international response of online fans as she explores various forms of reception and fan interaction online in "'Good Old Index'; or, The Mystery of the Infinite Archive." Recounting her own confrontation with the expanses of online fandom, Pearson contrasts the seemingly comprehensive knowledge gathering and overseeable fandom of Sherlockians with the overwhelming data flow of *Sherlock* fandom online with its rhizomatic structure and its ever growing contradictory approaches to the source text. Mirroring Holmes and Sherlock's differing approaches to research, Pearson moves from comprehensive data collection to a focus on organizational fannish structures and the way such structural protocols dominate and organize fannish infrastructure and, ultimately, content itself.

Despite its seemingly global reach, our awareness of the British context for Sherlock Holmes can only be heightened in Moffat's 21st century adaptation, and more specifically the series must engage with a specifically post-Imperial Great Britain. Moreover, as the contributors in this section illustrate, audiences are strongly aware of Sherlock's specific national and cultural identity, and thus different audiences indeed respond differently, not only based on their differing emotional relationship to Conan Doyle's canon or their familiarity with other intertexts, but also based on their own identity in relation to Great Britain. Paul Rixon looks at the British reception specifically in "*Sherlock*: Critical Reception by the Media." Analyzing the critical responses to *Sherlock* by the British national press, Rixon explores how reviews respond to paratextual publicity material and engage and reinforce a variety of underlying cultural values. In so doing, the journalistic press illustrates the way *Sherlock,* with its updated version of a quintessentially English hero, mirrors anxieties about national culture and identity as it cathects a nostalgic reminiscence of England's glory days. In contrast, Nicolle Lamerichs offers a specific case study of a group of foreign Holmes fans in "Holmes Abroad: Dutch Fans Interpret the Famous Detective." Using personal interviews, she explores how individual readers use their personal experiences, reading, and backgrounds to create specific and individual readings in a process she defines as "naturalizing." Unlike fans who often share interpretive communities with similar intertexts, Lamerichs' viewers show a diversity of responses, which are not clearly filtered through their similar national background, but which reflect their more individualized cultural repertoires. All three essays in this section, then, emphasize the interplay between official and unofficial, public and private, shared and personal media receptions; together, these essays paint a nuanced picture of how reception contexts influence viewer engagement.

Throughout this collection, contributors have addressed the changes that have or have not been wrought by transplanting the essentially British, fundamentally Victorian Holmes into the 21st century. Kustritz and Kohnen, for example, argue that *Sherlock* replicates central flaws of Conan Doyle's source text in terms of race, and Rixon showcases the way *Sherlock*'s critical reception plays out against the backdrop of a post-Imperial Britain in need of reclaiming a nostalgic identity. In Part Five, "Postmodern Sherlock," the contributors take seriously the notion of a *Sherlock* written and presented against a postmodern framework in order to explore where the show may ultimately find its limits, and where fan responses may indeed fulfill the project of Sherlock's postmodernity in ways the show itself cannot. Balaka Basu's "*Sherlock* and the (Re)Invention of Modernity" questions the seemingly postmodern facade of the new *Sherlock* and suggests that the show instead constructs a thoroughly nostalgic reclamation of an idealized retrofuturity. Drawing from visual aesthetics, characterizations, and narratives, Basu argues that the show is torn between respecting and updating Conan Doyle's canon in a way that prevents it from fully interrogating itself and its underlying ideology. Situating the fan writer in this modern/postmodern dynamic, Basu mirrors Hills' suggesting that ultimately Sherlock remains on the side of author(ity) rather than the postmodern freeplay of multiple authorships even as they pretend to embrace authorial multiplicity. Where Basu illustrates *Sherlock*'s failure to fully understand and ultimately acknowledge the fan, Francesca Coppa focuses on fan responses instead, showing how fandom uses the internal contradictions and complexities this Sherlock offers to create a truly postmodern, in fact, a Cyborgian protagonist. In "Sherlock as Cyborg: Bridging Mind and Body," she frames Doyle's narrative, consequent adaptations, and media fandom response within a modernist relationship of body/mind dichotomies. Confronting canon's belief in the power of Sherlock's mind with fandom's obsession with his body, Coppa complicates both the modernist dichotomy and the traditional focus on Holmes's mind only. In so doing, Coppa counters Polasek's more formal argument about *Sherlock*'s appeal to transformative fans by suggesting that it is that very conflicted and ambivalent relationship of mind and body that appeals to the predominantly female fan fiction fandom. A mind constantly at war with its body, Sherlock in her reading becomes the protagonist in a "literature written by (and for) the sexual mind and the intellectual body."

As we suggested from the outset, there are certain insights addressed and explored by most if not all of the contributors: the heretical fidelity to Conan Doyle's texts and the complex interplay both canon adherence and transformation create; the complex relationship of all acknowledged and unacknowledged influences of a TV show like *Sherlock*, be they national ideology, industry demands, fan expectations, or multimedial intertexts; the transmedial nature of not only the commercial presentation but also the internal logics within the show itself. At the same time, there are fundamental disagreements among the contributors, especially in terms of how successfully *Sherlock* balances its jump from 19th century Victorian London to its 21st century incarnation of a multicultural, metropolitan urban center and about how successfully creators Moffat and Gatiss handle and negotiate their authorial control. At its best, interpretation — like transformation — doesn't aspire to identifying a single truth, but instead thrives on multiplicities, complementarities and even contradictions. So even if we can't agree whether *Sherlock* has fully been successful in its 21st century adaptation, we can agree that fandom in all its myriad affirmative and transformative creativity has taken this modern Sherlock and made him fully and unapologetically postmodern, and in the process he has become a shared entity, potent in his very multiplicity.

Just as the fanvid "Brand New Way," with which we opened this introduction, brings to bear the productive transformativity spurred by our continued fascination with Sherlock Holmes, we hope that this collection reflects the dynamism of the multiple perspectives of its authors, woven together through the digital processes of peer-to-peer dialogue and debate.

Works Cited

Jenkins, Henry. 2006. *Convergence culture: Where old and new media collide*. New York: New York University Press.

Manovich, Lev. 2001. *The language of new media*. Cambridge: MIT Press.

Pearson, Roberta. 1997. It's always 1895: Sherlock Holmes in cyberspace. In *Trash aesthetics*, ed. Deborah Cartmell, I.Q. Hunter, Heidi Kaye, and Imelda Whelehan, 143–61. London: Pluto Press.

_____. 2007. Bachies, Bardies, Trekkies and Sherlockians. In *Fandom: Identities and communities in a mediated world*, ed. Jonathan Gray, Cornel Sandvoss, and C. Lee Harrington, 99–109. New York: New York University Press.

PART ONE

Transmedia and Collective Intelligence

Sherlock's Epistemological Economy and the Value of "Fan" Knowledge
How Producer-Fans Play the (Great) Game of Fandom

MATT HILLS

Abstract—This chapter analyzes the texts and paratexts of *Sherlock*, with a particular focus on "The Great Game" and on DVD commentaries involving showrunners Steven Moffat and Mark Gatiss. I argue that the series' representation of Sherlock Holmes develops Conan Doyle's depictions by portraying Sherlock himself as a coded validation of fans' "collective intelligence" (Jenkins 2006). This incarnation of Holmes engages with decentered and destabilized hierarchies of knowledge typical of networked culture. However, there are limits to the extent to which the figure of Holmes can incite fans' participatory culture as a cultural activator, since *Sherlock* specifically codes fan knowledge cut apart from fan affect. I then go on to consider how producer-fan discussion (on the DVD commentaries) both desegregates fandom and official production (Caldwell 2008) and simultaneously resegregates professional authorship and fan readings via what I term a discourse of "heretical fidelity." By distancing themselves from allegedly derivative fan works and prior transmedia adventures of Holmes, Moffat and Gatiss emphasize their creative autonomy, positioning and gendering the fan audience as knowledgeable "fanboys." Producer-fans thus enact a (para)textual disciplining of fandom, validating specific fan practices invested in knowledge (Hastie 2007).

Introduction

In this essay I want to focus on how *Sherlock* engages (extra-)diegetically with questions of fan knowledge and access to information. Writing rather presciently, media scholar Roberta Pearson suggested in 1997 that one might view "computers as the logical extension of Holmes' own practices and habits of mind" (1997, 144). Pearson argues that "computers and the Internet constitute the modern equivalent of Holmes' commonplace books, enabling immediate access to massive compendiums of facts" (1997, 155). *Sherlock* seemingly enacts the very equivalence put forward by Pearson, for as showrunners Mark Gatiss and Steven Moffat have observed:

> Sherlock Holmes was a man of his Age, and in the nineteenth century he was a modern man. He's constantly firing off telegrams, he's constantly receiving cables.... So we wanted him to be completely a man of now, and someone who has access to a vast store of knowledge. He would no longer really have an enormous system of box files, he would be intensely computer literate and very gadget happy [Gatiss 2010, ASiP DVD commentary].
>
> Well, the Internet is made for him, because one of the things he does in the stories, which is very rarely referenced in the films, is he reads the agony columns of the paper, the Agony Aunt stuff, to see what's happening out there. He was made to haunt Internet forums. I'm sure he's gone on all those forums looking for traces of Moriarty or something that's going on. He was absolutely born for this era [Moffat 2010, ASiP DVD commentary].

Contra production discourses which construct Holmes as "naturally" belonging to a world of Internet forums and computer literacy, it should be noted that Pearson's academic discourse is critically inflected: "In our ... era, the appropriation of Holmes as a hero of nineteenth-century rationalism may be motivated by a longing for a mythic and reassuring age, albeit one that has little relevance for contemporary life except by contrast" (1997, 154). If a contemporary, reimagined Holmes uses IT to solve crimes in the same epistemological mode as Conan Doyle's original creation, then far from web-based computing merely taking up the narrative role of the commonplace book, twenty-first century philosophies of knowledge may problematically be reduced to "nineteenth-century rationalism." We thus need to pay careful attention to the "epistemological economy" (Hastie 2007, 83) of *Sherlock* in comparison to the literary Canon, rather than wholly accepting *a production discourse of heretical fidelity*, where this Holmes is displaced into "non-period pastiche" (Ridgway Watt and Green 2003, 137) but supposedly remains true to the spirit of Conan Doyle's work at the same time, being "a man of now" and "born for this era." I will consider this contradictory discourse of heretical fidelity in more detail later. First, I want to set out a stronger argument about epistemology, approaching issues of knowledge not merely as a particular theme within *Sherlock*, but rather as a determinant of the show's twenty-first century success and incitement of fan cultures. Here, I am following Amelie Hastie's work on cult TV. She argues that shows such as *The X-Files*, *Twin Peaks*, and *Buffy the Vampire Slayer* are all "about investigation in some form":

Part of the reason that these series have become cult shows surely rests on the fact that they are all invested in knowledge; with their narrative tropes and their often open-ended nature, they invite fans to participate in this world of knowledge and to construct further "knowledge" about these worlds. This textual interest in investigation [also] appears to invite scholarly investigation.... Academics, though they may not identify with the typical "avid fan," participate in at least a parallel form of viewing and gathering of knowledge [Hastie 2007, 89; see also Hills 2002, 134–7].

Given the rapid emergence of scholarship (such as this collection) on *Sherlock*, we might similarly identify an epistemological economy within the series, again inciting fan and scholar-fan participation in (extra-)diegetic worlds of knowledge, through which the character of Sherlock and the textual values of *Sherlock* can be actively appropriated. Knowledge isn't just one theme among others in *Sherlock*—I am arguing that it constitutes a privileged component within the series' almost instantaneous cultification and fan embrace. Writing of cult texts within the context of convergence culture, and transmedia storytelling, Henry Jenkins draws on Pierre Levy's work to speculate over what kinds of texts would successfully incite and reward fan audiences:

The artwork will be what Levy calls a "cultural attractor," drawing together and creating common ground between diverse communities; we might also describe it as a cultural activator, setting into motion their decipherment, speculation and elaboration.... The most committed consumers [will] track down data spread across multiple media, scanning each and every text for insights into the [narrative] world [2006, 95].

Sherlock has proven to be just such a "cultural attractor," drawing together established Sherlockians, fans of the other work of executive producers Steven Moffat and Mark Gatiss (especially *Doctor Who*), readers passionately focused on the relationship between Sherlock (Benedict Cumberbatch) and John (Martin Freeman), and fan audiences drawn to Cumberbatch-as-Holmes, as well as to the show's use of contemporary styling such as its Belstaff coats or Spencer Hart suits, and its highly stylized televisuality, attributable to the directorial input of Paul McGuigan. But the show has clearly also functioned, in Jenkins' terms, as a "cultural activator," setting in motion the speculations and elaborations of fans such as at the (now defunct) Sherlocking forum, where an identification with the narrative world of *Sherlock* was rendered precisely as a verb, and hence a fan activity — from *Sherlock* to "Sherlocking." And as a "cultural activator" (see Ross 2008, 8–9), it is once more the question of (extra-)textual knowledge — of fandom as "collective intelligence" (Jenkins 2006, 27) — which comes to the fore. In what follows, then, I will investigate *Sherlock*'s diegetic uses of investigation, and how this epistemological economy is articulated with production discourses of fandom (Hills 2010, 58–78).

There is a major shift from the Canon's initial view of detection — exemplified by John Watson's humorous summary of Holmes' areas of expertise in *A Study in Scarlet*—to depictions of know-how in *Sherlock*. This can be glossed as follows: Conan Doyle depicts a world in which Holmes *knows what he needs to know*. By contrast — and it announces this most strenuously in "The Great Game"—*Sherlock* challenges any omniscient hierarchy of "useful" and "useless" knowledge. Always a matter of context, no form of knowledge can ever be consigned to the waste bin (or the Trash icon of Holmes's mind-as-computer). Trivia saves lives; gossip can be as valuable as a professorship, and indeed both modes of knowing — the untutored and the schooled — are instrumental to cracking the mystery of the Lost Vermeer. And so, too, is networked knowledge or "collective intelligence," as Sherlock scrolls through menu options on his smart phone, and goes online to learn from Connie Prince's fandom in "The Great Game": "fan sites. Indispensable for gossip."

"The Great Game" is, in fact, structured around a very specific rewriting of *A Study in Scarlet*. Whilst it is fair to say that Gatiss' script draws on a range of texts from the Canon, unlike Moffat's more singular reworking for episode one, this third TV episode is nevertheless premised on critiquing *Scarlet*. Its running gag, that Sherlock doesn't realize the Earth goes round the Sun, is meant to refer to events from "A Study in Pink," though it actually cites *Scarlet*, where Holmes announces of the Copernican theory: "What the deuce is it to me?... if we went round the moon it would not make a pennyworth of difference to me or my work" (III:34). Holmes even tells Watson, "Now that I do know it I shall do my best to forget it," in order not to clutter the attic of his mind with pointless "lumber" Conan Doyle has John list Holmes' knowledge of literature, philosophy and astronomy as "nil," whilst the detective displays an "immense" knowledge of Sensational Literature (III:32). This enumeration of Sherlock's limits is playful, perhaps aimed at eliciting a wry smile from the reader, but it is nonetheless set out as Holmes' rationalist approach to knowledge.

By contrast, "The Great Game" doesn't just joke about Sherlock's limits. It goes a step further and exposes them, making astronomy crucial to solving its key mystery and buying Sherlock a poolside meeting with Moriarty. Luckily, the "Van Buren" phenomenon is mentioned during the Planetarium presentation, enabling Holmes to make the link via empirical observation of detail and an exercise in memory. Freeman's Watson drives the point home, though, for us and for him — Holmes can't know in advance what will be relevant to his detective work. A world of fixed value, of "useful" furniture of the mind versus "lumber," no longer holds up in the media culture of the twenty-first century. Holmes even has to be "introduced to crap telly" when daytime TV forms a part of the investigation. No forms of know-how are now off-limits, or to be ultimately derided as valueless. Important forms of knowledge are all around, embedded in academia, astronomy, trashy TV — and fandom itself.

Speaking on the BBC DVD commentary (2010) for "The Great Game," showrunner and episode writer Mark Gatiss avers: "This, incidentally, is something I've wanted to do with Sherlock Holmes for years, which is a very, very undone thing, which ... stops him being a super human. He's incredibly ignorant about things that don't interest him." By emphasizing that this version of Holmes is limited, and that his scope of knowledge needs to be humanized and supplemented by John Watson, Gatiss recontextualizes Sherlock: no longer just the ideological bearer of pure rationalism and mythic cultural ordering (Knight 1980, 67), this Holmes is simultaneously brilliant *and* decidedly fallible — a representation of individualist "genius," but also a strong reminder of the need to be socially connected to others, in this case, Watson/the world of the media. The ideological project (Pearson 1997, 145) of the Gatiss-Moffat-Vertue Holmes is, I would say, one which valorizes social networks of friendship as much as social networks of information. Being networked is posited as an inherent social and cultural good which facilitates Sherlock's skills of deduction. As literary theorist Franco Moretti has observed of the Canon:

> All Holmes's investigations are accompanied and supported by the new and perfect mechanisms of transportation and communication. Carriages, trains, letters, telegrams, in Conan Doyle's world, are all crucial and *always* live up to expectations. They are the tacit and indispensable support of the arrest. Society expands and becomes more complicated: but it creates a framework of control, a network of relationships, that holds it more firmly together than ever before [1988, 143].

And communications are ever more ideologically "indispensable" to *Sherlock*'s ratiocinations in 2010, whether these are the texts of fan postings, or searchable weather data. The "network of relationships" engaged with by *Sherlock* is, however, not so clearly a modernist framework of control. It is, rather, a wiki world of dispersed, decentered, and distributed cognition (Booth 2010, 91–9), one where the required database or requisite expertise can be called up at the tap of a touch-screen. Embodied knowledge remains in the mix, to be sure, this time in the shape of the "Homeless Network" invested in by Holmes, but mediation is repeatedly central — a recording in the Planetarium, a news piece on the Vermeer glimpsed by Watson prior to the main story of Baker Street's explosion, or a moment drawn from Connie's TV show.

In "The Great Game," media texts are *always* meaningful: every bit of apparent mediated background is actually the plot's foreground. Gatiss may be following a screenwriters' rule of narrative non-redundancy, but the impression that's fostered is one of a media culture permeated with clues and vital knowledge, and a perfectly networked society that doesn't drop out of contact with itself, never so much as losing a mobile phone signal. *Sherlock* therefore intensifies the Canon's logic where, as Moretti notes, communications and technology always deliver the goods. Through this intensification, the twenty-first century TV series ultimately becomes a critique of Conan Doyle's "radiant empiricism," that world of detail awaiting Holmes' expert decoding (Atkinson 1998, 109). In the contemporary world, where all forms of knowledge can be archived and accessed via cloud computing, Conan Doyle's hierarchies of knowledge melt into air: unlike the 19th century rationalist, this version of Holmes *doesn't need to know in advance what he needs to know*, precisely because he's networked — he can consult digitally at the scene of the crime. As such, Cumberbatch's Holmes requires access to all forms of knowledge, all of the time, since anything and everything might furnish the contemporary detective's revelation. Even Copernicus. In today's narratives, Holmes really would be lost without his blogger — and without "indispensable" fan sites.

The epistemological economy represented by *Sherlock* is, thus, omnivorous rather than hierarchical. And by diegetically invoking the validity of fan knowledge, even if only in passing, *Sherlock* demonstrates itself to be a keenly "knowing" text, much in the spirit of Moffat's earlier reimagining of Robert Louis Stevenson's infamous "London Gothic" novella, *Jekyll* (Armitt 2011, 112). Where *Jekyll* incorporated psychoanalytic readings of *The Strange Case of Dr. Jekyll and Mr Hyde* via its invocation of the "Klein and Utterson Research Institute," *Sherlock*'s knowingness resides in how it intertextually reworks Conan Doyle's texts and hence hails Sherlockians, even while maintaining diegetically that Sherlock Holmes is a contemporary character, that is, that "he" has no existence as a prior historical fiction with an established cult following. *Sherlock* is thus structurally unable to refer textually to Sherlockians, and instead its mention of "fan sites" playfully gestures to Holmesian knowledge, suggesting that the exegesis of TV fans is valuable and worthy of the great detective's attention.

Given this diegetic prohibition on recognizing Sherlockian knowledge cultures — and their coded, knowing acknowledgment via a fictional fandom instead — it is perhaps unsurprising that extra-diegetically and extra-textually, official production discourses (over-)compensate for this structuring absence by appearing to be somewhat obsessed with interpellating real-world knowledge cultures circulating around the figure of Holmes. Nowhere is this more evident than in commentaries accompanying "A Study in Pink" and "The Great Game" on the BBC DVD release. These involve Mark Gatiss, Steven Moffat and Sue Vertue in the former instance, and Benedict Cumberbatch, Martin Freeman and Mark Gatiss in the latter case.

Derek Kompare has recently argued that "of all the paratextual forms of contemporary ... television authorship, the commentary track is paradoxically the most ubiquitous and least analyzed" (2011, 106). However, DVD box sets and their extras — especially commentaries — have been analyzed in relation to how they address fans (see, for example, Kompare 2005, 211; Hills 2007; Hunt 2008, 37–8). The DVD commentary can be considered as a paratextual site aimed both at disciplining audience knowledge, and responding to the fan audience's assumed desire to accumulate detailed information about a text. That is to say, the commentary track is explicitly about, and part of, a TV series' epistemological economy: it interpellates and serves an imagined audience's will-to-know. Commentaries therefore construct cult audiences, and require critical paratextual analysis rather than merely being taken at face value. Steven Moffat, for example, in his contribution to the "Study in Pink" commentary (2010) repeatedly refers to "Sherlock Holmes fanboys" when noting intertextualities in *Sherlock* which cite and rework details from Conan Doyle's work:

> Here's one for the Sherlock Holmes fanboys, and I bet there's a few of you out there listening. The name of this young fellow who's about to go back and collect his umbrella and die is James Phillimore, recorded in the original stories as one of Sherlock Holmes's unsolved cases ... we should quickly mention that, for you Sherlock fanboys out there, note the name on the coffee cup that Martin Freeman has been kind enough to hold by the burny bit of the cup, showing you it's called Criterion ... the two of them in the story, Stamford and Watson, actually met in the Criterion bar ... we wanted to honour that....
>
> Again, for the Sherlock fanboys, I reversed the logic here. In the original ... they find the word "Rache" on the wall and the police assume someone was interrupted while writing "Rachel".... This time round we invert it, she is in fact writing "Rachel" and the police think it's "Rache." So whatever you say with Sherlock Holmes in the room, he'll have the opposite view and he'll definitely be right!

Once again in marked contrast to production discourse, Roberta Pearson has argued that Holmesians typically disavow the label of "fan." She poses the rhetorical question "Sherlockians talk like fans and walk like fans but would they consider themselves fans?" (2007, 105) before noting:

> My knowledge of the Sherlockian worlds leads me to believe that most Sherlockians, like my ... respondents, would reject the label of "fan," even if ... they are fully aware of the cultural hierarchies at play. The terms they prefer — "admirer," "enthusiast," "devotee," "aficionado" ... dissociate them from the excessive affect and hormone-induced behavior connoted by fan [2007, 106–7].

This rejection of "fan" identity also stems from an "implicit hierarchization of the print media over the moving image media" (Pearson 1997, 160n11), although Pearson's observations here (and 2007) are based on a mobilization of personal, situated knowledge rather than a "fully articulated" ethnographic study (1997, 160n11). Nonetheless, it seems reasonable to assume that "fandom" would, at the very least, be a contested identity within Sherlockian culture. Moffat's "Sherlock [Holmes] fanboys" are hence a (re)construction and re-mediation of Holmesian knowledge culture; literary aficionados are reposi-tioned as a branch of media fandom, given that the term "fanboy" is typically linked to film and TV fan audiences. This challenges cultural hierarchies, rendering literary Sherlockians discursively equivalent to TV fandoms such as that for *Doctor Who*, but it also helps sustain a further equivalence — between showrunner and Sherlockian knowledge culture. Rather than recog-nizing the Holmes "aficionado" (as Beryl Vertue does in the making-of DVD extra, *Unlocking Sherlock*), Moffat's specific production discourse desegregates production knowledge and "fanboy" knowledge, objectifying them as one and the same while also gendering fandom — this is very specifically a world of paternalist showrunners and fan*boys*. Such a desegregating process corre-sponds with a significant aspect of contemporary TV production identified by John Thornton Caldwell in *Production Cultures*:

> the need to *desegregate* professional and audience activities ... popularizing for con-sumers ... kinds of self-referencing.... Professional knowledge about ... TV produc-tion now functions as a widespread cultural competence *and* consumer activity.... Production personnel also design productions vis-à-vis the parameters and con-straints of ... viewing environments that they personally know [2008, 333, 336].

Moffat's commentary works to popularize and highlight the ways in which *Sherlock* displays moments of "intertextual (sub)cultural capital" (Hills 2005, 179) by referencing Conan Doyle. The show's parameters are, to an extent, suggested by Moffat and Gatiss' own status as "Sherlock Holmes fan-boys," with this gendered identity being (problematically) extended to those assumed to be listening to the DVD commentary. Fan and producer identities are knowingly represented as mirrored, offering up the "fidelity" dimension of the "heretical fidelity" which structures much of *Sherlock*'s publicly acces-sible production discourse. Time and again it is stressed that the showrunners are carefully faithful to key aspects of the Canon, and via that act, to the pre-sumed expectations and passions of Sherlockian cultures:

> it's borne of a love affair with Sherlock Holmes ... it's also a purist's dream, I would like to think, because it is absolutely threaded with little nods to some of the most obscure stories ... it doesn't hopefully effect in any way your enjoyment if you're a casual viewer, but if you actually know your Sherlock Holmes there are lots of little things which hopefully bring a measure of delight [Gatiss 2010, TGG DVD commentary].

Likewise, Moffat speaks of wanting to "honor" the original stories, and inverting diegetic logic in the process of reworking, but nonetheless preserving the original's relationship between Holmes and the police force. Testifying to fidelity is important for the DVD commentaries and *Unlocking Sherlock*, as this reassures the Holmesian audience that the Canon remains as a sacred Ur-text, and that Gatiss and Moffat's updating emerges through a producer-fan "joy in writing" (Moffat 2010, ASiP DVD commentary) rather than merely as the result of a professional TV commission. This perfected symbolic collision of producer-fan identities occasionally stumbles, as for example when Gatiss misidentifies the source of a Conan Doyle quote in the commentary to "The Great Game," leading him to joke, "Don't worry, because we're going to go back, delete that [collective laughter]." Yet the error stays in, "reinforcing the impression of unmediated access" (Hunt 2008, 38) for DVD commentary audiences, and only momentarily disrupting Gatiss' performance of Holmesian expertise (Hills 2007, 56). Nonetheless, this lapse demonstrates that commentaries cannot be taken only or always as performances of showrunner authority; the subject who-is-supposed-to-know can display fallibility on occasion. Gatiss' error is recuperated as an exception which proves the rule of his Holmesian knowledge, and his fan cultural capital, by Martin Freeman's reparative interjection: "That was from *Study in Scarlet*. That'll be the only time I can correct you on Sherlock Holmes."

As well as desegregating production and fandom (in order to better target-market a text, and reassure an audience knowledge culture which might otherwise vehemently oppose *Sherlock* as textually inauthentic), producers and fans are also discursively segregated at the same time. The distinctions of media professionalism need to be conserved and defended, such that showrunners are always positioned as more than just fans: "These tendencies tend to *segregate* professional practices from audience activities, spotlighting their differences, by continuously redefining and re-valuing the otherwise uncertain futures of creative communities through expressions of professionalism" (Caldwell 2008, 331).

This discursive emphasis on professional, authorial identity is articulated with the "heresy" dimension of "heretical fidelity." Here, rather than being faithful to Holmesian expectations and the Canon, the showrunners position their creative labor as surprising, unexpected, and in violation of typical Sherlockian readings: "we preferred — of all the Sherlock Holmes movies — we liked the updated Basil Rathbone/Nigel Bruce ones best. Which is heresy. But just true" (Moffat 2010, ASiP DVD commentary). Producer "heresy" is important for its very disarticulation of producer-fan readings: *it functions to demarcate the authorial agency and autonomy of Moffat and Gatiss' version of Holmes*, that is, it supports their claims to authorship. If production discourse was one-dimensionally about faithfulness to Sherlockians and the Canon then *Sherlock* would move too close to the realm of fan fiction, lacking markers of professionalized and valorized official authorship. As such, the dual purpose of heretical fidelity is precisely to shore up "real gaps between cult TV fans and 'the powers that be' ... despite the discursive construction of the 'fan-producer'" (Kompare 2011, 111). *Contra* recent work on adaptation which has stressed, if not romanticized, continuities between professional work in the media industry and fanfic (Berger 2010; Marlow 2009), and where non-canonical fan writing can supposedly be folded back into canonical, professional screenwriting, *Sherlock* strongly refutes this concept of a "folding text." Official reboots, updates and reimaginings may tap "into a sensibility that most demonstrates the popularity and pleasure of adaptation in contemporary culture: fan fiction" (Marlow 2009, 52), but they do so while very much holding fanfic at a discursive and symbolic distance. A repeated trope in *Sherlock*'s showrunner commentaries is hence the notion of "blowing away the fog" of prior Holmes adaptations — hansom cabs, diegetic fog for period atmosphere, costume drama — and of producing a version that is "not about the trappings" (Gatiss 2010, Unlocking; Gatiss 2010, TGG DVD commentary). This distances the showrunners from slavish pastiche or imitation, and from merely reiterating a mythic Holmes celebrated by Sherlockians (Pearson 1997). At the same time, it further emphasizes authorial agency by distancing Moffat and Gatiss from the crowded field of other versions of Holmes:

> It's actually a reference [how we first encounter the character of Sherlock] ... this is one of the joys for us for doing this idea, as Steve said might sound heretical to dyed-in-the-blood addicts, is actually there are so many parts of the famous stories that have actually hardly ever been touched, sometimes like [Holmes's introduction thrashing corpses with a riding crop to determine the extent of bruising after death], never at all [Gatiss 2010, ASiP DVD commentary].

This captures the tensions of heretical fidelity perfectly; in the same "moment of television" (Kompare 2011), Mark Gatiss both acknowledges that creative decisions may be "heretical" to Sherlockians, but suggests that those self-same decisions can also display fidelity to Conan Doyle by highlighting the limitations, and textual inauthenticities, of previous adaptations. Television authorship is discursively produced as a matter of creative autonomy: fan expectations are disregarded, as are prior versions of Holmes, but fidelity to "the famous stories" is preserved. This positioning implicitly devalues types of fan activity, for example, transformative fan work and fanfic seemingly viewed as derivative, in favor of producers' alleged "heresy." Similarly, the portrayal of Sherlock himself as a validation of TV fan exegesis specifically values affirmational fan knowledge rather than fans' transformative work; there is a tacit hierarchy of (un)acceptable fan practices threaded through the textual and discursive moves of *Sherlock*.

Perhaps unsurprisingly, ideological faultlines fracturing heretical fidelity repeatedly threaten to surface in showrunner talk:

I think arguably, and we would argue quite strongly ... the detective stories are merely the surface, it's the story of the greatest friendship ever ... I find the joy in writing this is writing that friendship. ... It's subtext, but it really is right at the top level of the subtext, it's just about those two men and the fact they adore each other [Moffat 2010, ASiP DVD commentary].

Moffat and Gatiss' reading of the Canon has to be argued for "quite strongly," insofar as their authorial agency is again stressed. But any such "heresy" is immediately re-contained via a contradictory, awkward recourse to "fidelity"; they may be in the realm of subtextual and so highly contested engagement with the original Holmes, but "it really is right at the top level of the subtext." Hence these showrunners are seemingly in a perfect win-win position in relation to fan knowledge; their authorial agency can be secured via (implied or imagined) arguments with Sherlockian culture, but at the exact same time they are supposedly being objectively true to Conan Doyle. Heresy equals promoting an arguable subtext; fidelity equals the notion that it's "right at the top level of subtext."

The tensions of heretical fidelity produce a scenario where "everything was canonical ... every version, we're not just drawing on the stories but the Rathbone films, Jeremy Brett" (Gatiss 2010, ASiP DVD commentary). Yet some prior texts, for example, Conan Doyle's, evidently remain more canonical than others. In order to discursively secure their status as professional, autonomous creatives, these showrunners are required to (re)segregate production and "fandom," symbolically distancing themselves from certain Sherlockian readings and from Holmes pastiches (fixated on the "fog" of "trappings"). These accumulations and accretions of a mythic Holmes (Knight 1980, 104–5) are implicitly linked, I would say, to fanfic construed as overly reverential, but they are also explicitly linked to a range of prior adaptations. Heretical fidelity responds intertextually not just to the Canon, but to a plethora of different Holmes, whether Rathbone or Brett. Needing to clear away rival images of the character, *Sherlock* enters not only intertextual but also transmedia relations with literature, film, and other TV versions. However, as Roberta Pearson reminds us:

Fully kitted-out, narrativized virtual worlds such as *Star Trek*, *The Lord of the Rings*, and Sherlock Holmes seem to produce the widest range of commodities, but there's a distinction even here between copyrights vested in a single media franchise and those not; as a result, the first two examples give rise to more centralized production of commodities than the third [2007, 105].

Unlike the franchises of *Trek* and Moffat's *Doctor Who*, whose transmedia narratives generally cohere as part of designed, corporately-owned world-building across media platforms, the narrative world of Sherlock Holmes is fractured and fragmented across parallel versions — less a folding or unfolding text than a torn text. As such, Henry Jenkins' (2006) observations on transmedia storytelling call for some revisions here. Yes, *Sherlock* has a set of tie-in web sites, complete with mysteries for audiences to work out (www.thescienceofdeduction.co.uk) and even an "official" fan message board for Connie Prince (www.connieprince.co.uk), but as a transmedia story *Sherlock* nonetheless operates in relation to *rival versions across media* as much as it operates in relation to its own satellite texts. This may provide one explanation for the relative lack of emphasis on transmedia storytelling employed by *Sherlock*: rather than seeking to extend itself across multiplatformed iterations, the show is (inter)textually and extra-textually engaged in warding off rival Sherlock Holmes franchises.

Jenkins' focus is very much on singular narrative worlds (2006, 114) and transmedia points of entry into singular franchises (2006, 95–6); we might say that his work deals with one version of this process, that is, *de jure* transmedia where franchises are rationalized and consistently developed as unified, multi-platformed story worlds. Working very differently, the likes of *Sherlock* might be thought of as *de facto* transmedia where there is no guiding (corporate) hand compelling any unity across media and across narrative iterations, precisely because there is no singular franchise, but rather a network of intertextualities — some disavowed, others privileged — which contingently coalesce into the reinventions and extensions of cultural myth. In this case, even what can be counted as "text" and "paratext" is potentially destabilized; Holmesians might read *Sherlock*'s episodes as "paratexts to the [original] books' text" (Gray 2010, 125), whereas other audiences may render the TV series as "text" and Conan Doyle's stories as an optional paratext circulating around the Cumberbatch and Freeman realisations of Sherlock/John. Still others may read the Robert Downey Junior version of *Sherlock Holmes* as text, with *Sherlock* falling paratextually under its shadow. Textual pathways through *de facto* transmedia are far more plural and decentered than the possibilities offered by *de jure* transmedia, with its legally-bound authenticities of rights-owning franchise maintenance. And fandoms can be even more plural and multiple with regards to *de facto* transmedia: *Sherlock* may well have inspired its own cult following, but as a "cultural attractor" it will also play host to variant cult audiences possessing developed Sherlockian knowledge, for example, fans of other versions of the character beyond the Canon, as well as fans of other (historically) cult TV, for example, *Doctor Who*. Hence the need for production discourse, in the form of heretical fidelity, to declare every version of Holmes canonical so as not to alienate fans of other iterations of the myth. And hence also the overdetermined diegetic requirement to recognize fan knowledge ("gossip") only via a fictional coding (Connie Prince fandom) which is able to imply acceptance of divergent real-world fandoms, whether those surrounding Canon, Cumberbatch, or cult TV.

The "epistemological economy" that I have identified as acting diegetically — *Sherlock*'s networked relationships of knowledge where the individual detective-as-genius nonetheless has to rely on social networks of friendship (John most especially) as well as perfected media systems, signals and databases — stands in for, and incites, the variety of knowledge cultures that the series has drawn together as a cultural attractor/activator. This is more than a narrative of investigation inciting mimetic investigation among fans and scholar-fans (Hastie 2007), although it is this. In addition, *Sherlock* textually and diegetically recodes the conditions of contemporary fandom by representing the great detective as a magnifier of fans' "collective intelligence" (Jenkins 2006, 4). As Moffat asserts, this Sherlock was "made to haunt Internet forums. I'm sure he's gone on all those forums looking for traces of Moriarty." A connotative media fan — though certainly not denotatively so — the reversioning of Sherlock Holmes constitutes an "obscured" aesthetic invitation (Ross 2008, 8–9) to the speculations of multiple fandoms and aficionados. Stephen Knight has argued that

> an effective illusion allows the average reader contact with the hero's method [in Conan Doyle's work]. The contexts of medical science, the chemistry and the exhaustive knowledge of crime are only gestured at, and we are actually shown no more than a special rational process. This is, of course, closer to the powers of the mass audience, and so makes the detective more accessible in his heroism [1980, 86].

Sherlock also enacts this illusion — this reduction of expert knowledge in favor of a "special rational process" — but it goes further by constructing coded parallels between Sherlock's "accessible ... heroism" and networked fan activities/sociality (Booth 2010). Rather than simply finding a digital analogue for 19th century rationalism, *Sherlock* ideologically and narratively validates the practices of online fandom, but only up to a point. This incarnation of Sherlock may enact a form of connotative "forensic fandom" (Mittell 2009, 128), poring obsessively over data, looking for clues, and assembling evidence. However, given the need for John's humanizing guidance, this Sherlock nonetheless does so without displaying any analogue of fan affect. If he stands in for fandom's "collective intelligence," then it is as a specifically disciplined model of fandom — one that is intellectually rather than passionately engaged. The series validates gendered fan*boy* knowledge, but at the expense of implicitly disciplining and devaluing fan passion/affect.

Desegregation extends to the extra-diegetic discourse of heretical fidelity that also symbolically links showrunners (rather than Holmes) to "fanboys." But, again, the construction of such fidelities remains true only up to a point, for *Sherlock* is also premised (extra-)textually on segregating ordinary fandom from extraordinary discourses of showrunners' "heretical" creative autonomy and authorship. The great game of fandom played via the production discourses of Gatiss and Moffat remains, finally, in the service of professional, authorial distinctions, while textually-disciplined codings of affectively flat fandom imply that fan passions should be kept under masculinized control.

Work Cited

Armitt, Lucie. 2011. *Twentieth-century gothic*. Cardiff: University of Wales Press.

Atkinson, Michael. 1998. *The secret marriage of Sherlock Holmes and other eccentric readings*. Ann Arbor: University of Michigan Press.

Berger, Richard. 2010. Screwing aliens and screwing with aliens: *Torchwood* slashes the doctor. In *Illuminating* Torchwood: *Essays on narrative, character and sexuality in the BBC series*, ed. Andrew Ireland, 66–75. Jefferson, N.C.: McFarland.

Booth, Paul. 2010. *Digital fandom: New media studies*. New York: Peter Lang.

Caldwell, John Thornton. 2008. *Production culture: Industrial reflexivity and critical practice in film and television*. Durham: Duke University Press.

Gray, Jonathan. 2010. *Show sold separately: Promos, spoilers and other media paratexts*. New York: New York University Press.

Hastie, Amelie. 2007. The epistemological stakes of *Buffy the Vampire Slayer*: Television criticism and marketing demands. In *Undead TV: Essays on* Buffy the Vampire Slayer, ed. Elana Levine and Lisa Parks, 74–95. Durham: Duke University Press.

Hills, Matt. 2002. *Fan cultures*. London: Routledge.

_____. 2005. *The pleasures of horror*. London: Continuum.

_____. 2007. From the box in the corner to the box set on the shelf: "TVIII" and the cultural/textual valorisations of DVD. *New Review of Film and TV Studies* 5: 41–60.

_____. 2010. *Triumph of a Time lord: Regenerating* Doctor Who *in the twenty-first century*. London: I.B. Tauris.

Hunt, Leon. 2008. *BFI TV Classics: The League of Gentlemen*. Basingstoke: Palgrave Macmillan.

Jenkins, Henry. 2006. *Convergence culture: Where old and new media collide*. New York: New York University Press.

Knight, Stephen. 1980. *Form & ideology in crime fiction*. London: Macmillan.

Kompare, Derek. 2005. *Rerun nation*. London: Routledge.

_____. 2011. More "moments of television": Online cult television authorship. In *Flow TV: Television in the age of media convergence*, ed. Michael Kackman et al., 95–113. New York: Routledge.

Marlow, Christopher. 2009. The folding text: *Doctor Who*, adaptation and fan fiction. In *Adaptation in Contemporary Culture*, ed. Rachel Carroll, 46–57. London: Continuum.

Mittell, Jason. 2009. *Lost* in a great story: Evaluation in narrative television (and television studies). In *Reading* Lost, ed. Roberta Pearson, 119–38. London: I.B. Tauris.

Moretti, Franco. 1988. *Signs taken for wonders*. London: Verso.

Pearson, Roberta. 1997. It's always 1895: Sherlock Holmes in cyberspace. In *Trash aesthetics*, ed. Deborah Cartmell, I.Q. Hunter, Heidi Kaye, and Imelda Whelehan, 143–61. London: Pluto Press.

_____. 2007. Bachies, Bardies, Trekkies and Sherlockians. In *Fandom: Identities and communities in a mediated world*, ed. Jonathan Gray, Cornel Sandvoss, and C. Lee Harrington, 99–109. New York: New York University Press.

Ridgway Watt, Peter and Joseph Green. 2003. *The alternative Sherlock Holmes*. Surrey: Ashgate.

Ross, Sharon Marie. 2008. *Beyond the box: Television and the internet*. Oxford: Blackwell.

Winning "The Grand Game"

Sherlock *and the Fragmentation of Fan Discourse*

ASHLEY D. POLASEK

Abstract — For a century, the Sherlock Holmes fan community has engaged in an elaborate fantasy called "The Grand Game" which envisions Holmes and Watson as real people and the 60 Holmes stories as historical records. Through pastiche and pseudo-scholarship, "The Game" has informed the majority of fan discourse. However, The Game encourages fans to be suspicious of adaptations as it situates them as fictionalizations that, to varying degrees, misrepresent the "truth." Through contextual modernization, *Sherlock* has transcended this model and inspired new modes of fan discourse. With every new adaptation produced, the web of intertexts becomes more complex and contributes further to the conception of Sherlock Holmes as an amalgamation of visual cues, catch phrases, and Victorian trappings. The creators of *Sherlock* reject this conception, instead linking the show to the web of intertexts through an open acknowledgment of both the "Canon" and every previous adaptation as an influence on their work, challenging the fidelity fixation of The Grand Game. The fresh avenues of engagement that *Sherlock* offers to fan writers becomes apparent through a statistical analysis of all of the Sherlock Holmes-related material archived on the Internet's most active fan fiction web site, fanfiction.net. *Sherlock* is the inspiration for over half of all the pieces, and for well over two thirds of those based specifically on adaptations. Although this is certainly partly due to the overlap between the demographics of the site and the series — largely young people in both cases — it is also because the show is different enough from Conan Doyle's work to present themes for exploration that pastiche and Canonical fan fiction cannot, and offers an opportunity for writers to call upon their own experiences and historico-cultural contexts to engage with the characters.

Introduction

Sherlock is unique among the hundreds of adaptations of Sherlock Holmes because it has caused a fragmentation in the traditional fan discourse.

41

It has found acclaim both with new fans who are unfamiliar with the work of Sir Arthur Conan Doyle and with the most dedicated members of the established Sherlockian community who have largely guided the fan discourse for over a century. It is to these dedicated fans, the controllers of their unifying fan narrative, which is governed by an elaborate fantasy called "The Grand Game," that I refer throughout this essay when I use the term Sherlockian. Though they do not represent the largest portion of the fan community, they may be considered the authors and arbiters of the rules that generally outline the boundaries of "The Game."

This essay will be grappling with the tenets of The Grand Game and how it informs Sherlock Holmes fan discourse; in particular, I wish to turn attention to its negative influence on how Sherlockians perceive adaptations. I will look specifically at how *Sherlock* has broken this trend by loosening the rules of The Game and, in so doing, inspired new and different modes of fan discourse.

In section one I will analyze the traditional mode of Sherlock Holmes fan discourse known as The Grand Game and its effect on the reception of adaptations, including how *Sherlock* has transcended The Game. In section two I will address how Sherlockians engage with the intertextual nature of Sherlock Holmes and *Sherlock*'s place within the intertextual conversation. In section three I will offer an examination of *Sherlock*'s influence on the trend of Sherlock Holmes fan writing including a detailed study of the web site fanfiction.net and interviews with writers of *Sherlock* fan fiction.

Learning the Rules: Sherlock *and the Nature of "The Grand Game"*

The tradition of Sherlockian fan writing is older than many of the Sherlock Holmes stories penned by Sir Arthur Conan Doyle. Despite the often whimsical nature of the discourse, it tends to follow quite strict rules, which are enforced through a system of praise and censure within the fan community. Sherlockians engage in a complex fantasy called The Grand Game or simply The Game, in which Sherlock Holmes and Dr. Watson are envisioned as real historical figures and the 60 stories that comprise the Sherlock Holmes "Canon" are considered genuine records of their exploits, written by Watson. This fantasy necessarily relegates Sir Arthur Conan Doyle to a supplementary position and within the context of The Game, he is referred to as The Literary Agent.

It is worth briefly addressing the several connotations of the terms *Canon* and *game*. Canon is the term preferred by fans to describe the 60 Sherlock

Holmes stories written by Conan Doyle, particularly in reference to The Game. As The Game was originated by a priest and established to follow the basic formula of theological textual interrogation, the application of the word Canon is deliberate and significant. It not only situates the stories as works that are more than mere entertainment, works that can and should be analyzed, but it elevates them as well. It suggests that those who study them do so with a religious dedication and that the texts are treated with veneration. The word *game* defines an undertaking, the foremost purpose of which is entertainment. It also implies rules and boundaries that define acceptable behavior within the game's established context; one cannot play a game without knowing and abiding by its rules. These dual meanings are important to understanding The Grand Game as played by Sherlockians: it is certainly a form of play for fans of Sherlock Holmes; it involves literary and historical puzzles and a joyful engagement with much beloved characters. Sit in on a discussion with Sherlockians, and this sense of playful fun is immediately apparent. However, the rules are equally as vital and it is to an analysis of the nature and implications of these rules and their bearing upon fan engagement with *Sherlock* that I wish to turn in this essay.

The Game dates its origin one century ago, to Monsignor Ronald Knox's satirical essay "Studies in the Literature of Sherlock Holmes," first delivered at Trinity College, Oxford, in 1911. In the past hundred years, societies of Sherlockians around the world have sprung up and through them The Game has become thoroughly entrenched. Michael Whelan, the current head of the most exclusive Sherlock Holmes society in the world, the Baker Street Irregulars, rightly identifies it as "a literary phenomenon," inspiring thousands of essays (King and Klinger 2011, i). The continued relevance of this mode of discourse in the fan community is corroborated by the 2011 publication of a two volume anthology of Sherlockian pseudo-scholarship, itself titled *The Grand Game*. The Game has become inextricably linked to fan engagement with Sherlock Holmes, and thus has largely come to define Sherlockian fan discourse.

The Grand Game is played out by Sherlockians primarily through two types of fan writing: pastiche and pseudo-scholarship. The structure of the Holmes stories easily lends the franchise to pastiche. Conan Doyle's stories frequently made mention of "unpublished cases" and authors as diverse as Isaac Asimov, Neil Gaiman, Stephen King, and even Mark Twain, among hundreds of others, have produced Sherlock Holmes pastiche. It is common practice to adopt Conan Doyle's style, using Watson as the narrator and imitating the voice of the character to tell the story. Often, authors of Holmes pastiche will play into the fiction entirely, placing themselves in the role of editor rather than author of the text, and including a preface in which they recount how they happened upon this "previously unpublished" manuscript of Dr. Watson. Pseudo-scholarship is also produced in abundance in the Sherlockian community. Taking their cue from Knox, fans publish essays that attempt to reconcile inconsistencies within the original stories. The Game is the cornerstone of these essays, and manifests itself as aficionados, familiar with the Canon down to the last detail, seek to generate a single cohesive narrative that slots flawlessly into historical reality.

The Grand Game has a fascinating, though underexplored influence on how fans interpret and engage with adaptations of Sherlock Holmes. The Game certainly offers Sherlockians an outlet for transformative engagement, imagining, for example, that Watson or Holmes were women, that Moriarty was a drug-induced hallucination, or that Holmes fathered a child with Irene Adler. However, possibly as a result of The Game predating the Internet's massive influence on the scope and complexity of fan discourse, there is a strong affirmational tradition within the Sherlock Holmes fan community. Like many fandoms, it has established itself as the unofficial protector and guardian of the integrity of the texts. Fidelity is a complex issue in the field of adaptation studies, addressing the fundamental tension between an adaptation's subordinate position as a derivative work and its primacy established through the original qualities unique to its medium. Despite these complexities, fidelity is often the most important gauge of quality to a fan. Though fans often take texts in hand and stretch or alter them through fan fiction and other outlets, there is a general sense that an adaptation ought to bring the written characters to life, that, for example the movie should be like the book.

As a result of The Game, Sherlockians have an even more complicated relationship with the fidelity of adaptations than does the average critical fandom. According to Timothy Corrigan, "fidelity supposedly indicates a quantitative and qualitative measure of accuracy in how, for instance, descriptions of settings, the nuances of dialogue and characters, or the complexity of themes are moved from page to screen" (2002, 160). He rightly identifies this as an "impossible measure" as a result of the inherent differences between written and visual texts. Fidelity is further complicated by the manner in which Sherlockians engage with those settings, nuances of dialogue, characters, and themes. The conceit of The Game recasts Conan Doyle's written characters as real people; in this context, adaptations may be considered fictionalizations of historical events rather than a transfer of one fictional representation to another. The characters must be played by actors, the sets and costumes must be chosen and the words interpreted through directors, screenwriters, set dressers, and costume designers. Within the context of The Game, the final product, if successful, is more akin to a documentary or a re-enactment than to a traditional adaptation.

Conceptualizing the incarnation of beloved characters on screen as an act of fictionalization is largely a result of the specific transition from page to screen. In *Textual Poachers*, Henry Jenkins points out that "[texts] assume increased significance as they are fragmented and reworked to accommodate the particular interests of the individual" (1992, 51). The Sherlockian community does continuously fragment and rework the source text through pastiche and pseudo-scholarship; in such play rests the joy of The Game. Pastiche and pseudo-scholarship is distinguished from the Canon, though; through the lens of The Game, these texts are "a-historical." Adaptations should fall into this category as well, as they are technically derivative of Conan Doyle. The difficulty, however, lays in the adaptations' claim to primacy in their medium; they don't situate themselves as subordinate to the Canon. Robert Stam describes this view, opining instances when "the inter-art relation is seen as a Darwinian struggle to the death rather than a dialogue offering mutual benefit and cross-fertilization. Adaptation becomes a zero-sum game where film is perceived as the upstart enemy storming the ramparts of literature" (2005, 4).

This perception of the battle between source and adaptation was vocalized by Nicholas Meyer, himself an author of Holmes pastiche and the scriptwriter for the adaptation of his Sherlock Holmes novel *The Seven-Per-Cent Solution* (1974), in a keynote address at a Sherlock Holmes symposium in the early nineties. He noted that where Holmes adaptations are concerned, he has "never met a Sherlock Holmes movie [he] didn't dislike" mostly as a result of "the hideous capacity for film to ... inevitably get it wrong" (1996). The idea of "getting it wrong" springs from what is best termed an act of libel against fiction: a process by which fictional characters are seen by fans to be grievously misrepresented on screen. As a legally actionable act of defamation, libel cannot, of course, be perpetrated against a fictional character, but the boundaries between fiction and reality have become so blurred through the implementation of The Grand Game that though libel against Holmes and Watson may not be actionable in courts of justice, it is certainly an offense recognized in the courts of fandom. Rarely does a Sherlock Holmes adaptation appear that does not cause some fans to bemoan, for one reason or another, that the screenwriter, director, and/or actors were not familiar enough with the literary source, that if only the Canon had been consulted more often and more assiduously, the adaptation would not have contained so many errors or committed so many violations. The result is that instead of being judged on their inherent quality, adaptations are put on trial and often found guilty of criminal infraction against the Canon, regardless of how entertaining or insightful they may be.

Where adaptation is concerned, The Grand Game is a not merely the happy fantasy that Sherlockians generally perceive it to be. Its very nature predisposes fans to be suspicious of each new incarnation of their heroes, to which suspicions the speculation and fervor preceding the release of both Warner Bros.' big screen release *Sherlock Holmes* (2009) and BBC's *Sherlock* (2010) testify. *Sherlock* is a unique product for many reasons, but as regards the fan community, foremost among those reasons is its resistance to integration with The Game. The modernization of the text has created a world that is different enough from Conan Doyle to have passed beyond the realm of those reconcilable inconsistencies upon which The Game thrives. Unlike period adaptations, it cannot be envisioned as a re-enactment of historical events or the portrayal of historical figures. The show, in effect, needs no elaborate fantasy to reconcile the fictional and non-fictional elements of the source; it supersedes rather than integrates the source and therefore there is nothing to reconcile.

The omnipresent issue of fiction libel does not apply in the case of *Sherlock*. The show has effectively rewritten the "historical" Sherlock Holmes out of history; it therefore cannot be conceived as a representation of that history. Benedict Cumberbatch is not portraying Conan Doyle's or even, as The Game would have it, Dr. Watson's Sherlock Holmes, because in the context of the show that Sherlock Holmes necessarily cannot exist. Because it has written its own antecedent out of existence, viewers are obliged to engage with *Sherlock* as though it were a primary text. This does not mean that viewers don't recognize and appreciate that the series is an adaptation, but rather that it functions on a level equal to its source instead of as subordinate to it. The consequence of *Sherlock*'s innocence on the charge of fiction libel is a positive response from even the most discerning fans. *Sherlock* wins favor among Sherlockians because it has broken the rules of the game.

Playing the Game: Sherlock *and the Web of Intertexts*

Within the realm of adaptation studies, intertextuality is often considered to begin with the dynamic and multidirectional relationship between the source text and the adaptation. The act of interpreting a text affects future readings of that text; therefore, creating an onscreen interpretation not only involves an action of the source on the film, but also an action of the film on the source. When a franchise such as Sherlock Holmes involves the production of hundreds of unique adaptations of a single source, each one is an intertext, being acted on and acting upon both by the source as well as every other adaptation.

In his discussion of intertextuality in *Uncommon Cultures*, Jim Collins distils the term into two common interpretations: first, "it has been used to describe a free-floating intersubjective body of knowledge" and second, "it has been used to examine the explicit presence of other texts within a given work by focusing on the processes of citation, reference, etc." (1989, 44). Both definitions can be liberally applied to the body of Sherlock Holmes adaptations. Film is almost entirely responsible for the look and feel of Sherlock Holmes; the details of costume and setting have been constructed over the course of many incarnations and reinforced through repetition. It takes merely the vaguest silhouette of a man wearing a deerstalker hat and smoking a pipe to call the detective to mind and even those with no experience of Conan Doyle's stories or any adaptation at all have a subjective notion of the character and its context. As to the latter definition, the search for references within adaptations to elements of the Canon and to elements of other adaptations could be an endless pursuit, from the assimilation of a scene written for 20th Century–Fox's 1939 *The Hound of the Baskervilles* into the script of a version of the same story made in 2002, to the precise replication of the camera's track down Baker Street, lifted from the opening credits of Granada's television series and deposited wholesale into *Sherlock Holmes* (2009).

The "free-floating intersubjective body of knowledge" of Collins' first definition of intertextuality could easily be labeled "the idea of Sherlock Holmes." It involves a culturally invented collection of visual cues, catch phrases, and period referents that bares very little resemblance to Conan Doyle's character, and as such is often a source of frustration to Sherlockians. They never tire of reiterating that in the Canon, Sherlock Holmes was never said to wear a deerstalker, never said to smoke a calabash pipe, and never said to intone the words "elementary, my dear Watson." Mark Gatiss and Stephen Moffat have eschewed this "idea of Sherlock Holmes" and, as Gatiss says, made "an attempt to get back to the very essence ... and not [make it] about the trappings" (2010, TGG DVD commentary). They chose not to have Sherlock smoke a pipe and wear a deerstalker and the act of modernization itself eliminates the Victorian world of "pea-soupers," gas lamps, and steam trains. To Sherlockians, *Sherlock*'s rejection of these omnipresent Holmes referents appears to be a show of solidarity and an acknowledgment of the supremacy of the source text, though Moffat and Gatiss would almost certainly not view it this way. Regardless of the reasons, the rejection of these referents has led dedicated Sherlockians to argue that *Sherlock* "is in many ways truer to the spirit and heart of the original Canon than other recent adaptations" (Takenaka 2010, 20–21).

Sherlockians have a complex relationship with the intertextual conversation. They often judge the merit of an adaptation by the second of Collins' definitions, reveling in the search for Canonical references. Because The Game suggests that adaptations should be viewed as representations of a reality, the more they reference the Canon, the less likely they are to be libelous. It would be grossly inaccurate to suggest that Sherlockians are incapable of enjoying or appreciating any Sherlock Holmes adaptations. It is likely that most fans of Conan Doyle have a favorite incarnation of the character on screen. Interestingly, that favor often falls upon the actors who valued Canonical fidelity such as Jeremy Brett, who was famed for carrying a copy of the original stories on set and to script meetings, and Peter Cushing, who was himself a great fan of Conan Doyle and stated in his film studio biography that "the stories should be treated in traditional fashion, true to the spirit of Conan Doyle's original works" (Cushing, n.d.). Both actors insisted that their productions include as many direct and indirect references to the Canon as possible.

The cross-pollination of references from adaptations back into fan discourse is not as well received by Sherlockians. At the 2011 annual meeting of the Sherlock Holmes Society of London, crime fiction author and screenwriter Anthony Horowitz announced the upcoming publication of his own Sherlock Holmes novel. His speech underscored the tendency of the Sherlockian community to view adaptations as subordinate constituents of the intertextual conversation. He opened his speech by noting that his "notion of Sherlock Holmes is ... not escaping from circular saws or leaping into the River Thames; [he]'ll leave that to Robert Downey Jr." By insinuating that the Sherlock Holmes of the screen is not "the proper" Sherlock Holmes and should not be consulted as a source for interpreting the character, Horowitz could be confident that he would not break the most important rule that he'd developed for writing Sherlock Holmes pastiche: "try not to annoy the Sherlock Holmes Society of London."

Sherlock plays gleefully with both Canonical references and with references to adaptational intertexts. Mark Gatiss calls the show a "purist's dream" because it is "threaded with little nods to some of the most obscure stories ... if you actually know your Sherlock Holmes, there are lots of little things which hopefully bring a measure of delight" (2010 TGG DVD commentary). These references have delighted those that Gatiss and Moffat lovingly call "Sherlock fanboys." The show does not end its intertextual references with the Canon, however. In his commentary for the first episode of the series, Moffat states that they "decided early on that everything was Canonical, every version; we're not just drawing on the stories, but the Rathbone films and Jeremy Brett" (2010, ASiP DVD commentary). At a glance, this seems like fan-heresy, but it has not caused an uproar among Sherlockians the way that such a statement would have had it been used by Anthony Horowitz in describing his pastiche. This is likely because *Sherlock*'s context is so different from the traditional notion of Conan Doyle's Holmes and the countless Victorian incarnations on screen that the inherent fear of Sherlockians that an adaptation should displace or alter "the real" Sherlock Holmes is largely put to rest.

The creators' conscious elevation of *Sherlock* within the web of inter-texts — treating, as they do, all versions as equally worthy of reference and reverence — is the most powerful tool the series has for loosening the rules of The Game. Despite an abundance of Canonical references and episodes that are clearly adapted from specific stories, the show is also an original property. Because *Sherlock* does not have to submit itself to the same type of scrutiny The Game often places on adaptations, the series is able to offer a wider scope for unencumbered and much broader fan discourse.

Breaking the Rules: Sherlock *and the Tradition of Fan Writing*

The Grand Game provides the mode of engagement for traditional writ-ten fan discourse in the Sherlock Holmes fan community. It lends itself to pastiche, which has been the normative form of fan writing for over a century. The term *pastiche* describes a work that imitates another's style and may also incorporate parody. It is used by Sherlockians to describe their fan writing, as they seek to imitate the style of Conan Doyle, or what they would call, in the spirit of The Game, the Watsonian style. Pastiche is directly related to fan fiction, though their definitions do differ in two significant ways. Fan fic-tion is defined by the status of its author as an amateur rather than a profes-sional, which is not the case with pastiche. Like pastiche, fan fiction is based on existing characters; however, fan fiction is not restricted to an imitative style. Although the community of authors and readers, like the Sherlockian community, does direct the course of fan fiction through praise and censure, the rules are less strict and, importantly, authors of fanfic are free to engage with the texts they enjoy without adopting the style or tone of the source.

The differences between pastiche and fan fiction have generated tension within the Sherlockian community; because Sherlock Holmes fan writing considerably predates the Internet, the established fan community has a rep-utation for mistrusting online media. Before the Internet, authors had limited options for disseminating their work and traditional publishing methods have acted in a sense as quality control for pastiche. Various Sherlock Holmes fan journals provide outlets for fan-authored short stories; as submissions are cri-tiqued by other fans, these stories almost always conform to The Grand Game. Large publishing houses occasionally publish Sherlock Holmes books, banking on Holmes as a safe property with inbuilt demand. As the fan base is the core of the target audience, efforts are generally made not to alienate them, as Anthony Horowitz's rule attests. Ambitious Sherlockians may also seek to publish through Gasogene Press, an imprint of Wessex Books, which produces only Sherlock Holmes publications; though as the publishing house specializes as much in Sherlockian pseudo-scholarship as in Sherlockian pastiche, it is also heavily enmeshed in The Grand Game.

Fan fiction lacks the regulatory mechanisms that pastiche has enjoyed. Though vanity publishing has long been available, it was largely cost prohibitive until the birth of print on demand services that evolved as a natural consequence of digital publishing. Even print on demand requires certain financial and time commitments to one's work, however, and is thus a poor platform for the much shorter "one-offs" and "drabbles" that fill the archives of online fan fiction repositories. It is on these web sites, then, that amateur authors are able to give free reign to their imaginations with no financial outlay and little to no direct censure from the established fan community for taking liberties with the source material.

It is useful to employ some statistical analysis to understand the impact of *Sherlock* on Sherlock Holmes fan writing. It is certainly true that because traditional Sherlockian discourse has largely eschewed online publication, comparing Canonical fanfics to *Sherlock* fanfics must be accepted as evidence but not proof of this impact. It is also true that a generational gap is evident, with younger fans enormously more in evidence in online forums. It is nonetheless a useful analysis to undertake because it attests to *Sherlock*'s exceptional nature specifically among adaptations of Sherlock Holmes.

The largest and most popular archive of fan fiction on the Internet is fanfiction.net, which was founded in October of 1998. The first Sherlock Holmes fic to appear on the site was published almost exactly two years later, on October 22, 2000. The web site categorizes works first by the medium of the source text, then within that category offers a list of the sources that users have cited as the inspiration for their fics. The web site lists six sources in four categories that relate to Sherlock Holmes. Within the main category of "books," there is a section titled "Sherlock Holmes" which is the oldest and, until very recently, the largest repository of Holmes fan fiction on the site. As of, August 12, 2011, it lists 2,626 searchable published works; these account for 34.51 percent of Sherlock Holmes-related works in all the categories. There is also a small section for fan fiction based on Laurie R. King's popular Sherlockian novels, comprising just under 1 percent of total Holmes-related fan fiction on the site. There is one cartoon series, the 26 episode *Sherlock Holmes in the 22nd Century*, which aired between 1999 and 2001. With nearly 100 fanfics, the show has inspired just over 1 percent of the total number of Holmes fics on the site. There are only two Holmes-related sources under the "movies" category. This is perhaps surprising considering that hundreds of Sherlock Holmes films have been made. There are 319 works (4.19 percent of the total) inspired by the Disney film *The Great Mouse Detective* (1986), which is a loose appropriation of Sherlock Holmes, and 956 (12.56 percent) inspired by the 2009 Hollywood blockbuster, *Sherlock Holmes.* The final source is in the category of "TV": BBC's *Sherlock.* Despite being the most recent source to appear on fanfiction.net, first appearing following the show's premier in July of 2010, it has inspired an overwhelming 3,553 pieces — nearly a full half of all fan fiction related to Sherlock Holmes on the web site.

In light of these statistics, it would be difficult to deny that *Sherlock* has struck a chord with fans and is playing a major role in determining the current direction of Sherlock Holmes fan discourse. As further evidence of *Sherlock's* popularity and influence, it should be noted that hidden within the 2,626 fanfics labeled "Books: Sherlock Holmes" there are stories that claim other screen adaptations as their inspiration. According to the authors' summaries, 34 of the works were inspired by the 1984–95 series produced by Granada staring Jeremy Brett, four each were inspired by the modernized Basil Rathbone films produced between 1942 and 1946, and 1985's *Young Sherlock Holmes,* and one each claim to be based on *Sherlock Holmes: The Golden Years* (1992), *The Hound of the Baskervilles* (2002), *Sir Arthur Conan Doyle's Sherlock Holmes* (1968), *Sherlock Holmes* (1953), and *Without a Clue* (1988). If these statistics are further distilled and only works inspired by screen adaptations are taken into account, *Sherlock* leaps to an astonishing 71.58 percent of the 4,964 fanfics based on film and television sources. The online fan fiction community has been exempting its written discourse from The Game for over a decade, but no adaptation has become a primary source in its own right to anywhere near the degree that *Sherlock* has.

The authors of the fan fiction themselves seem best suited to define the qualities that make *Sherlock* the text that has inspired this influx of fans eager to engage in a different mode of discourse; several regular members of the online Sherlock Holmes forum holmesian.net were willing to discuss their motivations for writing. The forum is a community of fans drawn from across the globe and consists of both traditional fans who venerate Conan Doyle's stories and non-traditional fans who engage more, and occasionally exclusively, with adaptations.

Part of *Sherlock's* unique appeal is that it provides an outlet for Holmes fans who wish to write yet don't feel themselves capable or willing to write for any other incarnation of the character. According to fanfic author Zetared, it is "monumentally difficult to capture the right 'voice' for Canon! Holmes." She is clearly directly or indirectly influenced by The Game, as she claims that she "cannot write in the proper 'Watson' voice, nor [does she] feel like the Canon is properly captured in the third person" (February 15, 2011; www.holmesian.net). This need to imitate style makes her reluctant to turn to pastiche, which shows again how The Game has narrowed fan discourse into a single model. However, the less rigid structure of fan fiction paired with *Sherlock*'s unique ability to transcend The Game is allowing Holmes fan writers to work outside this model.

It is not only of interest to consider how fans may be attracted to writing *Sherlock* fics over Conan Doyle's Sherlock Holmes Canon fics; it is important to explore why *Sherlock*, among the multitude of adaptations that have been made, is the most utilized intertext for fan writers. Some writers of *Sherlock* fan fiction are also writers of fan fiction for the Canon, and yet they write for only those two incarnations. Lady Halle, a fan fiction writer who has published seven Holmes fics online ranging in length from a few pages to a 70-page story, is this type of fan. She says that while readers are likely to see similarities between her Canon Holmes and Jeremy Brett's television incarnation, she doesn't have Brett or anyone else in mind when she is writing fan fiction featuring a Victorian Holmes. When asked to consider why she hasn't written for any of the other screen versions of the character, she states that she doesn't "see any other version besides the contemporary *Sherlock* as being different enough from the original to warrant exploring. *Maybe* the premise of Sherlock fighting the Nazis, but [she] personally [doesn't] know a lot about that whole era" (February 15, 2011; www.holmesian.net). This illuminates the two main textual elements of *Sherlock* that make it a compelling source for fan fiction. First, the show is different enough from its own source that writers can use it to explore themes that they would be less able to explore through the Canon. Second, in order to write about characters in a contemporary setting, fans need only have knowledge and experience of the world around them, rather than specific historical knowledge, to engage with the context of the show.

Zetared asserts that *Sherlock* is appealing to write about because "there are issues one can write about that would have been examined and presented quite differently in the Victorian era" (February 15, 2011; www.holmesian.net). The abundance of new themes that are available to writers of *Sherlock* fan fiction is one of the show's main draws. Writers are often wary of foregrounding issues that would seem out of place in a narrative about Victorian England. The most popular "taboo subject" that is explored in all fan fiction is through the incredibly pervasive slash, a category of fic defined by same-sex romantic pairings. Slash is considerably less represented in fan fiction about the Victorian Sherlock Holmes than it is in fan fiction about *Sherlock*. According to fanfiction.net, only 19 stories of the 2,626 in the "Books: Sherlock Holmes" category are archived as slash, versus 179 of the 3,553 *Sherlock* fics, though this number is likely much larger in actuality, as not all authors choose to archive their fics under specific headings. According to Zetared, who identifies as primarily a slash writer, this colossal discrepancy is explained by the difference in the contexts of *Sherlock* and the Victorian Canon:

[T]he possible homosexual relationship between characters like Sherlock and John is simply more easy to write about in the modern era than it would be in the Victorian age. After all, a story about a homosexual relationship in the Canon-time would likely have to focus on issues like forbidden love, the hiding of affection, and the struggle of outwardly straight characters ... coming to terms with the "sin" of their attraction to a member of their own sex [February 15, 2011; www.holmesian.net].

Though the homoerotic subtext of the series is one of the most explored themes in *Sherlock* fan fiction, it is only one of many that allow writers to branch out from the Canon and more traditional elements of Sherlock Holmes narratives. Lady Halle adds that she "could see writers taking on the implications of various scientific or technological advancements — prejudice — terrorism — the rise of skepticism and atheism — things like that. Those types of themes would be more difficult to pull off in an 1890s version of Holmes" (February 15, 2011; www.holmesian.net).

The fog-shrouded, gas-lit world of Conan Doyle's Sherlock Holmes is often as mysterious as the detective's cases. People spoke differently, dressed differently, and lived differently; society itself was structured differently. To engage with Conan Doyle is, for a modern reader, to engage with an alien way of life. The Grand Game works to preserve the minutiae of this life and even non-traditional fan fiction writers seem reluctant to tamper with it. A quick cross reference of the publication dates and the synopses of Sherlock Holmes stories on fanfiction.net show that fan writers were finding ways to circumvent the challenge of writing stories set in an unfamiliar context by updating the characters long before Stephen Moffat and Mark Gatiss announced their intentions to do so in *Sherlock*. The show itself provides a framework for writers to do this without having either to invent a plot device to modernize the characters or to weave their own intricate modern context and modern mindsets for them. *Sherlock* gives writers a means to call on their own personal experiences as well as their own historico-cultural contexts, from the technology they use every day to pop culture references that permeate their lives, to create the foundations for their stories.

The qualities of *Sherlock* mark the show as a unique intertext. It is popular even among the Sherlockian elite largely because it has rejected the traditional mode of discourse. This mode of discourse is chiefly responsible for the habitual mistrust and occasional contempt that Sherlockians have for adaptations; because *Sherlock* doesn't engage with The Game, it has opened a path for fresh fan discourse that is uninhibited by a century of tradition. Fans who wish to write about Sherlock Holmes no longer need to consult Conan Doyle to learn what style they ought to use and they are free to explore any subject they wish with their writing. They are also able to call upon the world around them and their own experiences of the culture and society in which they live to write their stories. *Sherlock* is not numbered among the adaptations that have found themselves called before the courts of fandom to answer charges of libel; *Sherlock* is exceptional because it has transcended the game by refusing to play at all.

Works Cited

Collins, Jim. 1989. Towards a theory of intertextual arenas. In *Uncommon cultures: Popular culture and post-modernism*, ed. Jim Collins, 44–48. London: Routledge.

Corrigan, Timothy. 2002. Which Shakespeare to love? Film, fidelity, and the performance of literature. In *High pop: Making culture into popular entertainment*, ed. Jim Collins, 155–181. Malden, MA: Blackwell.

Cushing, Peter. n.d. Peter Cushing: Studio biography. Peter Cushing File. Margaret Herrick Library, Hollywood. Microfiche.

Horowitz, Anthony. 2011. Toast to the immortal memory of Sherlock Holmes, Speech to the Sherlock Holmes Society of London. Delivered January 15. London, UK.

Jenkins, Henry. 1992. *Textual poachers: Television fans and participatory culture.* New York: Routledge.

King, Laurie R., and Leslie Klinger, eds. 2011. *The Grand Game: A celebration of Sherlockian scholarship, Volume One 1902–1959.* New York: The Baker Street Irregulars.

Meyer, Nicholas. 1996. Sherlock Holmes on film: A personal view. In *Sherlock Holmes: Victorian sleuth to modern hero*, ed. Charles R. Pitney, Joseph A. Cutshall King, and Sally Sugarman, 2–9. Lanham, MD: Scarecrow Press.

Stam, Robert. 2005. Introduction: The theory and practice of adaptation. In *Literature and film: A guide to the theory and practice of adaptation*, ed. Robert Stam and Alessandra Raengo, 1–52. Malden, MA: Blackwell.

Takenaka, Kellie. 2010. *Sherlock*: 21st century digital boy. *The Sherlock Holmes Journal* 30 (1): 20–21.

PART TWO
Sherlock Then and Now

"But It's the Solar System!"

Reconciling Science and Faith Through Astronomy

Ariana Scott-Zechlin

Abstract — The scene in which Sherlock Holmes informs Dr. John Watson of his ignorance of the solar system is one of the most well-known from Sir Arthur Conan Doyle's original stories, and its translation into the BBC's modern adaptation *Sherlock* deserves attention. By comparing BBC's *Sherlock* with the original Holmesian canon, with particular attention to their individual uses of astronomy, this essay demonstrates how Sherlock Holmes has changed as a scientific symbol since the Victorian era. It also examines the 35 most popular fan fiction stories from Delicious for their reflection of these ideas, with particular focus on Candle_beck's "Space Travel." By investigating these three areas, this essay shows how Sherlock Holmes has changed from a symbol of evidence-based science's triumph over belief-based faith into a symbol of how science and faith must be reunited in order for humanity to progress.

Introduction

In 2010, the BBC series *Sherlock* gave the most famous literary detective of all time an update, taking Sir Arthur Conan Doyle's original characters and placing them a century away from their original late–Victorian setting. The change in time has altered more than just their wardrobe, however. While the Holmes of Conan Doyle's canon demonstrated the superiority of an evidence-based scientific mindset over a more irrational belief-based approach to seeking knowledge, the modern-day protagonist of BBC's *Sherlock* is shown to be incomplete in his pure rationality, requiring the new John Watson to guide him away from such a polarized approach and into a balance of both science and faith. This transition is well-reflected by the respective treatments of astronomy in both the original Holmesian canon and BBC's *Sherlock*,

56

demonstrating how the modern *Sherlock* serves as an advocate for a more unified approach in the discovery of knowledge, just as astronomy's rational explanations now serve to add greater wonder to the irrational mysteries of the heavens, effectively supporting faith through scientific discovery.

The Victorian Holmes

By the turn of the century in the Victorian age, Great Britain had seen an overwhelming surge of interest in both science and religion, especially in terms of defining the world and humanity's place in it. During this time period, the term *science* replaced what until then had mostly been called natural philosophy and natural history, while both universities and the upper classes encouraged the expansion of scientific education at every level. Religion, however, also continued to hold a significant place in the intellectual sphere, the Victorian populace having inherited a great deal of spirituality from the evangelical revival of the preceding century (Gilmour 1993, 71). Unfortunately, science and religion could not exist peaceably side by side, and God soon found His existence in serious debate as scientific scholarship flourished. Biblical scholarship, geology, and Darwinism all caused serious doubt as to the validity of Christian faith and the belief that God was the all-powerful creator. The great question became whether God or Nature was in charge; and if faith in God was no longer able to make sense of Nature's disorder, then what could replace it?

Enter the world's only consulting detective, the brilliant Sherlock Holmes, ready and willing to guide the British back to security with the illuminating light of reason. Sir Arthur Conan Doyle's first Holmesian story, *A Study in Scarlet*, appeared in 1887, detailing the meeting of Sherlock Holmes and Dr. John Watson and their first case together (III:5). Watson himself is just as lost and disillusioned as any of his fellow countrymen at the turn of the century, having suffered a bullet wound while fighting in the Second Afghan War and a case of typhoid fever while recuperating in India (III:7, 13). He has "gravitated to London, that great cesspool into which all the loungers and idlers of the Empire are irresistibly drained," but London's streets offer him no solace from the hardships that the greater world has inflicted upon him (III:14). It is only by meeting Holmes that Watson may finally find a home for himself, with Conan Doyle keeping the art of punning well-alive. That Holmes' name is a pun on "home," rather than the word "house," is significant, as Holmes does not merely offer Watson physical shelter, but also mental shelter from the greater dangers knocking at Britain's door. Though Watson knows little of Holmes' character, aside from his clear interest in the scientific, he immediately accepts Holmes' offer of shared rooms, suggesting that Holmes' appreciation for scientific reasoning is testament enough to his moral character. While Victorian society had, since the evangelical revival, constructed a moral code of the proper and humane way to live and treat other people from religious writings, here we see morality instead associated with scientific logic. Holmes needs no faith, nor ever expressly confesses to any within the canon, for "the universe of Sherlock Holmes is a Darwinian one in which change prevails," as does the science that accompanies it (Frank 2003, 143). Throughout the Conan Doyle canon, Holmes acts as a guiding light of reason for both the characters around him and for his readers. It is no coincidence that many of the original illustrations, including the original cover of *A Study in Scarlet*, consist of Holmes holding up a light to illuminate his surroundings (III:2). Things are never as they appear in a Holmesian mystery, and the only means by which the falsities can be stripped away is through Holmes' "Science of Deduction and Analysis," as the consulting detective clearly assumes the role of hero for his enraptured followers (III:40). Watson remains constantly in awe of his friend's deductive powers, as do we, and Holmes almost never fails to see justice served. In fact, Holmes is so endowed with integrity that he even occasionally steps outside of British law to deliver his own judgment and sentence, as in "The Adventure of the Abbey Grange" when he judges the actions of the murderer to be morally sound and lets him flee (II:1187). Admittedly, Holmes has his faults, including the occasional drug habit and a general arrogance when dealing with the police (III:213, 61). Yet these faults are some of Holmes' most treasured features, demonstrating to his readers that he is so unusual, so far above the norm in his mental capabilities, that he must rely on recreational drugs to inject some color into our tediously normal lives or that his incredible rational mind entitles him to openly criticize the police in a way no average citizen ever would. Combined with Holmes' constant restoration of the moral balance, this emphasis of Holmes' intellectual prowess through his faults creates a scientifically-minded, larger-than-life hero, providing the answer for every question and more just than even the English law. For a Victorian Britain, questioning its faith in God and unsure of science's capacity to replace that faith, Holmes offers proof that science can not only show answers where there previously were none, but can also support a higher moral code.

What is curious, therefore, is that astronomy is one area of science completely dismissed by Holmes as having any value whatsoever. Watson finds to his surprise that his new acquaintance is "ignorant of the Copernican Theory and of the composition of the Solar System," information of which "any civilized human being in this nineteenth century should ... be aware" (III:32). Astronomy seems to be one scientific field in which Holmes possesses absolutely no knowledge at all, having at least a limited knowledge of botany and geology (III:34). It seems almost a gross oversight that he should lack any understanding of the order that centuries of astronomical observation and deduction have managed to give the heavens, especially considering that Holmes is such an all-encompassing symbol of the power of science and reason to make sense of chaos. Yet Holmes' claim that "if we went round the moon it would not make a pennyworth of difference to [him] or to [his] work" appears to be entirely justified, for there is no point within the Holmesian canon at which Holmes' lack of astronomical knowledge causes him any hardship or prevents him from solving a case (II:34).

Astronomy had, in fact, made quite a few significant achievements during the 19th century. There had been improvements in telescopes, an abundance of new observatories, as well as "the development of celestial photography and multiple improvements in cataloguing, measuring and theorizing the heavens" by the end of the century (Schroeder 2002, 3). Astronomy itself was often associated with detective work in various turn-of-the-century texts, as both used motive, evidence, and deduction to bring reason to bear on observed phenomena. Many of the most popular astronomical essays often used "detective" language, with the canals of Mars described as a "'riddle' to be answered," as well as "a 'mystery' to be solved, and a 'secret' to be revealed" (Schroeder 2002, 188). Therefore, the question still stands: why would Conan Doyle have chosen to exclude astronomy from Holmes' scope of knowledge? It is thus important to realize that Holmes was not just a symbol of science's power but rather its specific power to *protect*. The far reaches of space were not seen as a threat by the British populace, for even if scientists were speculating about life on other planets at the turn of the century, these theories were understood to be speculation only, hardly proof of an alien threat soon to descend upon British soil. "Home" was what needed protecting, and "home" for Britons was still confined to the shores of their small island. Despite astronomy's popularity in the late Victorian period, it had no part in Sherlock Holmes' heroic embodiment of science, as there was no localized British mystery which astronomy could solve. The far-off mysteries of the heavens would have to wait the better part of a century before a consulting detective deemed them worthy of his attentions.

The Modern-Day Sherlock

With the last story belonging to the Holmesian canon published in 1927, more than eighty years passed before 2010 witnessed the arrival of BBC's *Sherlock*. Literature's most easily recognizable detective has come a long way from his origins, yet co-creator Mark Gatiss claims in the "A Study in Pink" commentary that the character of Sherlock "was absolutely born for this age" (2010, ASiP DVD commentary). However, it is important to note that the modern Sherlock's characterization has clearly emphasized particular aspects of both his personality and his relationship with John. These accentuations, combined with the role of astronomy in "The Great Game," result in a portrayal of Sherlock that suggests that science is no longer superior to faith, as it was in the Holmesian canon. Instead, the two are of equal importance and must be reconciled and combined to create a man who is not just a powerful calculating machine, but also, as Lestrade hopes Sherlock might one day become, "a good [man]" (ASiP).

Sherlock is quick to establish that our new Sherlock remains an intellectually distant character, far above our mundane everyday lives. He is cold and utilitarian in his approach to other human beings, at times seemingly lacking in all human kindness. Also, he has an addictive personality, willing to do nearly anything, including risk his own life, to stave off boredom. Combined with his abundant egotism, these myriad faults make it sometimes seem as though Sherlock's massive intellect is in fact the only worthwhile thing about this self-categorized "high-functioning sociopath." With such blatant character flaws in mind, the question is whether this modern-day Sherlock is still a hero to be admired and mimicked by his audience. Conveniently, Sherlock himself answers this very question, saying to John, "Heroes don't exist, and if they did, I wouldn't be one of them." The romantic worldview that still existed during the Victorian era is now being deconstructed, bringing Sherlock down to a very flawed and *un*heroic level. This new Sherlock lacks the inherent sense of right and wrong that Conan Doyle's Holmes possessed, relying constantly on John to explain the baffling rules of social interaction to him, completely at sea when it comes to the humane and considerate treatment of other people. Yet the modern-day hero is incontestably a man of flaws, as well established by James Joyce's *Ulysses* and countless novels since, which suggests that, while this Sherlock might not be a hero by Victorian standards, he is the perfect hero for our modern-day world. The lighting of *Sherlock* also reflects the world and role of the new Sherlock, being much darker and subdued than usual for a television program, for Sherlock and John are still living in a dark and confusing time. While the heroic light-bearing motif of the original stories is not exactly mimicked, Sherlock himself is usually lit to appear brilliantly pale against the darkness that surrounds him, thus carrying on the idea that Sherlock brings the light of scientific reason with him so that others may see.

Just like his predecessor, however, Sherlock is still completely lacking when it comes to knowledge of the solar system, once again declaring that "if we went round the moon, or round and round the garden, like a teddy bear, it wouldn't make any difference." This much adored scene from *A Study in Scarlet* is resurrected in *Sherlock*'s "The Great Game," but rather than being a passing reference to the original story, Sherlock's lack of knowledge about the solar system is a crucial lack which leads to his near defeat by Moriarty, narrowly averted by his assimilation of the astronomical knowledge necessary to solve the case. This alteration demonstrates adaptability on Sherlock's part, but also, most importantly, a new willingness to acquiesce to John's judgment of what is truly important. BBC's modern Sherlock is willing to change, even if it requires a few childish tantrums along the way, and John Watson acts as his teacher, the doctor harmonizing his caring faith with Sherlock's cold science to make Sherlock into the "good man" Lestrade believes he can become.

There is a subtle change in the tone of John and Sherlock's argument over the relative importance of the solar system in *Sherlock* as compared to that of Conan Doyle's original, which demonstrates how John is no longer the one submitting to Sherlock's judgment of what is and is not important. In *A Study in Scarlet*, Watson is shocked at such a gap in Holmes' knowledge, but then lets the matter drop with relative ease, with Watson's view of Holmes as a mature, well-educated man intact (III:34). Yet in *Sherlock*, the argument is clearly one that has happened before, and John's incredulity seems more a result of the fact that "it's primary school stuff." John's depiction of Sherlock as an ignorant child is quickly corroborated by Sherlock's childish teddy bear imagery, delivered in a juvenile mocking tone. Likewise, both Lestrade and John remark in John's fictional online blog on how, "like a child, he just doesn't understand the rules of society" (February 7, 2010; www.john watsonblog.co.uk), and Sherlock himself constructs a view of London populated with villains and archenemies, as if he were the hero of a storybook.

Sherlock's childishness, however, rather than being a fault, may in fact be his greatest strength. While a young child may currently be ignorant, they can easily learn new information and new ways of thinking, just as it is often easier for young scientists who have grown up with a new way of viewing the world to accept a radical theory than their forbearers, as in the eventual acceptance of Copernicus' heliocentric universe, Newton's gravitational theory, or Einstein's special theory of relativity. When Sherlock is eventually required to rely upon astronomical knowledge to solve a case, he learns that astronomical knowledge does, in fact, "matter" and is very "important" indeed (TGG). In addition, the admittance that Sherlock is in fact initially ignorant regarding essential information also suggests that perhaps a lack of omniscience is not so debilitating. After all, if Sherlock is depicted as fallibly human, then his skills are human skills and can be learned by anyone in order to make sense of the dark and baffling world around them.

Yet if Sherlock is not omniscient, then he must continue to learn, and it is John Watson's role to teach him. Throughout Series 1, John takes an active role in curbing Sherlock's most inhuman eccentricities, not only through his argument for the value of astronomical knowledge, but also through his coaching of Sherlock through social situations and his prevention of Sherlock's plan to take the possibly fatal pill at the end of "A Study in Pink." It is true that John is not a shining example of a well-balanced personality, being quite the adrenaline junkie and frequently putting himself in harm's way. However, John's embodiment of just behavior is unquestionable in consideration of his shooting the cab driver in the first episode. The viewer is clearly intended to support John's actions, thus endowing the doctor with the right to judge whether a man deserves to live or die and implying he possesses enough understanding of right versus wrong to make the proper choice. When he shoots, John puts a stop to Sherlock's self-destructive actions at the same moment in which he displays this command of moral behavior, guiding Sherlock away from the life-threatening place to which his extreme rationality has led him. While Sherlock may adamantly claim to have known which pill was which, the viewer is not so sure, suspecting that the only reason Sherlock is still alive is because John was there to stop him. John is just as flawed as Sherlock, certainly, but he is vital in countering Sherlock's purely scientific mind with more irrational, yet more human considerations, beginning the process of turning Sherlock into Lestrade's "good man."

The main opposition to Sherlock in this modern adaptation takes the form of Jim Moriarty. In the original canon, Professor Moriarty is an accomplished astronomer of great genius (III:636). In BBC's *Sherlock*, Jim Moriarty is no longer a professor, but still clearly has a good knowledge of astronomy if he is able to almost defeat Sherlock with knowledge of the Van Buren supernova. Of greater importance, however, is his impression of being all-knowing and omnipresent throughout all three episodes of Series 1, unlike the original Moriarty who only appeared in three stories of the entire Holmesian canon. Jim Moriarty is not known to Sherlock or the audience until the final scene of "The Great Game": there is "never any real contact," "just messages" and "whispers," and yet he still has the ability to control Sherlock's almost every move, saying, "I like to watch you dance" (TGG). Spoken of but not witnessed, able to command the actions of others from afar and even determine whether they live or die, Moriarty has the appearance of a mysterious, all-powerful God. However, it is important to note that this Godlike presence is combined with evident scientific deductive powers to rival Sherlock's, with Moriarty able to create puzzles of sufficient complexity that only Sherlock is capable of solving them. Thus, in keeping with Moriarty's remarks throughout "The Great Game" of the similarity between the two of them, Moriarty, like

Sherlock with John's guidance, combines both rational science and irrational faith in one character.

Yet, unlike the gradual, humanizing, and positive combination of these two opposite approaches progressively embodied in Sherlock, science and faith in Moriarty's case seem to be almost tearing him apart, separating him from humanity rather than bringing him in closer. This instability can be seen most obviously when Moriarty suddenly returns into the swimming pool, saying, "Sorry, boys! I'm *so* changeable!" Moriarty is unpredictable, swinging back and forth between incredibly rational behavior and inexplicable eccentricities, such as his extraordinary planning of his entire "great game" with Sherlock that is then revealed as a mere attempt to avoid being bored. Unlike Sherlock, Moriarty's Godlike presence and scientific mind are pulled to extremes, giving him both his "word of God" ineffability and his ability to design puzzles of deduction that nearly outwit even Sherlock Holmes. However, in their extreme power, this unbalanced mixture of science and faith's central concepts has resulted in a destructive combination. Moriarty's actions and words are almost always characterized by negation, whether in the extermination of human life or the undercutting of other people's claims, as when Sherlock says, "I will stop you" or even just "Catch you later," and Moriarty replies, "No you won't!" Furthermore, Moriarty's warring personality is accompanied by complete isolation, as he himself declares, "No one ever gets to me," with his extreme power keeping him cut off from any real human contact, unlike Sherlock with John Watson faithfully at his side. This uneven integration of science and faith well-represents the relationship between these two apparent opposites during the Victorian era when science and religion were often seen as unable to coexist, with rationality eventually becoming the dominant approach through its gradual undercutting of religion's support. Thus, while Sherlock represents the postmodern harmonious combination of science and faith, Moriarty represents the incompatible relationship of the past, which BBC's *Sherlock* now suggests should be left behind.

Moriarty and Sherlock share many obvious similarities, with Sherlock showing great admiration for Moriarty's tactics and Moriarty remarking, "We were made for each other, Sherlock." Yet Sherlock has John Watson there to keep him human, with the doctor's presence preventing him from turning into a similarly omnipotent figure, completely isolated from all human kindness. As previously mentioned, John frequently acts as a morality check for Sherlock, made particularly evident over the course of "The Great Game" as John becomes increasingly angry with Sherlock's cold rationality in approaching each case, at one point inquiring if Sherlock even remembers that there is a woman's life on the line. However, it is made clear in the final confrontation between Moriarty and Sherlock that Sherlock's one weakness is John, because John is the only person whose endangerment finally makes Sherlock visibly upset. After Moriarty leaves them, Sherlock removes the explosives from John's person in a panic and then quickly dissolves into frantic pacing, fidgeting, and stammering. The Sherlock of this scene is no longer so calculating and rational, so far above the rest of humanity due to his great intellect. While Sherlock's comment at the beginning of "The Great Game" that he'd "be lost without [his] blogger" may be a sarcastic one, it is proven true by the end of the episode. Without John to guide him, Sherlock *is* Moriarty — inhuman and indifferent, caring only about puzzles and never people. Sherlock's science is combined with his faith in John to create a new balance between those two supposed opposites, with that balance relying upon connection with and trust in another human being. Because Moriarty remains isolated from all human contact, he also remains inhuman and destructive. Sherlock may appear to be the weaker of the two, brought down by human failing in his concern for John, but he is also now clearly the "good man" which Lestrade envisions, rather than just the "great man" which Moriarty still remains. Within BBC's *Sherlock*, Sherlock Holmes serves as an example of how the power of human reasoning should be combined with human faith to create a better man, as opposed to the polarized antagonism between the two approaches embodied so destructively by Moriarty.

Fan Fiction and the Modern-Day Sherlock

Although the relationship between science and faith in fan-created works may be expressed through different means than in the canon material of BBC's *Sherlock*, the resolution of these two opposing forces remains present, demonstrating how these themes have been absorbed and interpreted by the show's viewers. Astronomical imagery, in addition to themes of science versus faith, appears in a variety of fan-created works, including fan art, fan videos and fan fiction. However, fan fiction has a particularly straightforward gauge of these works' relative popularity in the form of Delicious, which is frequently used in fandom as a recommendation database; thus, each story's ranking serves as a fairly reliable indication of its popularity among readers. Therefore, this discussion will be limited to the 35 most bookmarked fan fictions on delicious.com as of February 23, 2011.

Throughout *Sherlock* fan fiction, the greater part of plot focus is given to the relationship between Sherlock and John, and unsurprisingly so, as the vast majority of such stories are slash and thus primarily propelled forward by the growing intensity of Sherlock and John's romantic relationship. While *Sherlock* itself may not go quite as far in physical intimacy, similar attention is already given to Sherlock and John's relationship in the source material, as Mark Gatiss remarks that the show is "much more [about] getting back to the original friendship between these two unlikely men" (BBC 2010). The most common character-related assumption among fan fiction authors comes from the show itself in the depiction of Sherlock and John as the unlikely complement to one another. The author Wordstrings has a series of popular stories, three of them within the top 35 on Delicious, all of which feature a Sherlock who goes past sociopath and into the realm of the dangerously psychotic, his relationship with John characterized by obsession and violent need. Yet even in such an extreme case, John remains the only person who seems to possess any understanding of his flatmate. In "The Death and Resurrection of the English Language," for example, he responds to Sherlock's "When I met you at Bart's that afternoon, I wanted to open up your skull and see inside," with a casual "That's more or less what it felt like, yep" (September 23, 2010; www.livejournal.com). No matter what John discovers Sherlock to have left sitting in the fridge (with each author unfailingly providing their own delightful suggestions), the doctor's understandable frustration never fails to be superseded by his appreciation for the excitement and unpredictability Sherlock brings to his life. For his part in the relationship, John largely acts as a stabilizer for Sherlock, grounding him in practicalities such as having central heating that functions, as in the case of Libraryofsol's "The Second Law of Thermodynamics," or taking out the rubbish bins, as in Rageprufrock's "Homemaking." Thus, Sherlock and John are generally portrayed as a harmonious relationship of an eccentric genius balanced by a more calming and practical individual. Sherlock gives John a greater enjoyment of life and an appreciation for the wonders of rational thought, while John pulls Sherlock up from the depths of his own thoughts and out into the real world populated by real people, as opposed to fanciful archenemies.

In fact, in many of the scenarios written by fan fiction authors, Sherlock seems to be learning how to be human with John as his guide, uniting his rational scientific mind with John's more irrational but humane considerations for both the welfare of others and supposedly useless knowledge, such as the layout of the solar system. Irisbleufic's "Profit and Loss" (August 31, 2010; www.livejournal.com) depicts Sherlock and John traveling to Bruges at Mycroft's insistence after the confrontation at the end of "The Great Game," in the hopes that the distance will put Moriarty off their tail. When asked by John to research tourist activities in which he would normally have no interest, Sherlock remarks upon how "he must learn to accept that what John thinks is relevant, *is*, in fact, relevant." Much as how John in *Sherlock* informs Sherlock when he has overstepped a line of humane behavior, even with just a quiet, "Bit not good," the doctor also appears in fan fiction to illuminate for

Sherlock what is and is not acceptable human behavior. In personal correspondence, the author Candle_beck remarked that she believes "the darker sides of Sherlock's antihero persona are going to be tempered by his continuing relationship with John" within *Sherlock* itself, especially "considering we're only three episodes into the BBC's version of canon" (February 19, 2011). In short, John's humanization of Sherlock in fan fiction is a prediction of the same course the show will eventually take, already begun in Series 1. John's role as teacher for a childish Sherlock is reiterated in Candle_beck's "Space Travel" (August 21, 2010; www.livejournal.com) when John compares him to "a child who hadn't yet learned not to ask why people were in wheelchairs." A number of works casually reference Sherlock's ignorance of what John refers to as "primary school stuff," the passing nature of such comments indicating that Sherlock's incomplete knowledge is an accepted and perhaps even essential part of his character. Thus, as seen in earlier discussion of *Sherlock*'s canon material, fan fiction affirms the notion that John is a necessary complement to an otherwise incomplete detective, as it is indeed difficult to imagine Sherlock Holmes without John Watson by his side. Yet fan fiction also repeatedly emphasizes how John is not only the appreciative witness and cataloger of Sherlock's adventures, but also a critic of Sherlock's actions during them, seeking to improve his flatmate's behavior and turn him from a brilliant but inhuman symbol of scientific thought into a more irrational but more complete human.

The fact that John serves as an instructor for Sherlock, however, does not mean that Sherlock loses his own role as a guiding light for both his friend and his avid viewing audience. Fan fiction still abounds with references to Sherlock as an illuminating guide, easily providing answers that previously seemed unfathomable to John's limited gaze. In fact, one of the works most concerned with depicting Sherlock as a guiding light for John is Candle_beck's "Space Travel" (August 21, 2010; www.livejournal.com), the most astronomy-centered work to be found among Delicious' 35 most bookmarked stories. The description of Sherlock as an "alien" is common throughout a number of works of fan fiction, usually as a passing indication of Sherlock's incomprehension of social interaction and normal human behavior. However, rather than describing Sherlock's "alien" appearance in order to emphasize his lack of understanding, Candle_beck instead equates his "unearthly" appearance with his guiding role, being thus "easy to follow, impossible to lose." The central metaphor of "Space Travel" has John waking from the dream of chaos and suffering into a new and alien world, "a different planet" where "Sherlock Holmes [knows] his way around." While John begins the story with parts of his mind "still asleep," he slowly starts to make sense of the strange new world in which he finds himself with Sherlock's guidance. John leaves one nonsensical world only to enter another, but on this new planet he has someone on whom he can rely and to whom he can entrust his well-being, someone who can make sense of the world for him and open his mind to new methods of understanding.

The Sherlock of Candle_beck's story is more than a guide, however; he becomes a metaphorical source of life itself in John's eyes, "[bringing] gravity in with him," with "oxygen here, and sunlight." This imagery of Sherlock as a life-giving force is also combined with the description of looking at Sherlock being like looking at the star-dusted universe, "staring again. Still. Always. On and on," out into the farthest reaches of the infinite black. John imagines the distance between them "on a cosmic scale," characterizing Sherlock as something beyond his limited reach. Thus, Sherlock has been put on the same level as God as a result of his close association with the illuminating power of science. While most of this comparison is largely rooted in the visual imagery Candle_beck provides, in "Space Travel" Sherlock also possesses an all-knowing Godlike presence when he guesses what John is thinking before John gives the slightest hint toward the matter, a trick which Sherlock actually pulls in "A Study in Pink" when he assumes John has come to ask about the flat at Bart's. Although Candle_beck may have taken her own artistic liberties in her descriptions of Sherlock as an omniscient guiding light, they clearly arise from the original source material. While Sherlock is memorably shown in "The Great Game" to have no understanding of the scattered stars of the universe, he is still placed up among them in "Space Travel," as if he is the only one who could come close to understanding them, assuming he actually cared enough to try. Interestingly, when John asks Sherlock near the end of "The Great Game" for an admission that some familiarity with the solar system would have helped him solve the mystery of the fake painting more quickly, Sherlock replies, "Didn't do you any good, did it?" only to have John reply, "No, but I'm not the world's only consulting detective." Even though John is essential in pointing out to Sherlock what knowledge is truly important, Sherlock is the only one in both BBC's *Sherlock* and its fan fiction that can then use that information in a meaningful way. Sherlock must be the one to draw science and faith together, for the two cannot remain separated between himself and John and still create a significant progression. It is not enough for Sherlock to simply call on John as his guide to the ways of humanity; Sherlock must eventually become human enough that he can make the decisions of a "good man" without first requiring John's advice.

Such imagery depicting Sherlock as Godlike is not limited to "Space Travel" alone. Phantomjam's "The Perils of Urban Warfare" (July 28, 2010; www.livejournal.com) chronicles John's therapist's attempts to get him to realize that Sherlock is an unhealthy influence and that John needs to stop skipping out on his therapy sessions in favor of attending crime scenes with his flatmate. When John receives a text on his way out of 221B Baker Street on the way to his appointment with his therapist, the text consists solely of Sherlock's command that John "look up," only to see Sherlock gesturing at him from the window, beckoning for John to follow him not only further into a shared life of danger but also into a closer relationship. This association is even more explicit in Orange_crushed's "The Dangerous Book for Boys" (October 12, 2010; www.livejournal.com), an alternate universe story in which the two boys meet at secondary school. As John lies in a hospital bed, recovering from injuries after their encounter with Moriarty's men, he describes Sherlock's gaze as "familiar and safe, like Sherlock is making sure that everything's still in order," ensuring that "God is in His Heaven and John Watson is right with the world." Despite the fact that these stories also continue to describe Sherlock as flawed, with dark and unsettling aspects to his personality, they still set him on the same level as God.

In *Sherlock* fan fiction, the heavenly is shown to be within human reach through two means: Sherlock's comparison to God and John's ability to connect to the Godlike Sherlock by the end of every story. Even though John reflects on the seemingly cosmic distance between the two of them in Candle_beck's "Space Travel," he still manages to close that distance by the end of the story with physical intimacy. Similarly, as John compares staring at Sherlock to staring at the cosmos, he also realizes that on "this strange kinder planet — Sherlock [is] staring back" (August 21, 2010; www.live journal.com). In the realm of *Sherlock* fan fiction, God is subject to human comprehension as Sherlock pulls his followers out of their chaotic postmodern worlds with the light of reason, much like Conan Doyle's Holmes of the Victorian age. However, in keeping with *Sherlock*'s unification of science and faith, Sherlock's all-knowing rational mind is clearly dependent upon John's irrational faith in him to balance it, with the similarly Godlike yet psychotic and cruel Moriarty serving as the warning for what Sherlock would become without John by his side, helping him discern right from wrong, human from inhuman. Even if fan fiction authors are not actively trying to depict an interdependent relationship between Sherlock's science and John's faith, the fact that such themes are still present in their stories shows how essential that relationship is in the canon material. The centrality of Sherlock and John's balancing relationship in *Sherlock*'s fan fiction also clearly expresses a prevalent desire among *Sherlock*'s viewers for Sherlock to not be just an incredible rational mind but rather for him to become a more humane and considerate human being through his deep connection with John, showing widespread support for the current direction of the characters' relationship within the show itself.

Conclusion

When Sir Arthur Conan Doyle wrote the original Holmesian canon, he was responding to a time in which faith often seemed to have been replaced by doubt, and the Victorians were searching for a new guiding principle that would restore order to their world. Sherlock Holmes was portrayed as a guiding light for the Victorians, showing how rationality could protect them from the unknown outside world they so feared. Astronomy was not a realm of science that could help reassure the British public, especially as it remained almost as far from mankind as God himself. It was thus of no importance in the world of Conan Doyle's canon. In our modern world, however, the dangerous and chaotic outside world beyond Britain's shores has become the inside world, and God's domain has been opened to human exploration. If the greater threat faced by mankind embodies our concern for the state of humanity itself, then the means by which Sherlock must now protect us is to restore our faith in mankind and a greater order. Science must be shown as more than a destructive force that negates our previously sacred beliefs or causes us to question our faith, whether in God or in each other. *Sherlock* depicts a detective who embodies just as much dark as he does light, and yet is rescued from his isolating pure rationality by the irrational faith in another human being with which the good doctor provides him. As demonstrated in both BBC's *Sherlock* and its related fan texts, Sherlock Holmes can no longer be a man of singular scientific thought, but instead must rely on John Watson to take him beyond just one method of understanding. In its redefinition of Conan Doyle's main characters as the union of both science and faith, the modern-day Sherlock Holmes thus suggests we look toward the stars, where man and the great unknown now meet in the heavens.

Works Cited

BBC. 2010. *Stephen Moffat and Mark Gatiss Interview.* July 16, 2010. www.youtube.com.

Frank, Lawrence. 2003. *Victorian detective fiction and the nature of evidence: The scientific investigations of Poe, Dickens and Doyle.* New York: Palgrave Macmillan.

Gilmour, Robin. 1993. *The Victorian period: The intellectual and cultural context of English literature, 1830–1890.* New York: Longman.

Schroeder, David. 2002. A message from Mars: Astronomy and late–Victorian culture. PhD diss., Indiana University.

Terror, Nostalgia, and the Pursuit of Sherlock Holmes in *Sherlock*

ELLEN BURTON HARRINGTON

Abstract—*Sherlock* casts Moriarty as Sherlock Holmes's greatest fan, ironically invoking the original Holmes's legendary fan culture through the portrayal of his nemesis. Whereas Conan Doyle portrays Holmes as a decadent genius who admires Moriarty's intellect but pursues him because he represents an affront to Holmes's effective management of crime, *Sherlock*'s Moriarty explicitly flirts with Sherlock, enticing him with a series of scripted cases. Despite the violence of the cases Moriarty proffers, he tempts Sherlock to admire crime amorally and for the sake of its craft. *Sherlock* creators Moffat and Gatiss, longtime Sherlock Holmes fans themselves, have created a Moriarty who is cast in their mold as fan author, audaciously pursuing Sherlock and writing new cases for him; in emphasizing Moriarty's scripting of these crimes, they connect the criminal-author with the fan author as well as the official author, since, like Moriarty, both Moffat and Gattis effectively keep Sherlock relevant by giving him more work to do. By making Moriarty a terrorist-author, scripting cases for Holmes, Moffat and Gattis highlight the ambivalent position of the fan author who challenges as well as engages the original text. Furthermore, *Sherlock*'s portrayal of terror as localized in Moriarty and often personal in its motivation can be turned back to illuminate Conan Doyle's stories, which also tend to depoliticize crime, having Holmes discover personal rather than political motives for crimes. Ultimately, *Sherlock*'s treatment of Holmes's "arch-enemy" reminds us of the pleasures of using fiction to escape from the reality of crime and terror, thus nostalgically evoking the original stories' escapist function.

Introduction

"This is a turn-up, isn't it, Sherlock?" asks John Watson, continuing, "Bet you never saw this coming" in a sally that might be directed at the audience as well. In the final scene of *Sherlock*'s "The Great Game," Sherlock Holmes goes looking for Jim Moriarty and finds John Watson. Of course, this teasing doubling is actually Moriarty's way of making the game personal.

70

Sherlock logically presumes that the complex and artful series of crimes by the serial bomber must be motivated by the desire to possess the Bruce-Partington plans, but Moriarty makes it clear that his interest is not political or even mercenary, but personal. By making John the final suicide bomber and the voice of Moriarty, he forces Sherlock to be engaged personally in the case, a case that Sherlock had regarded with admiration, as a complex and well-crafted puzzle. "What would you like me to make him say next?" John asks as the unwilling vehicle for Moriarty, who has brought the terror of John's wartime experience back to London, echoing other recent terrorist attacks in style rather than substance, since Moriarty sends out suicide bombers as victims, purely for his own satisfaction.

In *Sherlock*, Moriarty becomes the new face of terror, peppering his crimes with gratuitous killings and bombing threats and enjoying the personal power that ensues. *Sherlock* repeatedly features acts of terror that are all too familiar in contemporary society, but these are all enabled and sometimes staged by Moriarty. By attributing such a divergent series of crimes to the versatile Moriarty, *Sherlock* evokes Sir Arthur Conan Doyle's Sherlock Holmes stories' compelling fictions about social order and invites a kind of Victorian nostalgia. This approach in *Sherlock* implies that there is an underlying order to criminal enterprise that defies fears of anarchic, urban violence and global terrorism, and that Sherlock can duel Moriarty to stop it.

Moriarty has an assured place in contemporary culture as Holmes's nemesis, though Professor Moriarty plays a limited role in the original stories, appearing in "The Final Problem" only to die allegedly locked in struggle with Holmes on Reichenbach Falls, apparently conceived as a vehicle for Conan Doyle to eliminate the character of Holmes. *Sherlock* offers a bold rendering of Moriarty as a showman, not just the restrained force that Holmes reads between the lines, but an outrageous and violent personality who takes pleasure in engaging Sherlock in a clever, dueling interpretation of Reichenbach Falls. "A Study in Pink" and "The Blind Banker" allude to the elusive figure of Moriarty as an ominous presence behind the crimes that Sherlock solves, and the third episode, "The Great Game" centers on Moriarty's aggressive pursuit of Sherlock. In Conan Doyle's story, Moriarty threatens Holmes only when Holmes actively pursues him and nearly places him in the custody of the police, but, in *Sherlock*, Moriarty appears fascinated by the detective, first meeting him in a disguise that emphasizes the erotically tinged flirtation that Moriarty will pursue as he challenges Holmes. While Conan Doyle's Holmes is a recognizably decadent figure, *Sherlock*'s Moriarty seems to resemble the *fin-de-siècle* aesthete more than Sherlock, since the dapper and flamboyant Moriarty propagates his crime as a kind of art, proffered for Sherlock's appreciation and independent of morality. Framing Moriarty as a Wildean figure for whom crime is a seductive, dangerous art, makes him a figure for the author; Moriarty is a criminal who lures the detective-reader with his carefully crafted clues.

In *Unlocking Sherlock*, the *Sherlock* creators, Steven Moffat and Mark Gatiss, disclose their fascination with Sherlock Holmes and his adaptations, as well as their longstanding desire to revisit the Holmes stories in this project. Their reinvention of Moriarty as the villain in pursuit of Holmes, Moriarty as a proactive rather than a reactive force, reflects their own fascination with the cult figure of Sherlock Holmes. The creators portray themselves less as official authors of the series than as fan authors (a deliberate stance, as Rixon examines in the volume), who are fascinated by Sherlock and enjoy scripting his role, much as Moriarty does for Sherlock in the last episode. Distancing themselves from their "official" authorial role, Moffat and Gatiss establish a kind of authorial legitimacy by strategically associating themselves with the stories' immense fan culture and its rewritings of the canon. Their Moriarty playfully crafts new plots (nostalgically inspired by the original stories) for this version of Sherlock. Moffat and Gatiss allude to the familiar model of detective as reader, wherein the detective reconstructs the narrative of crime for and alongside the reader, and in so doing casts the criminal as author, and even more specifically, as fan author. Moriarty is not merely the individual responsible for these crimes; he is the author of a series of compelling cases that lure Sherlock at his own peril. Indeed, Moriarty becomes a kind of sensational writer whose desperate victims are forced to parrot his words to Sherlock in a kind of eerie parody, thus emphasizing Moriarty's role as puppet master for so many lesser criminals and ultimately for Sherlock himself. Moriarty's terrorism reflects the ambivalent position of the fan author, since writing these new plots can be construed as not just engaging but challenging the original and thus making *Sherlock* relevant for the contemporary viewer.

Sherlock's portrayal of terror as individually localized and often personal in its motivation in turn illuminates Conan Doyle's stories, inviting the reader to revisit the milieu of the stories and their response to the terror present in late 19th century London. The Holmes stories also were conceived amidst anxiety about violence and terrorism following the Ripper murders and in a London beset by Fenian and anarchist bombings. Yet the stories do not deal specifically with serial killings and bombing outrages, instead emphasizing the criminal disorder associated with problematic colonial subjects, criminal conspiracies, and "private wrong[s]" (III:199). The original Holmes stories respond to increasing anxiety over crime, including violence from abroad, offering a reassuring vision of order restored that validates the status quo, albeit via a detective with many decadent qualities. Yet the crimes Holmes investigates are repeatedly proved to be personal rather than political (Thomas

1999, 224), a theme recalled in Sherlock's misreading of Moriarty's motivation in the final scene of "The Great Game." Even crimes that initially resemble anarchist or Socialist violence in Conan Doyle are shown to concern individuals rather than political movements, though such distinctions ultimately break down to show the connection between the personal and the political (Thomas 1999, 224–25) and enable social critique. While *Sherlock* masters fears of terrorist bombers and serial killers by tracing them back to the playful and deadly hand of Moriarty, the Holmes stories do not deal with these fears directly, but supplant them with something else altogether, eliding the concerns about violent anarchists to depict instead a wronged lover in *A Study in Scarlet*, for example. By keeping Holmes's work apart from larger political movements or unrest, Conan Doyle ensures that Holmes's genius in problem solving remains at the forefront of the narrative, thus providing a pleasurable escape from larger social concerns. Similarly, *Sherlock* uses Sherlock's investigation of Moriarty and his unwilling suicide bombers to allow viewers to escape from contemporary, post 9/11 fears about willing bombers and larger political threats. Ultimately, *Sherlock* invites the viewer to revel in the knowing, nostalgic refiguring of a familiar character, allowing us to enjoy Sherlock's rivalry with Moriarty and the satisfying way that this representative villain might be challenged and potentially defeated. By making Moriarty both an admiring, playful fan author and the series' terrorist-villain, Moffat and Gatiss highlight his ambiguity; the crimes that Moriarty scripts fascinate Sherlock, but the gleeful violence he perpetrates alludes to the human toll of uncontrolled terror.

Degeneracy and Decadence in Conan Doyle

Since the character of Moriarty does not appear until "The Final Problem," the irresistible figure of Holmes's criminal double is thus rather tangential to the success of the stories, which had achieved legendary popularity in *The Strand* magazine long before any reference to Moriarty. In "The Final Problem," Holmes intriguingly alludes to an ongoing battle of wits with Moriarty, who "is the organizer of half that is evil and of nearly all that is undetected in this great city" (I:719). Conan Doyle crafts an irresistible counterpart to Holmes in Moriarty, a character who matches Holmes's intelligence and energy yet realizes the darker implications of Holmes's decadent character. As Holmes describes Moriarty, Holmes tempers the "good birth and excellent education" of the former professor with this diagnosis: "A criminal strain ran in his blood, which, instead of being modified, was increased and rendered infinitely more dangerous by his extraordinary mental powers" (I:718). Touching on phrenology, Holmes here offers a medicalized assessment of Moriarty, in accordance with turn-of-the-century criminal anthropology. Yet, the reader also glimpses Holmes's own atavism in "The Boscombe Valley Mystery" when Watson describes a "transformed" Holmes on the chase: "His face flushed and darkened," and "His nostrils seemed to dilate with a purely animal lust for the chase" (I:121). Indeed, Holmes's addiction to his work seems to trump any other passion; as Ed Wiltse notes of Watson's description of Holmes here, "coming at the moment of Jekyll and Hyde, the appearance of this snarling, dark-skinned beast where the aesthete had been must have been a transformation indeed" (1998, 116). By making Moriarty a double for Holmes, seemingly his intellectual match, Conan Doyle alludes to Victorian concerns about degeneracy as manifest in the detective as well as the criminal.

Alongside his detective genius, Holmes himself is a recognizably decadent figure in the contemporary understanding of the term, since, for example, he takes cocaine to alleviate his ennui, taking pleasure in the sensations of the drug, and he surrenders himself to music in his consummate skill at violin and his pleasure in attending concerts. Holmes's professionalism is generally paramount, yet he acknowledges to Watson in *The Sign of Four* that his work is the ultimate stimulant and, without the "mental exaltation" of it, he takes morphine and cocaine to relieve his "stagnation" (*Novels* 2005, 216). In addition, Holmes pointedly does not take part in family life in the way that a solid British citizen like Watson does, apparently forgoing romantic relationships in his desire not to upset the balance of his mind, as Watson famously explains at the beginning of "A Scandal in Bohemia." This combination of the disciplined professional and the decadent genius as framed by Watson's narration and his character reminds the reader that Holmes more resembles Moriarty than he does the staid Watson. Holmes acknowledges, "My horror at his crimes was lost in my admiration of his skill" (I:719), emphasizing Holmes's appreciation for Moriarty's art despite Holmes's ethical objection to it, an acknowledgment of the doubling between Holmes and Moriarty in the narrative.

Sherlock *and the Great Game*

The Sherlockians call the fiction of Holmes's actual existence and the rich fan culture that ensues "The Grand Game" (treated in this volume by Polasek), so titling the third episode of *Sherlock*, which features Moriarty most prominently, "The Great Game" alludes to his position as fan author in relation to Holmes. However, in Conan Doyle's time, "the great game" would indicate espionage, notably the contest between Britain and Russia for parts of Asia, including Afghanistan, which is famously portrayed in Rudyard Kipling's *Kim* (1901). The use of the 19th century phrase, which did not appear in Conan Doyle's stories, in *Sherlock* alludes in part to the kind of sporting contest we see in *Kim*, whose title character and protagonist is a lighthearted youth with an effortless ability to disguise himself effectively to retrieve information and, thus, function as the perfect spy. Certainly, Moriarty of *Sherlock* resembles Kim in his playfulness, his talent at disguise and concealment, and his ability to locate and use important information. *Sherlock* plays on the horrifying notion of a sporting contest that has life-and-death consequences for the individuals that might get caught up in it unknowingly, an underlying issue in *Kim* as well.

Of course, because of his clear professional ethics and his paternalistic commitment to stability and the rule of law — if sometimes through extralegal means — Kim also shares significant qualities with Sherlock Holmes. In Conan Doyle's stories, Holmes is frequently in disguise, gleaning crucial information from unsuspecting witnesses, and he usually reveals himself unexpectedly, to Watson's utter amazement. In *Sherlock*, however, the emphasis on disguise has moved from Sherlock to Moriarty. While Sherlock does flirt stiffly with Molly Hooper for information and access to the morgue in *Sherlock*, perhaps a mild reference to Holmes's unscrupulous courtship of a housemaid in Conan Doyle's "The Adventure of Charles Augustus Milverton," he does not appear in disguise in *Sherlock*'s first season. Interestingly, Moriarty more effectively and unscrupulously seduces Molly for information and access to Sherlock, and it is Moriarty who uses disguise and concealment repeatedly in "The Great Game," targeting innocent victims to serve as his voice and carry his bombs, and also posing as Molly's boyfriend in order to meet and observe Holmes. Enigmatic references to Moriarty in the first two episodes foreshadow his authorship of the alluring plots of "The Great Game," which he structures specifically to engage Sherlock, personally addressing him in the diverse voices of the victims Moriarty has compelled to wear his bombs. In his pursuit of Sherlock through these forced suicide bombers, Moriarty performs a parody of Sherlock's desperate clients and perhaps of Sherlock Holmes's adoring public. Moriarty's status as Sherlock's fan, featured pointedly in the series, is considered further in Basu's essay in this volume.

The enigmatic Moriarty featured in both the stories and the BBC series becomes the principle source of crime, a single man who might be cast out or killed to restore order. For all Moriarty's high intellect, he represents the crudest human inclinations: cruelty, greed, sadism, egotism, self-gratification; and these are portrayed most vividly in *Sherlock*. In contrast, Sherlock Holmes works to regulate his inclinations (for example, his humorously excessive use of nicotine patches in *Sherlock*) to allow him to succeed as a detective. G.K.

Chesterton famously characterizes the detective or "the agent of social justice" as "the original and poetic figure, while burglars and footpads are merely placid old cosmic conservatives, happy in the immemorial respectability of apes and wolves" (1974, 6). Chesterton's characterization of the detective invites us to read Sherlock Holmes as a maverick, upholding civilization by opposing mankind's baser instincts. Importantly, Sherlock Holmes's partnership with John Watson frequently serves to keep Holmes's impulses in check, from Watson worrying over Holmes's alternation of morphine and cocaine at the beginning of Conan Doyle's *The Sign of Four* to John's anonymous shooting of the serial killer at the end of "A Study in Pink" to save Sherlock from his own weakness. John Watson, a kind of idealized British everyman, is shown to be brave and often intelligent in the stories and *Sherlock,* as well as a moderating influence, though his character is doomed to be a dullard in comparison with the agile, creative intelligence of Sherlock Holmes. Chesterton enticingly describes morality as "the most dark and daring of conspiracies" that works against the natural inclinations of humanity (1974, 6). This portrayal recalls the decadent qualities of Sherlock Holmes, though, for all of his protestations against the police and his occasional outmaneuvering of its officers, he must be recognized as a conservative force that works to reinforce and perpetuate the social order and, in the stories, the class hierarchy. If he occasionally admires the dark side of humankind, Sherlock Holmes also recognizes it to police it.

"I have made up my mind to kill Sherlock Holmes"

"One would think we were the criminals," Watson complains during his frantic flight with Holmes in Conan Doyle's "The Final Problem" (I:731). Ironically, Holmes's greatest threat here is not Moriarty but Conan Doyle, who uses Moriarty to orchestrate the detective's premature — and ultimately temporary — demise. Conan Doyle's growing animosity against his famous popular character is well documented; he discussed his frustrations with his mother among others, and Henry Lunn, who was traveling with Conan Doyle when he visited Reichenbach Falls, later reported that Conan Doyle told him in Lucerne, "I have made up my mind to kill Sherlock Holmes; he is becoming such a burden to me that he makes my life unbearable" (qtd. in Lycett 2007, 203). Despite the immense profitability of the stories, Conan Doyle found Holmes a distraction from his other writing projects. Referring to Conan Doyle's memoir, Wiltse characterizes his relationship with his fictional character as a kind of addiction: "As countless twentieth-century narratives of addiction have taught us to expect, alongside Doyle's discourse of resolution is one of resentment, of his habit's power and the possibilities it has foreclosed (1998, 109). In this analysis, Holmes's creator's addiction might be a stronger version of the one felt by his fans. Of course, after a break of some ten years, Conan Doyle, lured by the immense profits, went back to producing Holmes stories. Conan Doyle's marked ambivalence towards his most beloved and enduring creation sheds light on his own literary aspirations, mirrored in Holmes's repeated derision of the sensationalism of Watson's literary efforts, efforts which are, of course, ostensibly the stories themselves.

Celebrating the Holmes stories and the interpretations they inspire, *Sherlock*'s rendering of Conan Doyle's characters and plots inserts itself self-consciously into the pursuit of Sherlock Holmes. In re-envisioning Conan Doyle's serious Professor Moriarty as a playful, youthful, dapper man, mockingly concerned with John's wrinkling his Vivienne Westwood suit while threatening his life, *Sherlock* capitalizes on the pairing of Sherlock and Moriarty, bringing the eroticism of their death-duel into the very dialogue. *Sherlock* has thematized the uncertainty of Sherlock's sexuality, as John negotiates his place with Sherlock and the space in the apartment, Sally Donovan highlights the erotic charge that Sherlock gets from a good case and the violence it might entail, and Moriarty masquerades as Molly's new boyfriend whom Sherlock immediately pegs as gay. While the stories offer a dogged pursuit initiated by Holmes because of Moriarty's affront to Holmes's policing of London, *Sherlock* makes it clear that Moriarty writes the scripts that lure Sherlock. Moriarty's "flirtation" with Sherlock is obviously gratifying to both men, more so because of the high stakes involved in their intellectual joust.

Early in the last episode, "Jim" leaves Sherlock his number as a come-on, a joke since Moriarty knows the real come-on for Sherlock is not a man's number, but the intricate, highly crafted puzzles that he offers Sherlock anonymously. Moriarty's very outrageousness, a marker of a kind of caricatured queer identity, reminds the viewer of Sherlock's queerness, an uncertain identity that he never fully reveals, even to the earnest John, longing to understand and demonstrate his acceptance of his new roommate. Knowing Sherlock's enthusiasms, Moriarty crafts cases bracketed by the time pressure of a ticking bomb, again exposing Sherlock's unseemly pleasure in his cases and detachment from the consequences. John's disgust at Sherlock's detachment highlights the decadent aspect of his genius; like Moriarty, with a kind of Wildean sensibility, Sherlock admires the craft of the crime largely without judging its morality. Sherlock openly takes pleasure in the texts he has been invited to read, the range of clues Moriarty has laid, perhaps a witty take on the maxim "art for art's sake" of the decadent movement.

Readers of detective fiction are familiar with this analogy between detective and reader, since the detective's role is to read the clues, retelling the fragmented story of the crime in a logical, linear way and identifying the criminal: Peter Hühn follows Tzvetan Todorov, explaining "through the development of the second story [investigation] the absent first story [crime] is at last reconstructed in detail and made known" (Hühn 1987, 452). Thus, the detective recounts the narrative of crime, and the investigation that solves the crime becomes the subject of a second narrative, like Watson's narration. Again, the criminal is actually the author of "the first story" or the crime, as the detective discovers the true meaning of the clues to recount the events of the crime. Hühn examines the analogy of criminal to author:

> In a manner of speaking, the criminal writes the secret story of his crime into everyday "reality" in such a form that its text is partly hidden, partly distorted and misleading. But although he tries to subject the whole text to his conscious and, as it were, artistic control, some signs usually escape his attention and inadvertently express their "true" meaning (his criminal authorship). So, even if the criminal as a skillful author has managed to rewrite the story of his crime in the coherent form of a different story, these unmanageable signs tend to disrupt the appearance and create a mystery [1987, 454].

For Moriarty, the test of his skill is not only dissociating himself from his crimes so effectively (already a feat), but also creating a series of clues that can be read only by Sherlock and that would bewilder other less insightful detectives, like Lestrade or John. Here, the confidence of the criminal is so great that he does not simply obfuscate his criminal role, but he authors a series of clues specifically for Sherlock, a kind of sensationalized narrative of crime that serves as a character sketch for the criminal, a diverse résumé of crimes, starting from his boyhood murder of another boy. This audacity makes Sherlock and Moriarty members of an elite community with regard to crime — one composed of these authors and readers of crime — a kind of testament to their complementary genius. (In her consideration of science and faith in the series, Scott-Zechlin further considers this doubling between the two men and examines Moriarty's God-like pose.) Even as Moriarty longs to destroy Sherlock, Moriarty considers Sherlock a fellow connoisseur and also longs for his admiration, and Sherlock relishes the case. While Watson acknowledges in Conan Doyle's "The Final Problem" that he and Holmes have become the prey, *Sherlock* takes it a step further as a seduction of Sherlock, a seduction that began in "A Study in Pink" as Sherlock longed to consume the tablets in the vial to demonstrate his confidence in his ability to "read" the serial killer.

The admiring relationship between Sherlock and Moriarty explicitly evokes the relationship of Moffat and Gatiss to Sherlock Holmes. Ostensibly through Moriarty, they write a series of cases that legitimate a 21st century Holmes. These stories desire to seduce Holmes and, through him, the viewer, renewing interest in the striking figure in a deerstalker hat from more than a century ago who survives in so many diverse interpretations. Unlike Conan Doyle in his attempt to kill off the character, they seek to revive him, celebrating, rather than disparaging, his popular appeal. Moffat and Gattis are familiar with the transition from fan appreciation to textual production, having already made the transition from *Doctor Who* fans to writers for the series. In each case, they have moved from enjoyment of the original texts to sanctioned cultural production — new *Doctor Who* episodes for BBC or the BBC version of Sherlock Holmes — that continues the cultural life of the original. Sherlock Holmes has a long history of blurring reader/author distinctions through pastiche, and even Conan Doyle spoofed Holmes (see "The Field Bazaar" and "How Watson Learned the Trick" in Conan Doyle 2003). Moffat and Gatiss might be characterized as audacious fans, like Moriarty, who move to producing authorized narratives that perpetuate and transform these "cult" characters and perhaps revive their popularity, reinterpreting them for new audiences. Their status as fans legitimizes their connection with these characters, allowing them to pursue Sherlock Holmes and reinvent him, all the while unabashedly following Conan Doyle's detective formula and including the sort of nostalgic details that reward fans of the original series. Through Moriarty, they author cases to extend the career of Sherlock Holmes, rejecting Conan Doyle's own sense of the stories as an unseemly addiction that sidetracked his writing career.

Terror in Conan Doyle and Sherlock

As the preeminent plotter in *Sherlock*, Moriarty is well versed in the language of contemporary terrorism, which he appropriates for his own purposes. Conan Doyle's Moriarty, who claims to be first annoyed, then threatened by Holmes's aggressive pursuit of him, responds by finally pursuing Holmes and Watson to the Continent to Reichenbach Falls. This Moriarty can be relied upon to supply a highly effective assassin for hire, for example, as in the resolution of *The Valley of Fear*. However, in the relatively few glimpses the reader gets of Moriarty in the stories, he seems to operate his consulting practice with intelligence and efficiency, independently of Holmes. In contrast, in *Sherlock*, terror orchestrated by Moriarty plays a role in each of the episodes as Sherlock contends with criminals who hide in plain sight

Sherlock begins in "A Study in Pink" with a serial killer who forces his various victims, the presumably random occupants of his cab, to commit suicide. Presumably, Moriarty cannot get much tangible benefit from sponsoring these random killings, except perhaps the way they occupy the police and the public, yet he funds the murders. Here, even that staple of contemporary thrillers, the serial killer, is part of Moriarty's conspiracy, perhaps gratifying his taste for control, cloaked in chaos. In comparison, the Orientalist plot of "The Blind Banker" with its smuggling, cryptic messages, and gang violence seems to be a much more practical plot for Moriarty, who stands to gain financially from the successful smuggling of antiquities. "The Great Game" represents a departure for Moriarty, since he becomes deeply involved in the threatened bombings in a fashion that he generally eschews. In a 21st century context, these bombs represent a kind of urban terror in the major metropolises of the West associated with recent political bombings in New York, London, and elsewhere. Certainly, when the elderly bomb-bearer begins to describe Moriarty and he detonates her bomb, the image of a large chunk blown out of an apartment building recalls a familiar image and a familiar fear for a 21st century viewer.

The very concept of a suicide bomber seems inextricably linked to politics for a contemporary viewer. Yet this bomber, Moriarty, for all his disregard of life, does not appear to have a political motive. He is perhaps, as Sherlock avers, bored, but he is not beholden to any cause beyond his own power and enrichment, harkening back to Chesterton's idea of criminals as "cosmic conservatives" (1972, 6). Moriarty enjoys violence and plotting as a kind of self-gratifying art as well as a business. Even as he is detached from his victims as individuals, Moriarty is invested clearly in the satisfaction that the series of outrages represents, inviting Sherlock's admiration, stimulating his intellect, taking his time. By using John as the final bomb-bearer, Moriarty raises the stakes for Sherlock. *Sherlock* invites the viewer to mistake John for Moriarty, until the viewer realizes that John, like the other victims, has been co-opted to be the voice of Moriarty, literally in reading out Moriarty's challenges to Sherlock and figuratively in serving as an unwilling suicide bomber. Thus, Moriarty has challenged Sherlock's detachment by making the final scene a personal, rather than intellectual, threat. The terror that Moriarty represents finally has reached Sherlock more directly through John. Yet, this personal conflict means that the villain can be clearly identified, effectively dueled, and potentially cast out, which harkens back to Victorian nostalgia. Presumably, a world featuring an "arch-enemy," as John describes him with deliberate, ironic sensationalism, is a world of moral certitudes wherein Moriarty's own plots, the crimes he authors, enable the villain's downfall.

Here again, Moriarty's position as fan author connects with his role as criminal mastermind. Though the terrorist Moriarty longs to destroy Sherlock and John, doing so would eliminate the only individuals in a position to admire (and thus legitimate) his work, so Moriarty continues to play with them, assuming he can keep the upper hand. Moriarty's sometime hostility toward Sherlock is tempered by his need for Sherlock's admiration. Moriarty's relationship with Sherlock mirrors some of the ambivalence of the fan author's relationship with his or her source text; even as the fan author alters and reinterprets the source, the connection to the original legitimates the fan texts he or she produces. This very ambivalence in the relationship of fan author to source recalls Conan Doyle's sometime hostility toward his own creation.

This emphasis on terror in *Sherlock* seems to be a thoroughly contemporary touch, orchestrated by the enigmatic villain that only Sherlock seems to have perceived fully. Yet the Holmes stories were written and published during a time of terrorist incidents that resonate with our current sensibility, notably a series of attempted terrorist bombings, some successful, in London: "For instance, in London in 1884, terrorist plots were foiled by the discovery of bombs at Charing Cross, Paddington, and Ludgate Hill Stations, and in Trafalgar Square, but there were explosions at Victoria Station, the Junior Carlton Club, Scotland Yard, and London Bridge" (Knowles and Moore 2000, 12). Certainly, the contemporary milieu for the stories would involve fears of terrorism and anarchists in London; however, this context is notably missing in the stories. Likewise, the stories of the most influential of detectives make no reference to the Jack the Ripper murders in Whitechapel, though this case became a media sensation on both sides of the Atlantic. Since the Holmes stories famously treat colonialism and related issues, generally taking a New Imperialist position on empire, the decision not to address contemporary political bombings and the figure of the serial killer as revealed in the Whitechapel killings seems to be a deliberate one, though, of course, this historical context can inform the stories without playing a direct role in the plot.

The murder at the heart of *A Study in Scarlet* initially appears to be a political one, but Holmes rapidly dismisses the "RACHE" scrawled on the wall in the murderer's blood (a clue revised for Conan Doyle fans in *Sherlock*'s "A Study in Pink"): "it was simply a blind intended to put the police on the wrong track, by suggesting Socialism and secret societies" (III:68–69). Holmes realizes that the writing was intended to look German, but "[i]t was simply a ruse to divert inquiry into the wrong channel" (III:69), and he seeks a "more specific and personal accounting" for the crime (Thomas 1999, 224). The criminal smashing busts of Napoleon in "The Adventure of the Six Napoleons" is not, as a shopkeeper avers, part of "a Nihilist plot," because "No one but an anarchist would go about breaking statues" (II:1043–44). Instead, the smasher is a thief trying to locate the "black pearl of the Borgias" that he hid in the wet plaster of the bust shortly after it was crafted (II:1059). Mentions of socialism and anarchism are rare in the stories, despite their topical relevance. In his consideration of the Holmes novellas, *A Study in Scarlet* and *The Sign of Four*, Ronald R. Thomas examines the way that Holmes solves crimes which appear to be political by finding them to be personal: "Like the emerging criminological literature that explicitly sought to medicalize crime and marginalize the impact of social conditions, the outcomes of Holmes's investigations are inclined to make each crime a case unto itself rather than a manifestation of a more general political or social condition" (1999, 224). Ultimately, this distinction breaks down in *A Study in Scarlet*, and Thomas argues that the personal and the political are irrevocably linked: "the case may be more accurately regarded as an expression of the essentially political nature of any personal matter" (1999, 225). Thus, having Holmes investigate an anarchist bombing would work against the premise of the stories, which tend to understand and present crime as a personal issue. This is perhaps a kind of strategic plotting on Conan Doyle's part: superficially, personal battles seem easier to contain, though such plotting suggests anxiety about the politics inherent even in "personal" solutions.

Similarly, perhaps it is the way that the never-solved Whitechapel killings fail to lend themselves to comforting resolution that keeps such serial killings from being addressed in the Holmes canon. Christopher Pittard comments on the omission of the serial killer in the stories: "The Holmes stories, often regarded as the point of origin for the aesthetics of late–Victorian crime narrative, certainly had little contact with Ripper mythology," going on to cite Franco Morretti's caution that is would be "unwise" for the "omniscient detective" to go to Whitechapel (2008, 42). Certainly, the Ripper case had become a morass of botched clues and investigative dead ends, nothing Conan Doyle would want to associate with the genius of Sherlock Holmes. But for *Sherlock*, the serial killer has become a familiar part of the landscape of crime fiction, no longer a legendary monster like Jack, but a dishearteningly commonplace aspect of the contemporary environment. In tying the cab driver's killings to Moriarty in "A Study in Pink," *Sherlock* makes them part of the bourgeois business of crime, less about gruesome self-gratification for the killer (though that is one aspect of the case) and more about providing a pension for his family.

Nostalgia, Resolution, and the Pleasures of Sherlock

When Moriarty asks Sherlock, "What would you like me to make him say next?" (TGG), forcing John to be his mouthpiece, Moriarty invites us to consider his position as criminal, author, and terrorist. Slyly inviting Sherlock's complicity in the subjugation of John, Moriarty mirrors Sherlock's aesthetic appreciation of artful crime and his detachment from its victims. This offer highlights the link between Sherlock's coldness and Moriarty's cruel disregard for humanity. It also reflects the viewers' own voyeuristic bloodlust; like

Sherlock, we long for a good, scripted crime to engage us, to help us escape from the banalities as well as the horrors of daily life. *Sherlock* recasts the serial killer as a worker earning a pension and the suicide bomber as the innocent victim of a flamboyant crime boss. Like Conan Doyle's stories, each of these plots demystifies crime and makes a mysterious criminal agency material, yet *Sherlock* also follows Conan Doyle in recasting apparently political crime as personal. By making suicide bombers not fervent jihadists but victims of Moriarty, terror becomes localized and containable rather than diffuse. Also, revealing terror to be a plot of Moriarty's devising makes this plotting into something pleasurable. Moriarty's construction of multiple narratives of crime, his careful arrangement of clues as he authors these crimes, and his anticipation of Sherlock's and the police's understanding of his crimes remind us of the work of the fan authors, Moffat and Gatiss, in adapting the Holmesian characters and plots. Conan Doyle found Holmes both addictive and suffocating and plotted to kill him. Reflecting the role of the fan author, Moriarty both invites Sherlock's admiration with his artful plots and seeks to vanquish him with his superior skills. Befitting all this plotting, the first season ends with a cliffhanger, inviting the viewer's addictive response to all this dueling between the detective and the plotter, which leaves the viewer longing for season two.

Sherlock enjoys the sensationalism and self-conscious fictionality of its project, recreating a world where Holmes has an arch-enemy, a figure who ties myriad crimes together through his impressive network, and who can be dueled with and quelled. *Sherlock* develops Moriarty into a dynamic character who, in pursuing Sherlock, reveals much about the decadent side of Sherlock himself. By making Moriarty into a figure for the fan author, Moffat and Gatiss consider the complex ways in which an adaptation challenges its source as well as reinvigorates its cultural life. Moriarty admires Sherlock and scripts his cases, but he still longs to kill him, much as Conan Doyle did. By acknowledging the omnipresence of terror in a contemporary society concerned with suicide bombers, serial killers, and targeted violence, *Sherlock* also offers us the fictional reassurance of a character that can locate the principle of order in apparent chaos and act to save society. In acknowledging the pleasures of its fictional world, *Sherlock* implicitly endorses the pleasures of fannish enjoyment of these texts as a relief from the 21st century environment, thus harkening back to the popularity of the original series and its similar endorsement of readerly enjoyment.

Works Cited

Chesterton, G.K. 1974. A defense of detective stories. In *The art of the mystery story*, ed. Howard Haycraft, 3–6. New York: Carroll and Graf.

Conan Doyle, Arthur. 2003. The field bazaar. In *The Complete Sherlock Holmes*, Vol. 2., 671–73. New York: Barnes and Noble Classics.

_____. 2003. How Watson learned the trick. In *The Complete Sherlock Holmes*, Vol. 2., 674–75. New York: Barnes and Noble Classics.

Hühn, Peter. 1987. The detective as reader: Narrativity and reading concepts in detective fiction. *Modern Fiction Studies* 33 (3): 451–66.

Knowles, Owen, and Gene Moore. 2000. Anarchism. In *Oxford reader's companion to Conrad*, 12–14. Oxford: Oxford University Press.

Lycett, Andrew. 2007. *The man who created Sherlock Holmes: The life and times of Sir Arthur Conan Doyle.* New York: Free Press.

Pittard, Christopher. 2008. The real sensation of 1887: Fergus Hume and *The mystery of a Hansom cab. Clues: A Journal of Detection* 26 (1): 37–48.

Thomas, Ronald R. 1999. *Detective fiction and the rise of forensic science.* Cambridge: Cambridge Universtiy Press.

Wiltse, Ed. 1998. "So constant an expectation": Sherlock Holmes and seriality. *Narrative* 6 (2): 105–22.

Decoding the Industrial and Digital City

Visions of Security in Holmes' and Sherlock's London

ANNE KUSTRITZ AND MELANIE E. S. KOHNEN

Abstract — Both the original and BBC Sherlock Holmes rely on the science of deduction to solve crimes and dazzle audiences. Emerging in times of cultural transformation, both characters offer reassurance about safety in the city by decoding people and places using contemporary technologies. In industrial Victorian/Edwardian London, Holmes relies on emerging sciences of social and criminal typology to classify residents into proper British subjects and deviant criminals. In millennial London, Sherlock links crimes to perpetrators by utilizing digital media to filter modern informational chaos. Sherlock's intellectual brilliance and mastery of technology offer viewers an appearance of familiarity, which ultimately stems from long-standing cultural tropes that structure narratives about securing urban space, and separating criminologists from criminals. Despite updates, we argue that problematic aspects of Conan Doyle's stories linger in *Sherlock*: 19th century ideas about hereditary deviance resurface in Sherlock's self-diagnosed sociopathy, and Orientalist renderings turn Chinese culture into the one mystery that Sherlock's mastery of digital technology cannot unravel. Indeed, perhaps *Sherlock*'s true innovation is found in moments of doubt about Sherlock's ability to decode and fit into a heterogeneous society. Despite the insistence that digital technology and social typology help master 21st century life's informational overload, at the series' conclusion even Sherlock himself escapes and defies categorization.

Introduction

The first time Sherlock Holmes and John Watson meet in the BBC's *Sherlock* registers as both familiar and new to viewers acquainted with Sir Arthur Conan Doyle's works. Like previous incarnations of the famous detective, Sherlock uses the science of deduction to ascertain John's background and motives. Analyzing little details like tanning patterns, a slight limp, and rigid posture, Sherlock correctly deduces that John recently returned from military service in Afghanistan or Iraq and seeks a place to live in London. Yet, Sherlock misreads one detail by assuming the engraved "Harry" on John's smart phone indicates a brother, rather than a sister named Harriet, with an estranged wife. This brief scene encapsulates the pleasure in (re)discovering the figures of Sherlock Holmes, John Watson, and the ever-changing London metropole, and the promise and pitfalls associated with using social typologies and digital technology to understand urban life. After all, in contemporary London people like Harriet defy even increasingly heterogeneous social norms and thus upset Sherlock's carefully crafted idea of the world around him.

In his original incarnation, Sherlock Holmes functioned as a virtuoso reader of people and places; he thus provided assurance that the newly expanded industrial city remained understandable and therefore safe by shoring up faith that scientific skills and an analytic mind can thwart the dense physical and social geographies of Victorian and Edwardian London. Holmes ushered in a "golden era" of detective fiction, but also plied his craft against a real world backdrop in which the social typologies of the detective, social scientist, and born criminal also emerged. Thus, as *Sherlock* reassembles the canon for a modern audience, its exclusions, revisions, and adaptations reveal contemporary cultural anxieties, stubborn continuities, and transformations in the city's structure and politics from industrial to post-industrial, imperial to neo-colonial, and scientific to digital. Watching both Sherlock's virtuoso and his failed attempts to navigate and read digital London offers viewers an opportunity to reconceptualize the safety, comprehensibility, and predictability of contemporary urban life. In doing so, *Sherlock* simultaneously invests in and undermines older systems of racialized criminal typology, represented in the guise of modern neurobiology and digital technology, as the key to safety in the city.

Of Sociopathy and Social Control: Imperial and Millennial Politics of the Science of Deduction

While both the original Holmes and BBC's Sherlock famously employ the science of deduction, a network of assumptions about the city of London and a predictive model of human behavior underlie the method, with profound political consequences. In the original stories, Holmes' assumptions reflected and encouraged growing concerns about cultural and racial purity within the British Empire, and the emerging consensus on the physicality of racialized criminal "types." The BBC's reimagined version offers a picture of an increasingly multi-cultural, heterogeneous London; at the same time, it re-presents some startlingly similar stereotypes based on race, class, nationality, and criminal typology, all of which would not have been out of place at the turn of the 20th century. Both Conan Doyle's original and the BBC's *Sherlock* rely on the technology of social typology to make the chaos of the city comprehensible, but while Conan Doyle offered a new scientific hero as the solution to security in London, *Sherlock* often reveals the illusory nature of such fantasies of social control.

Conan Doyle relied upon his readers' shared beliefs about how people live in order to make his characters' behavior seem predictable enough for Holmes' deductions to function plausibly. For example, "The Adventure of the Blue Carbuncle" begins with Holmes' conclusions regarding the likely owner of a lost hat, many of which no longer make sense to modern audiences. At first Watson protests when Holmes states that the hat demonstrates its owner has lost his wife's love, but Watson agrees with his friend's reasoning when Holmes describes how his inference derived from the hat's accumulated dust. He explains, "When I see you, my dear Watson, with a week's accumulation of dust upon your hat, and when your wife allows you to go out in such a state, I shall fear that you also have been unfortunate enough to lose your wife's affection" (I:203). In this case Conan Doyle requires that his readers share the same assumptions about gender and marriage; the deduction only makes sense if readers can believe that all wives take care of their husbands' hats. Even more glaringly strange for modern audiences, Holmes asserts that the owner must be intelligent because of the large size of his head. A reference to the now debunked pseudosciences of phrenology and cranial measurement, Holmes explains, "It is a question of cubic capacity ... a man with so large a brain must have something in it" (I:202). Yet, at a time in which skulls and facial measurements featured prominently in Alphonse Bertillon and Cesare Lombroso's revolutionized policing through the definition of physical markers of criminality, as well as the increasing popularity of eugenic and anthropological explanations of innate racial difference, Conan Doyle could count on his readers to follow Holmes' reasoning and assume that the size and shape of the skull reflects the thoughts it holds.

Each of these small deductions indicates a set of concepts about human behavior with wide-ranging consequences, one socio-cultural and the other bio-racial. The first deduction requires an improbably homogeneous view of life in the city, and exemplifies a class of deductions that depend on the assumption that all people would behave the same way in the same circumstances. "The Adventure of the Blue Carbuncle" thereby constructs heteronormativity

and gender compliance as dominant in Conan Doyle's era, and similar inferences throughout the Holmes works alternately suppress and Other London's
multiculturalism. While modern audiences would dismiss the notion that a
dirty hat presents irrefutable proof of the loss of a wife's love, characters' normative characteristics still remain unmarked and unremarked upon. Thus,
even in modern London, *Sherlock* may depend upon contemporary viewers
to accept that men can't carry pink cases, or that giving oral sex degrades
women but not the men who receive it.

Yet, while relying on a deductive method based upon social uniformity,
Sherlock must repeatedly grapple with a population whose habits fail to conform to one homogenous life path, including his own. The one type of deduction Sherlock repeatedly miscalculates involves sexuality, both because of his
reliance on heteronormativity and social stereotype and because of his own
sexual nonconformity. Thus, Sherlock's "reading" of John's phone proves true
in every respect apart from the gender and sexuality of John's sibling. Sherlock
begrudgingly dismisses the error, frustratedly declaring, "It's always something" (ASiP), but the subject of sexuality continues to foil him throughout
the series, indicating a pattern rather than a fluke. Later, Sherlock "plays gay"
to entice a suspect, but subsequently falls for an enemy's use of the same
tactic, misrecognizing a performance for a sincere proposition and missing
an early opportunity to catch the villain. Thus, by assuming that particular
underwear and mannerisms equate with a desire to sleep with men, he demonstrated an inability to differentiate between stereotypical symbols of gayness
and actual lived experience, which takes many forms.

These incidents position non-heteronormative desires and lives as "difficult to read" and mark Sherlock as an earlier era's archetype adrift in a sexually diverse city with few tools to appropriately understand this strange new
world. Yet, Sherlock also distances himself from the prospect of either a girlfriend or boyfriend, characterizing himself as "married to my work" (ASiP).
While perhaps an allusion to Holmes' status as a dedicated bachelor, a phrase
often used in Victorian representations to indicate men with same-sex desires,
it also offers at least two other readings: either Sherlock's marriage to his work
precludes all romantic and erotic interest, or, as his work involves violent
crime, his admission associates the desire, passion, and commitment of marriage with murder. Thus the text positions Sherlock as sexually illegible, as
either asexual or criminally perverse. In either case, Sherlock's inability to
decode sexuality, along with his own non-normative desires, present modern
London as sexually heterogeneous and thus opaque; hat caretaking can no
longer be taken for granted.

With regard to Holmes' deductions about the hat owner's intelligence,
Conan Doyle functioned within the rise of "scientific" explanations for human

behavior derived from race and heredity. This sort of deduction assumes that behavior can be predicted and social order maintained by classifying people into definable types, as each type exhibits a recognizable and dependable behavioral pattern. As Alison Moore notes, typologizing the criminal in the late 1800s as an inherently different and genetically inferior kind of person linked criminality to racial inferiority by associating sadism and amorality with primitive urges that civilized people evolved beyond (2009). These theories suggested that governments could control criminals, and other "racial degenerates," by visually identifying them and engineering the city and the Empire to keep them separate from respectable families (Siddiqi 2006). Thus, Napoleon rebuilt Paris to create a revolution-proof city that thwarted barricading and the gathering of visually impenetrable crowds, and colonial settlements strictly limited and controlled the movements of both colonial agents and subjects (Stoler 2002). The winding alleyways of the medieval city slowly gave way to broad boulevards, but where they remained a concomitant social contagion remained: the fear of visual impenetrability and the seething crowd which might act *en masse* or disappear entirely at any moment, undermining typologization's imposition of urban legibility and security.

Despite the ridiculousness of Holmes' assertion about the size of the hat for modern audiences, the underlying notion that criminals have distinct biophysical properties, or that biological factors associated with race cause crime, still emerge in new or altered forms in contemporary politics and representation; thus the integration or non-integration of racial Others into the (neocolonial) city remains fraught in *Sherlock*. "The Blind Banker" opens upon Sherlock and a robed figure in a turban engaged in swordplay inside 221B Baker Street; the facial covering not only ties the figure to modes of Orientalist representation wherein the "orient" appears mysterious and dangerous, but also renders him completely anonymous, foreshadowing his utter irrelevance to the plot as the fight and the figure never reappear. The episode actually revolves around a Chinese smuggling ring run by acrobats, reminiscent of the Andaman Islander, Tonga, featured in "The Sign of the Four," known for his inhuman agility and archaic, amoral code of honor; the acrobats exhibit both as they enter supposedly impregnable buildings, exhibit sadistic pleasure in others' terror, and mercilessly kill family members who break the group's code of honor. Like the opening's veiled figure, most of the Chinese characters in "The Blind Banker" remain anonymous, using aliases; Sherlock and John thus repeatedly fail to deduce which individuals in a crowd of Chinese people pose a threat, which are criminals, and which are properly incorporated British subjects. Most strikingly, when John and Sherlock visit London's Chinatown, the camera pans across a stream of anonymous faces, creating a visual equivalence between members of the crowd as mutely homogeneous in their racial difference from the protagonists. The chief villain stands among the crowd filming John and Sherlock without raising their suspicions, then seamlessly disappears within it. *Sherlock* thus presents the masses of London as criminal, frightening, and opaque — as long as that crowd is primarily Chinese.

Yet, although not all criminals in *Sherlock* are racial others, the series represents crime itself as an essentialized, speciated, heritable personality trait, which offers the promise of safety in the city through the removal of these "bad people," particularly for a class of "master criminals," which includes the chief villain, Moriarty, as well as the sadistic Chinese acrobats' leader. Because the notion of evolutionary, heritable criminality reached its clearest articulation in the original stories' time, within the original Conan Doyle narrative Holmes represented a civilizing figure of order, as did the British Empire throughout the world. While not himself an aristocrat, Conan Doyle's Holmes takes his racial and cultural *noblesse oblige* seriously and believes in his duty to protect the innocent and punish those who continue to threaten social order. Again from "The Adventure of the Blue Carbuncle," Holmes reminds Watson that an innocent life hangs in the balance of their current case, and lets the villain go, because he predicts that the young man will not return to crime, acting as an ultimate moral arbiter. In its reinvisioning, *Sherlock* undermines these distinctions by updating the concept of inherent criminality with modern psychological constructions of personality disorder. Security in London therefore becomes not simply a question of controlling the (racialized) lower classes, but controlling all psycho-genetic deviations which unpredictably emerge from within the body politic, and even within the heroic figure himself.

While maintaining the racial purity of Empire structured the city in the original Holmes' time, *Sherlock* takes place in the wake of a decade long overhaul in the British government's approach to policing space through criminal psychology, culminating in the creation of two new classes of citation and detention: the Anti-Social Behavior Order (ASBO) and Dangerous and Severe Personality Disorder (DSPD) order, which both typologize crime as inherent and inheritable. The term ASBO appears in *Sherlock* when a graffiti artist and informant of Sherlock's leaves John holding his spray can when the police arrive. A few scenes later John angrily tells Sherlock that as a result of the incident, "They're giving me an ASBO!" This seemingly incidental reference illuminates profound changes in millennial London's social and political geographies caused by Prime Minister Tony Blair's neo-liberal-inflected New Labor government. A crown jewel of New Labor politics, Blair intended the ASBO to deal with public concerns about disorderly youth and a new class of "sub-criminal acts." Thus, despite the name and attendant pathologization, the ASBO does not address true Anti-Social Personality Disorder, but rather may be issued by police at their discretion, with a lower threshold of proof, for behavior deemed "non-conforming to social norms." Particularly because New Labor slowly defunded many social services, and any member of a household's ASBO citation may revoke existing social services including public housing, ASBO policies replace a social safety net with punishment, which reliably falls most heavily on minorities and the poor, thereby criminalizing and pathologizing poverty and racial difference in the name of crime prevention (Rodger 2006; Squires 2006). *Sherlock* alludes to and elides this bundle of racist, classist, and criminally essentialist social policy by casting a white youth as the actual target, and white, educated, professional class John as the default target of an ASBO order, erasing the actual social violence perpetuated against London's new "underclasses." While London's homeless briefly appear as Sherlock's informants, the narrative offers no commentary on the origins of their plight within a political era of personal not social responsibility, or the condition of contemporary homelessness amidst the spectacles of wealth and spaces of capitalist production highlighted by the plot. Instead Sherlock uses the homeless for information, and then blithely and brutally dismisses them in the language of social contagion, citing a need to "disinfect [him]self" (TGG).

In the London where Sherlock lives, psychological nonconformity provides the only necessary clue to deduce future crime, under the assumption that crime derives from stable, inborn personality traits and, like Holmes' deductive method, the government uses that belief to make predictions about future behavior. Thus, policing related to actual Anti-Social Personality Disorder falls under DSPD policy, which allows for preventative incarceration based on some anti-social diagnoses either in the absence of a crime or as an additional amorphous term of confinement which ends only upon recovery from an ailment defined as incurable. Yet numerous clinicians and legal theorists question the validity, reliability, and predictive value of the current diagnostic criteria for anti-social personality disorder and psychopathy, its subclassification, as well as the government's right to deny liberty for ascribed future crimes (Haddock et al. 2001; Hammel 2006). When Sergeant Donovan warns John away from Sherlock with the prediction that he will eventually kill just like the murderers he hunts, and later calls Sherlock a psychopath to his face, Sherlock responds not by denying her claim but by reclassifying himself as a "high functioning sociopath" (ASiP) accepting his place as mentally disordered, but separating himself from psychopaths, who fall under DSPD policy. Such a thin demarcation relies merely on semantic sleight of hand, as clinical and lay definitions of sociopathy and psychopathy vary widely. Sherlock does indeed qualify for many of the criteria listed on the standard Hare Psychopathy Checklist and constructs himself as incapable of empathy yet uniquely qualified as a detective due to the psychological disorder he shares with criminals. Unlike the original Holmes who solved cases to protect the innocent, he thus repeatedly tells John that concern for victims is irrelevant, and miscalculates when deductions require empathy, like the longstanding emotional importance of a stillbirth which provides a password in "A Study in Pink." As such, his liberty in contemporary London remains subject to the police's discretion; although played for humor by the series, the police's good will toward him varies as they search his home without evidence and alternately rely upon and deride him due to his supposedly inborn lack of empathy. Sherlock most clearly relates to psychopaths including Moriarty and the first episode's villain, a genius cab driver, while relational drama derives from John's constant attempts to bridge the emotive gaps between them, attempting to explain to Sherlock why he should care about other people, and how "normal" emotions function. The series thereby appears to reinforce the social perceptions necessary to garner public support for the preventative incarceration of people diagnosed with psychopathy and/or anti-social personality; *Sherlock* supports the belief that the most dangerous criminals' behavior results from such extreme innate bio-psychological differences that they become or are born as monsters who normal people cannot understand, and that because they consequently lack that which makes a person human, namely empathy, a social services approach or rehabilitation will fail while only permanent incapacitation will stop them. The concomitant promise of both New Labor's DSPD and ASBO politics and Victorian criminal typologies assures the public that safety in the city can be purchased at the price of these deviants' liberty.

However, *Sherlock* also incorporates moments of doubt and contradiction regarding the construction of Sherlock and his foe Moriarty's mirrored anti-social characters. In a scene capturing the strange postmodern symmetries of reboots which must simultaneously repress and embrace the franchise's past, Sherlock describes Moriarty as "something new" (TGG). And yet, while new to Sherlock, the audience of previous Holmes works is well acquainted with Moriarty. Within the narrative Sherlock describes Moriarty as "new" due to his unique *modus operandi* as a "consulting criminal," solidifying his role as the dark mirror to Sherlock's "consulting detective." However, here too the classification as "new" stutters, because the character himself references an earlier era, as does the concept of a master criminal, and the practice of goading others into performing violent acts, known as anti-social by proxy. Moriarty's pattern of helping and pushing others into murder may seem like the perfect apologia for the DSPD model as a new type of criminal who exceeds traditional policing and thus requires a new kind of bio-psychological treatment and preventative incarceration. Yet calling such behavior "new" performs exactly the postmodern excision of history inherent to pastiche, deliberately forgetting that such figures have long existed, from mafia bosses to Shakespeare's Iago, and that Moriarty himself is anything but new.

Perhaps most tellingly, the season builds toward a climactic final scene wherein Sherlock must choose between capturing Moriarty and saving John's life. By this point, the little hints constructing a picture of Sherlock's sociopathy intensify until John directly challenges Sherlock's inability to care about other people, take responsibility for his own actions, or feel human emotion. Thus if the clinical and lay reasoning behind anti-social personality validly and reliably predicts behavior, Sherlock should have no problem sacrificing his "friend" to gain the greater satisfaction of outwitting his intellectual equal. Yet, he does not. Instead, he puts himself in danger to save John, and prolongs that danger to ascertain John's well-being. In a telling moment, Sherlock and Moriarty banter about whether or not he will sacrifice John; while Sherlock insists that he has no heart, once again self-diagnosing his pathologically monstrous lack of empathy, Moriarty insists, "We both know that's not true." The series thereby ends by affirming the primacy and depth of Sherlock's attachment to and affection for John, against all odds and contrary to Sherlock's own self-diagnosed bio-psychological limitations.

Thus, while the bulk of the season reinforces a vision of the city and human behavior suggesting that safety relies upon simply typologizing and removing "bad people," the last few moments of *Sherlock* provide a glimpse of a very different, very unsettling understanding of human nature: one that is subject to completely unpredictable change. Although Moriarty does not dedicate his life to good, the fact that Sherlock can feel emotion, and that Moriarty knows it and thus does understand emotions, strongly suggests that he is psychologically and biologically capable of doing so but he chooses not to. Anti-Social behavior disorder and the government's approach to dealing with it suggest that bad people commit crime because they are inherently bad, and good people do not commit crimes, because they are inherently good. The very end of *Sherlock* suggests on the contrary — that people have the capacity for both heroism and evil, and that we make meaningful choices between many possible behaviors. Thus our behaviors are not predetermined by genetics or environment, but instead are subject to change based upon our decisions. While the striking emergence of the older Holmes' social typing based on racial heredity found in ASBO and DSPD policy appears to suggest that contemporary London remains readable and thus controllable to specialists trained or born to understand it, fissures of doubt mar this picture of security and closure. Repeatedly, the heterogeneity of the postmodern city foils attempts to uniformly apply social typologies, even when Sherlock utilizes them to understand himself. Thus it is to digital technologies that the narrative turns to fill these gaps, offering not a new kind of man, but a new kind of technology as the answer to the impermeability and constant change within the digital city.

The Place of Technology in Sherlock

The incorporation of digital technology in *Sherlock* provides the most visible line of demarcation between the BBC series and the original stories. At first glance, integration of contemporary technology offers a clean transition from problematic aspects of Conan Doyle's stories. Yet the digital slots comfortably into the place once occupied by science. Thus, Sherlock fulfills a similar cultural role to Holmes: both extraordinary men reassure us in a time of cultural and social transformations. While Holmes' scientific knowledge reassured 19th century readers that order could exist in the industrial city, Sherlock's technological expertise eases 21st viewers' anxieties about the digital city and information management.

At first sight, Sherlock appears to be a typical member of the millennial generation. He prefers texting to calling, is permanently attached to his smart phone, and maintains a web site called "Science of Deduction." One might think that Sherlock fits right in with "the young and the digital" who gather on social networking sites to maintain social relationships (Watkins 2009, 47). Yet, Sherlock is uninterested in social relationships — he only goes online to acquire information that allows him to establish the missing links between the various clues he has deduced. In Sherlock's first analysis of a crime scene, he accesses local weather reports via his phone and deduces that a moist coat signals the victim traveled from Cardiff (ASiP). Throughout all three episodes, this pattern repeats: Sherlock proves himself an excellent reader of people and places, but he often relies on information gathered via online sources to render his deductions into a coherent picture. We can relate to Sherlock because digital technology occupies a central part in his everyday life as it does in so many of ours, and at the same time we can admire the ease with which he navigates and searches digital networks. Ultimately, Sherlock's technological mastery of, and occasional struggle with, digital London both fascinates and reassures.

Digital London

The incorporation of digital technology in *Sherlock* structures the representation of London. London manifests in *Sherlock* in two interrelated ways: as an assemblage of recognizable and mediated landmarks and as a network of information. Digital London is a map of visual information that can be reproduced, organized, and accessed via technologies of transportation, surveillance, and visualization, and thus becomes a safe, easily navigated cityscape.

The filming of London in *Sherlock* constructs a view of the city's architecture, and thus of the city's political organization, only available through media technology. This mediated perspective reinforces Michel DeCerteau's argument that all urban cartographies are also socio-political geographies (1984). *Sherlock*'s credits artfully mix shots of well-known landmarks, like the London Eye, with close-ups of Sherlock's investigations. Likewise, many wide-angle establishing shots place Sherlock and John in front of easily recognizable places around London, including the National Gallery. Even viewers who have never visited London can identify landmark locations and thus feel reassured that the characters traverse familiar spaces. Television, film, and photography have captured countless images of London — as with many other global cities, the "famous" parts of London have become recognizable to modern audiences through endless repetition in the media. Thus, just as Sherlock himself is composed of familiar parts with a new veneer, the historical icons of London mix with steel-and-glass architecture to create a pastiche of old and new.

London's vista serves as a stunning backdrop to Sherlock and John's travels, but they only experience the city through careful mediation, glimpsed through and mirrored in the windows of taxis. One the one hand, taxis serve as visual confirmation of Britishness and as reference to Victorian hansom cabs. On the other hand, reliance on taxis removes Sherlock and John from the hustle and bustle that they would experience on the Tube. Traveling in a taxi allows them to survey the city without being in direct contact with its people. The taxi thus separates them from the more "undesirable" parts and inhabitants of London. Long takes of Sherlock and John traversing London in a taxi align the audience with the technological mastery of the city made possible by the camera.

There are brief moments in which London issues a challenge to Sherlock and John. In the first episode, they lose track of a taxi speeding off into traffic, but Sherlock's accurate mental map of London projects an alternate route through back alleys and across roofs that eventually allows them to catch up. The visual rendition of Sherlock's mental map alludes to the layout of digital maps and suggests that a digital network overlays the physical structure of the city. Much like a computer calculates a route from Point A to B, Sherlock visualizes the fastest way to catch up with the taxi. The viewer witnesses Sherlock's visualizations in real time as they are intercut with Sherlock and John running down dark streets. Unlike the taxi and the computer, however, Sherlock's mental map is not confined to streets. While fixed physical maps allow some measure of control over the city, Sherlock's grasp of unmapped areas allow him to navigate all of London with confidence. Thus, even seemingly unruly dark alleys and rooftops become comprehensible in the logical system of Sherlock's mind.

Sherlock's ability to recalculate his route through the city in real time echoes the possibilities of digital mapping, which translates physical space into data that can be parsed and calculated. Sherlock once again appears as a relatable but also superior citizen of digital London: the way he maps his way through the nooks and crannies of London looks familiar to us, but in contrast to us, Sherlock does not need to rely on a computer to calculate a route through urban space. Significantly, *Sherlock* portrays digital mapping as beneficial, and not, as some critiques of Google maps and Google street view argue, as invasive (Wray 2009; Holliday 2010). A later scene in "A Study in Pink" highlights these benefits when John tracks the pink phone's GPS signal to find and save Sherlock from the murderous cabbie: the constant stream of information becomes the crucial set of data that saves Sherlock's life. In both cases, it is the digital mapped onto the physical that allows Sherlock and John to move around the city with ease. In fact, loss of digital surveillance represents the real danger. Sherlock's brother Mycroft uses his position in government to turn the city's network of cameras away from John, implying that anything might befall him once outside the camera's eye. The narrative thus momentarily invokes the horror of the unknowable that lies beyond the urban legibility facilitated by social and digital control.

In addition to maps and GPS, Sherlock taps into other networks of information that overlay the geography of London. Across the series, Sherlock regularly searches for weather data, high tide of the Thames, and police reports, all of which he accesses via his smart phone. Sherlock is an expert at efficiently searching these digital networks of information and he knows how to navigate the overwhelming information that an Internet search can produce better than the average user. We could say that Sherlock has learned to master the art of the Internet search: he navigates the terrain of the world wide web with the same sure footing that allows him to navigate the streets of London. As such, Sherlock offers reassurance that we can make sense of the information we have accumulated and that constantly surrounds us. If Sherlock can find patterns in the chaos of data, so can we.

Sherlock manages the informational chaos of 21st century life by discarding extraneous information. When confronted about his ignorance regarding the solar system, Sherlock explains that he "deletes" irrelevant information from his brain, stating, "This is my hard drive and it only makes sense to put things in there that are useful, really useful" (TGG). This exchange between Sherlock and John is a direct callback to the Conan Doyle stories. In the original *A Study in Scarlet*, Holmes compares his brain to an attic and explains that "the skilful workman is very careful indeed as to what he takes into his brain-attic" (3:32). Much like Holmes' brain attic, Sherlock's mental database only stores information relevant to solving cases. Sherlock's smart phone serves as a crucial extension of that mental database and saves the day when Sherlock needs to date the appearance of a supernova, proving that access to searchable data trumps memorization. Throughout all episodes it becomes clear that Sherlock depends on mobile storage and access to information. For example, Sherlock researches Interpol's Most Wanted list and local missing person reports while standing on the bank of the Thames in "The Great Game," which allows him to identify the body as a museum guard without ever leaving the crime scene. Indeed, the information Sherlock accesses online often provides the crucial last piece in Sherlock's deductions.

While we haven't seen Sherlock without access to his external hard drives (his smart phone or laptop), it is apparent that even Sherlock Holmes might be lost without access to the Internet. Online searches without useful results frustrate Sherlock as much as the rest of us. The most striking example of this occurs in "The Great Game" when Sherlock receives a photo-based clue from Moriarty and he immediately identifies the location, observing, "View of the Thames. South Bank, somewhere between Southwark Bridge and Waterloo." Yet, the significance of this clue eludes Sherlock's deductive skills. Via his phone, Sherlock researches the location, which is visually rendered on the screen for the viewer. He quickly moves from "Thames + High Tide + River-side" to "Thames Police Reports: Duty Log" without finding satisfying results. Sherlock appears irritated when the Internet doesn't provide answers and calls Lestrade for help (since we know that Sherlock prefers texting to calling, this person-to-person call is clearly a last resort). The overall portrayal of Sherlock's relationship to digital networks affirms that Sherlock is deeply embedded in them. Moreover, while he knows how to master these networks, he also clearly depends on them — when the Internet fails Sherlock, he is (momentarily) lost. Sherlock thus navigates between two poles of contemporary technology-related anxieties: on the one hand, the fear that the amount of data we encounter on a daily basis is too overwhelming; on the other hand, the fear that we would be lost without access to this data.

A telling exception to the technological legibility of digital London occurs in "The Blind Banker" when the Internet does not provide the crucial missing links that Sherlock needs to bring his deductions to a successful conclusion. Rather, the series of "cyphers" that John and Sherlock encounter and trace through various sites in London prove to be outside the realm of modern databases and thus appear illegible. Perhaps ironically, it is in this introduction of illegible communication that *Sherlock* shows most clearly its backward-looking allegiance to 19th century logics of Orientalism. The missing links that finally allow Sherlock to identify them as Chinese characters are provided by one of Sherlock's informants and by chance when John turns over a tea cup in a store in Chinatown. Indeed, as Sherlock observes,

> the world's running on codes and cyphers, John.... Cryptography inhabits our every waking moment ... but it's all computer-generated. Electronic codes, electronic cyphering methods. This is different. It's an ancient device. Modern code-breaking methods won't unravel it [TBB].

Whereas many details of the Conan Doyle stories are translated into a 21st century setting, the idea that Chinese characters exist in a pre-modern world outside of technology retains late nineteenth-century Orientalism. The Orientalist rendering of Chinese characters as "illegible" cyphers that appear throughout London constitutes a slippage between the digital and the industrial city, as though Chinese culture alone remains unchanged from Holmes' to Sherlock's London. As such, the depiction of London's Chinatown represents the most direct link to the ideologies that characterized the original setting of Conan Doyle's stories.

At the same time, the clear separation between digital London and Chinatown elides the way in which Orientalism has fueled our perception of digital spaces. The idea of the digital as a navigable space, for example, first appears as "cyberspace" in novels such as William Gibson's Asian-influenced, exoticizing *Neuromancer* (1984). Gibson's novel drowns its characters and readers in information, little of which is explained, but physical and digital spaces remain mappable through Orientalist tropes. Wendy Chun argues that "*Neuromancer*'s global or cosmopolitan future depends on stereotypical descriptions of raced others who serve as 'orienting points' for readers and the protagonist" (185). The future spaces imagined in *Neuromancer* thus remain mappable and decodable through the integration of a historical landscapes and racialized tropes. While digital spaces and the Internet as mass media were only a futuristic fantasy in 1984, the digital is part of our present. Nevertheless, as *Sherlock*'s representation of Chinese culture demonstrates, we still rely on Orientalism to provide points of orientation in the digital city.

The Orientalist representation of Chinese culture in "The Blind Banker" serves as another way to affirm Sherlock as a 21st century figure. Sherlock can read the digital city, but he cannot read the "cyphers" that seem to exist outside of the modern sphere. Curiously, once Sherlock and John identify the cyphers as Chinese characters, Sherlock can access a large quantity of knowledge about the inner workings of Chinese smuggling rings. One might say that maintaining narrative suspense constitutes the main reason for Sherlock's blocked knowledge. If he had identified the cypher as Chinese characters early on, the suspense would have evaporated. But the continued air of mystery surrounding all things Chinese, even after the identification of the cyphers, speaks to Orientalism as the fundamental location of narrative suspense. The smuggling of Chinese antiquities, Soo Lin's job in a museum, and the Chinese circus all mark Chinese culture as something different and separate from 21st century digital London.

Moreover, the representation of Chinese culture as fundamentally alien to modern Britain places the viewer in a spectatorial position complicit with Orientalism. Positioned outside of and in opposition to an "unreadable" Chinese culture, the imagined viewer, much like Sherlock himself, cannot identify the "cyphers." This imagined viewer is thus by implication a non–Chinese viewer. While much of *Sherlock* invites the viewer to share Sherlock's experience of digital London, the exclusion of Chinese culture and viewers from this digital modernity suggests that only specific viewers may partake in the decoding of the city: namely those who occupy a position of normative Britishness. Thus, even though the presence of digital technology in *Sherlock* is part of other signals that are supposed to mark the program's diegesis as cosmopolitan and progressive, the depiction of China underlines the lingering presence of Orientalism that shaped the representation of Imperial London in the original Conan Doyle stories and that shaped the emergence of the digital as a mappable and navigable space. While digital technology in *Sherlock* offers a masterful visual and organizing principle for understanding and controlling the rapidly evolving digital city, it continues to function at the expense of those deemed too different and too deviant for the mechanical eye of power to sort, map, and render. In other words, the series' inclusion of digital technology suggests a progressively modern vision of Sherlock Holmes and London, but this vision can only be sustained by reactivating the processes of exoticization and othering at work in the original Doyle canon.

Works Cited

Chun, Wendy Hui Kyong. 2006. *Control and freedom: Power and paranoia in the age of fiber optics.* Cambridge: MIT Press.

DeCerteau, Michel. 1984. Walking in the city. In *The practice of everyday life*, 160–175. Berkeley: University of California Press.

Haddock, A.W., Peter R. Snowden, Mairead Dolan, Julian Parker, and Harvey Rees. 2001. Managing dangerous people with severe personality disorder: A survey of forensic psychiatrists' opinions. *Psychiatric Bulletin* 25:293–296.

Halliday, Josh. 2010. Google committed significant breach over street view. *The Guardian*, November 3. www.guardian.co.uk.

Hammel, Andrew. 2006. Preventative detention in comparative perspective. In *Annual of German & European Law, volumes 2–3*, ed. Russell A. Miller and Peer Zumbansen, 89–115. New York: Berghahn Books.

Moore, Alison. 2009. The invention of sadism. *Sexualities* 12:486–502.

Rodger, John. 2006. Antisocial families and withholding welfare support. *Critical Social Policy* 26:121–143.

Siddiqi, Yumna. 2006. Cesspool of empire. *Victorian Literature and Culture* 34:233–247.

Squires, Peter. 2006. New labor and the politics of antisocial behavior. *Critical Social Policy* 26:144–168.

Stoler, Ann. 2002. *Carnal knowledge and imperial power: Race and the intimate in colonial rule*. Los Angeles: University of California Press.

Watkins, S. Craig. 2009. *The young and the digital: What the migration to social-network sites, games, and anytime, anywhere media means for our future*. Boston: Beacon Press.

Wray, Richard. 2009. Google launches street view in UK. *The Guardian*, March 19. www.guardian.co.uk.

PART THREE

Adaptations and Intertextuality

Shaping Sherlocks
Institutional Practice and the Adaptation of Character

Elizabeth Jane Evans

Abstract — This essay considers how the BBC's adaptation of Sherlock Holmes
as a character is shaped by its institutional policy. In 2010, film and television
audiences were offered three very different versions of Holmes. Warner Bros. created Holmes as an action star; mockbuster company The Asylum offered a mild-
mannered, monster-fighting Holmes; the BBC transplanted Holmes to the modern
world, surrounding him with laptops, mobile phones, and GPS. Even though all
three were based on Conan Doyle's work, each approached its adaptation in
unique ways, privileging certain aspects of Sherlock's personality, appearance, and
personal relationships, whilst reducing or ignoring others. Focusing on the BBC
series specifically, this essay argues that such choices are shaped by institutional
policy and practice. After establishing the link between institutional practice and
character construction through the Warner Bros. and Asylum versions, it moves
on to examine *Sherlock* and its relationship to the Corporation's role as a public
service broadcaster in a global television market. The BBC's Sherlock is detached
from the modern world he inhabits, bringing an air of Victoriana to an otherwise
contemporary diegesis. In doing so, the series combines two traditions of "Quality" television. The first is the U.S.-focused model of high production values,
layered narratives, and psychologically deep characters. The second is the British
tradition of "prestige" drama that privileges literary adaptations and the working
through of Britain's cultural heritage, something inherent to the BBC's charter.
By incorporating both, *Sherlock* encompasses the BBC's need to compete within
a global television drama marketplace dominated by U.S. quality drama whilst
still fulfilling its public service remit and role within the British broadcasting
ecology.

Introduction

A burly street boxer hunts a sadistic, aristocratic villain with claims of
the occult, finally confronting him atop an incomplete Tower Bridge. A short,

thin, mild-mannered detective seeks to discover the origins of several mystical monsters that have been attacking the underbelly of Victorian London society. A haunted, self-confessed sociopath liaises with a put upon Metropolitan police force, solving grisly murders with the help of GPS and smart phones whilst taunted by a sinister figure via his web site.

The above descriptions could easily have applied to three different fictional detectives. In 2010, however, they applied to just one: Sherlock Holmes. In January, Robert Downey Jr. played Holmes in Warner Bros.' *Sherlock Holmes*, while the unknown Ben Syder appeared in straight-to-DVD exploitation company The Asylum's mockbuster version *Sir Arthur Conan Doyle's Sherlock Holmes* (*SACDSH*). Later that year, as the rest of this collection explores, Benedict Cumberbatch played the role in the BBC series *Sherlock*. When it comes to the numerous screen adaptations of Conan Doyle's novels it quickly becomes apparent that the traits of the literary Holmes are not universally applied. The individual physicality and performance of actors, alongside production choices that change narrative events and settings, all contribute to multiple Holmeses.

This essay explores the way in which the BBC's version of Sherlock Holmes is shaped by the corporation's institutional policy and practice. The BBC's need to compete in a global television market whilst simultaneously fulfilling its public service requirements to promote Britain's cultural identity and heritage manifests through the character's appropriation of two traditions of quality television. The first is the growing proliferation of U.S. quality drama series on British screens, something the BBC has been forced to compete with. The second is the tradition, common in British broadcasting, of privileging literary adaptations and cultural heritage.

The Other Holmeses: Institutional Practice and the Adaptation of Character

Roberta Pearson argues that television's complex, repetitive form of engagement means that "[t]elevision characters are to some extent autonomous beings; autonomous, that is, of the televisual codes and individual scenes/episodes that construct them, existing as a whole only in the minds of the producers and the audiences" (2007, 43). Characters exist beyond individual moments, with specific scenes, lines, or moments of performance building to create a whole that is greater than the sum of its parts. Using David Bordwell's work, she identifies six components of televisual characters: "psychological traits/habitual behaviors; physical characteristics/appearance; speech patterns; interactions with other characters; environment; and biography" (2007, 43). Such a model acts as a useful starting point for considering the construction of Sherlock Holmes as a character in the BBC series; however, it is crucial to acknowledge that he is not the creation *of* that series. In fact it is precisely because he is adapted from an independent source text that the relationship between institutional practice and character construction can emerge. The differences evident in screen adaptations of Holmes indicate how the same character, from the same source texts, can be shaped to particular industrial ends.

In the books, the narrative role of Dr. Watson allows Conan Doyle to step outside of the diegesis and provide explicit descriptions of Holmes that fill many components in Pearson's model. In *A Study in Scarlet* he is physically described as follows:

> In height he was rather over six feet, and so excessively lean that he seems to be considerably taller. His eyes were sharp and piercing ... and his thin, hawk-like nose gave his whole expression an air of alertness and decision. His chin, too, had the prominence and squareness which mark the man of determination [III:29–30].

Conan Doyle goes on to identify a number of personality traits in a convenient, numbered list:

1. Knowledge of Literature — Nil.
2. Philosophy — Nil.
3. Astronomy — Nil.
4. Politics — Feeble.
5. Botany — Variable. Well up in belladonna, opium and poisons generally. Knows nothing of practical gardening
6. Geology — Practical, but limited. Tells at a glance difference soils from each other. After walks has shown me splashes upon his trousers, and told me by their color and consistence in what part of London he had received them.
7. Chemistry — profound.
8. Anatomy — Accurate, but unsystematic.
9. Sensational Literature — Immense. He appears to know every detail of every horror perpetrated in the century.
10. Plays the violin well.
11. Is an expert singlestick player, boxer, and swordsman.
12. Has a good practical knowledge of British law [III:34–35].

Such sections give the screen adapter a cheat sheet of physical appearance and psychological traits/habitual behaviors for creating a cinematic or televisual Sherlock Holmes. Of course, in doing so, the narrative codes used to present him are automatically different; the character is constructed not through written words but through a combination of script, direction, costume, performance, and stardom. However, this shift does not prevent any of the features listed above appearing on screen. Instead, it is necessary to consider other factors that may determine how his character is adapted.

One such factor is historical specificity. Sarah Cardwell discusses the importance of history when dealing with classical literary adaptations when she acknowledges both "the relationships through time that an adaptation might bear to other adaptations" and "the historical gap that separates the source novel from the adaptation in question" (2002, 14). A century of social/cultural/political change and of different Holmes adaptations sits between the stories and the BBC series, all of which may shape the way he is constructed.

Similarly, there is the complex issue of medium specificity. Holmes has appeared in radio dramas, theatrical plays, a musical, films, television series, comic books, board games, and video games. However, as I have argued elsewhere, a medium involves multiple components encompassing technology, textual form, and industry (Evans 2011, 175), and each of these may individually shape the tools available to the Holmes adapter. Comparing the different cinematic versions of Holmes that Warner Bros. and The Asylum created allows the opportunity to consider the function of industrial (and especially institutional) factors within adaptation. Both appeared within weeks of each other, thus sharing the same historical context. Although one is a cinematic and the other a straight to DVD release, they share the same narrative conditions in terms of length and narrative closure. Yet despite these contextual similarities, differences still emerge, ones that can be linked to the different priorities of each institution.

Warner Bros.' Action Star

Warner Bros. released *Sherlock Holmes* in the heart of the Christmas blockbuster season, and the character is constructed to reflect his position in a large-budget mainstream film. Within the film and its promotional surround, Holmes is clearly the central narrative agent. He features in most scenes and is the most prominent figure in marketing materials, positioned at the front and center of posters and as the focal point of trailers. Although Watson (Jude Law) also features heavily, he remains clearly secondary; his literary role as narrator is removed and he vanishes for many of the narrative's key moments. Holmes is alone when he fights the gigantic Dredger (Robert Maillet), deduces the truth about the film's core mystery, and finally confronts nemesis Lord Blackwood (Mark Strong). The investigation is clearly structured with Holmes as the central figure and Watson as his sidekick.

The physicality of the film and the casting of Robert Downey Jr. not long after the success of *Iron Man* (2008) constructs Holmes as an action figure in ways that the casting of another, similarly high profile actor may not have done. Sarah Cardwell argues that, "when we watch actors performing, they can never wholly disappear beneath their roles.... Actors, especially well-known ones, which in classic-novel adaptations is often the case, can never simply be viewed as the characters they play" (2002, 89; see also, Pearson 2009). Downey Jr. helps to privilege a particular interpretation of Holmes and shape him as an action hero. His role as *Iron Man*'s genius superhero Tony Stark establishes connotations of characters that are highly intelligent but ultimately action stars. At five foot eight, he is significantly shorter than both the literary Holmes and Law's Watson; however, the film constantly highlights his physicality. He is introduced mid-foot chase with the first shot of his face coming out of a forward roll, later seen combining intellect and pure physical strength in a boxing match, and succeeds in his final confrontation with Blackwood because of his fighting ability as much as his ability to outwit him. At several points in the film, he appears fully or semi-naked, emphasizing his physical body and muscled physique. The highlighting of Holmes' physical attributes and the emphasis on habits that support his action credentials, such as boxing, over others, such as the various topics he is ignorant of, constructs this particular cinematic Holmes as an action hero. As such Downey Jr.'s Holmes fits the strategies of a large Hollywood studio, seeking the viscerally engaging spectacle of a tent pole end-of-year release.

The Asylum's Sci-Fi Sidekick

Less than a month after the blockbuster hit was released in cinemas, B-movie/exploitation company The Asylum released its own version (*SACDSH*, 2010) with director Rachel Goldenberg. The Asylum's brand identity is firmly entrenched in the low-budget science fiction market, based on combining mutant monster films, such as *Mega Shark vs Giant Octopus* (2009), with mockbusters that mimic the story lines of mainstream blockbusters, such as *Transmorphers: Fall of Man* (2009). Unlike other Asylum productions, however, *SACDSH* is not just a parody of a blockbuster film that must evade the copyright issues I.Q Hunter identifies as a central part of exploitation films' narratives (2009). It is also an adaptation of a well known, crucially out of copyright, literary character. Whereas the studio's other releases must rely on generic and vague situational similarity, in this case the studio is able to use the same character and, in adapting him, to demonstrate their broader institutional priorities.

In some aspects, The Asylum's version of Holmes is recognizable. He remains highly intelligent, capable of deducing numerous facts about a situation or person instantly. His relationship with Watson (Gareth David-Lloyd) is intellectually uneven, with Watson often doubting Holmes' assertions until Holmes proves himself correct. In other aspects, however, this Holmes differs significantly from both the stories and the Warner Bros. version. Physically, Ben Syder is slighter than Downey Jr., and throughout the film any sense of physicality is reduced. He is much shorter and thinner than the other actors around him, most noticeably David-Lloyd. Holmes' martial arts skills, which figure so prominently in Downey Jr.'s Holmes, are entirely absent. Scenes that require physical action, including climbing down a cliff face and chasing after nemesis Thorpe's (Dominic Keating) robotic accomplice are performed by Watson, with Holmes taking a more advisory or intellectual role. Holmes' small stature makes him seem meek, and his soft speech patterns, even though the words being spoken are deductively correct, give him an air of uncertainty. Many of his idiosyncrasies such as violin playing and cocaine addiction are absent, appearing merely as a slight inability to get on with other characters, rather than any concrete eccentric habits.

These differences in how Holmes is constructed are compounded by the relative status of other characters, most notably Watson. As in the novels, Watson serves as the key narrator and framing device, narrating a missing section from his diaries on his deathbed; he is heavily involved in key narrative sequences and took a prominent role in promotional material, figuring heavily in the trailer and being given top billing, followed by the film's villain, Thorpe. The reasons for this emphasis become apparent when considering The Asylum's association with science fiction markets. Whereas the recent success of *Iron Man* made Downey Jr. the most well-known cast member of the film, Syder is unknown. In contrast, the actors playing Watson and Thorpe, Gareth David-Lloyd and Dominic Keating, were already established within science fiction fandoms (*Torchwood* and *Star Trek: Enterprise*, respectively). Whilst Robert Downey Jr. brought extratextual meaning to the role of Holmes, Syder is the exact opposite; instead it is Watson and Thorpe that bring the marketing and extratextual meanings linked to known actors. By privileging David-Lloyd and Keating, The Asylum aligns its adaptation of Sherlock Holmes with a pre-established genre audience.

Institutional Practice and Character Adaptation

The multiple differences between adaptations of Sherlock Holmes position him alongside figures such as James Bond, Robin Hood, and Batman, in

Bennett and Wollacott's model of a "popular hero" that, they argue "break[s] free from the originating textual conditions" (1987, 14). They discuss such figures as transcending their original source materials, with character acting as a central narrative point with more import than events or setting. This sets such adaptations apart from franchises that privilege narrative events and settings, such as *Lord of the Rings* (2001–2003) or *Harry Potter* (2001–2011). Whilst some Holmes adaptations followed Conan Doyle's actual stories, most notably the Granada series (1984–1994) and various adaptations of *The Hound of the Baskervilles* on film, radio, and television, it has tended to be the *character* rather than individual story lines that is adapted. It is, then, perhaps natural that different Holmeses emerge. Uri Margolin argues that "[a]ll texts are finite, while each [character] can be specified with respect to an indefinite number of attributes. Consequently, textually created characters are radically incomplete as regards the number and nature of the properties ascribed to them" (2007, 68). He goes on to write: "any given character may be amenable to a whole range of alternative individuations, all of which are none the less compatible with the original" (2007, 69). While the literary Holmes may be incomplete to begin with, screen Holmeses are incomplete versions of that incompleteness and in turn may privilege different aspects of his personality. But, to follow Margolin's argument, each one is as legitimate as the other, because no individual text could ever offer a fully complete Holmes (including Conan Doyle's stories).

The differences between 2010's two film versions of Sherlock Holmes demonstrate the relationship between each incomplete version of Holmes and the institutional policy of its source. Whilst some allowances should be made for the individual creative decisions of production personnel, such decisions take place within a complex industrial context. Trisha Dunleavy has explored the difficulty of discussing authorship in television, arguing that "the 'lone talent' model of authorship" fails "to confront the industrial realities of TV production as a linked chain of four main collaborative processes–concept design, scriptwriting production, and post-production" (Dunleavy 2009, 35). Unlike novels and short stories, films and television programs are produced from an industrial and institutional context that involves multiple inputs from various personnel. Anthony Smith (2010) has demonstrated how comic book narratives have been shaped by their institutional context, and Warner Bros. and The Asylum similarly indicate how each institution's practice and policy functions to shape the character's construction. Decisions about casting, script direction, and performance reflect the particular industrial positions and priorities of the institutions behind them. Comparing each Holmes' physical appearance, personality traits and relationship to other characters, and to Watson in particular, leads to the recognition of very different characters, each with different narrative roles and status. Warner Bros.' is a Hollywood blockbuster Holmes; The Asylum's is one that is slighted in favor of science fiction elements. Against this backdrop, we can now consider how the BBC's 2010 version of Sherlock Holmes reveals the nature of his institutional origin in a contemporary public service broadcaster operating in an increasingly competitive global television marketplace.

Sherlock's *Sherlock: A Thoroughly Modern, Victorian Holmes*

The most obvious way in which the BBC's version of Holmes differs from the ones by Warner Bros. and The Asylum is in what Pearson refers to as "environment." Unlike the two filmic versions, which maintain a late 1800s setting, the BBC's Sherlock is transplanted into the 21st century. State of the art technology, including smart phones and GPS, features heavily throughout the series, often proving central to solving the episode's mystery or catching the perpetrator. Certain idiosyncrasies are modernized, with tobacco substituting for the now less-acceptable cocaine. His sexuality, something that is predominantly absent in the stories, is presented ambiguously, with an awkward conversation between Sherlock and John Watson (Martin Freeman) alluding to the possibility, though not confirmation, of a more fluid sexual identity, that sits more easily now than in the overtly conservative Victorian period. This modernizing is translated into the characters at the most basic level with the shift from Holmes to Sherlock and Watson to John, a more modern, casual mode of address, something underlined by the series title. However, this surface modernizing sits uneasily with the series' construction of Sherlock as a character. The BBC series privileges traits from the source stories that position Sherlock as slightly out of touch with the world around him. Although his use of modern technology echoes the use of early forensic science in the original stories, the BBC series emphasizes a disconnection between Sherlock and the world around him, one that speaks to his literary and historical origins.

Sherlock's first appearance immediately positions him within both the modern world and the late 19th century. In his opening scene he is seen repeatedly beating a dead body with a riding whip in order to monitor the development of post-mortem bruising. Whilst such an act is in line with the context of Victorian criminology, it seems somewhat archaic in a post-forensic science, post–*CSI* world. His specialized but limited awareness of contemporary general knowledge is not only maintained, but becomes a key plot point in "The Great Game" when John is appalled at Sherlock's inability to recall primary school facts and a young child almost dies because of his lack of interest in astronomy. The series' mise-en-scène provides Sherlock with an aesthetic air of Victoriana. Laptops and smart phones sit within a flat that is furnished with cluttered antique furniture and decorated in dark, patterned wallpaper. In comparison to John, whose cotton shirts, jeans, and waist length jackets position him as a sartorial everyman, Sherlock's tendency towards silk fabrics, high collared long coats, and suits (but no tie), position him as visually distinct. He is not the casually dressed everyman but he is equally not the tailored businessman. He is both a part of the modern world and detached from it.

Cumberbatch's physicality fits the original description of Holmes very closely, far more so than either Downey Jr. or Syder, and thus contributes to this sense of modern Victoriana. Executive producer Steven Moffat refers to Cumberbatch's physical appearance as a key factor in his casting, saying, "[a]s soon as we saw the film *Atonement*, we saw Benedict Cumberbatch thinking 'oh he looks like a Sherlock Holmes'" (Unlocking). At over six foot, he is not only significantly taller than Martin Freeman, but also taller than nearly any other actor who appears within the same frame as him. Cumberbatch's height is often emphasized by his placement in the front and center of frames, with other characters positioned behind and to the side; a number of acute camera angles shoot him from above or below, elongating his body, in particular his face. In doing so, he is physically set apart from the other characters, becoming distorted from the world around him. He speaks quickly, often ending sentences abruptly before moving away suddenly and leaving other characters lost. His sharp-toned upper middle class accent similarly distinguishes him from Freeman's lower middle-class John. The casting of Cumberbatch also contributes to the character's straddling of the 19th and 21st centuries in terms of the associations he brings from previous roles. Although not quite as well known to audiences as Freeman (thanks to the latter's role in *The Office* [2001–03]), Cumberbatch was still recognizable from a mixture of films and television series that straddled period pieces, including *Atonement* (2007) and *The Other Boleyn Girl* (2008), and modern-day settings, such as *The Last Enemy* (2008) and *Stuart: A Life Backwards* (2007). As with Downey Jr., Cumberbatch too brings extratextual references with him, and more specifically he contributes an association with a mix of modern and period-set dramas.

This sense of disconnection from the world around him also figures in his relationship with John, indicating Roberta Pearson's assertion that "as with real people, fictional people derive identity partially from the social roles that they enact in the home, in the workplace" (2009, 150). The BBC series constructs the men's relationship as a mutually reinforcing partnership of opposites and in doing so emphasizes Sherlock's detachment from modern social mores. Despite his extraordinary back story in Afghanistan, John is presented as the everyman, and his few extraordinary skills (beyond being a good shot) and general confusion about the situations he finds himself in positions him as the audience's key touchstone of the familiar. This everyman role stands in contrast to Sherlock, making the latter seem out of touch with the modern world. John is practical, whereas Sherlock is more fanciful, as demonstrated in opening to "The Blind Banker" in which John is shopping and Sherlock is fending off an assassin in an elaborate, but comical, fight. John is in tune with other characters' emotions, whereas Sherlock is often oblivious and completely unconcerned about his emotional disconnect, as evidenced in his interaction with morgue attendant Molly (Loo Brealey). If John is the modern man in 21st century Britain, then Sherlock is the echo of Victoriana in it.

The marketing for the series also reflected this mix of heritage and the contemporary, often to contradictory ends, positioning this construction of Sherlock as a wider strategy for the series and the BBC. The DVD packaging proclaimed on the front that *Sherlock* gave viewers "a new sleuth for the 21st Century," suggesting that the character contained within represented a break from the long history of detectives that had come before (including, of course, previous incarnations of Sherlock Holmes). The back cover, however, emphasized not only the character's long existence, but his specific Victorian origins by referencing the London fog that permeates literary and cinematic representations of London in the late 19th and early 20th centuries: "The world's favorite detective has emerged from the fog ... this is Sherlock for a new generation." Such publicity material seeks to make this Sherlock new and innovative, but without losing the cultural heritage and cache he brings with him. This mix of modernity and heritage reflects not only any personal intention on the part of the series executive producers to update a classic hero, but also the Corporation's broader position and practice. Dunleavy's model of television authorship recognizes the complexity of intentions at play in television production (2009, 35). In addition to the agency of individual production personnel, forces at the institutional level must also be taken into account. The BBC must agree to fund and broadcast the series, and, as a public service broadcaster with a clear remit, must ensure that it fulfils that remit. *Sherlock*, and the construction of the central character especially, embodies a combination of modernity and heritage that brings together two traditions of "quality television": the U.S. tradition of glossy, psychological deep and complex drama and the UK tradition of "prestige" through heritage and literary adaptation. This combination in turn reflects the BBC's attempts to maintain its public service purposes whilst competing in a global television market.

Character Construction and Institutional Practice: Quality, Prestige, and the Global Public Service Broadcaster

Definitions of U.S. "quality" television drama have ranged from institution-focused ones that examine the concept as a reaction to technological and industrial competition (Feuer, 1984) to textual models that ascribe particular narrative and aesthetic characteristics (Thompson 2007, xvii), to an amorphous model that shifts within the context it is used in (Nelson 2007). The most consistent argument is that quality television is distinct from 'normal,' run of the mill television (Jancovich and Lyons 2003, 2). There is general agreement amongst scholars that "quality" (and similarly loaded and evaluative terms) should not suggest that such content is better or more valuable than other televisual content, but that quality texts are positioned as distinct by industrial and popular critical discourses. However, this distinction often runs in line with a number of textual features, including an engrossing cinematic visual style, complex narratives, and psychologically deep characters (see, for example, Thompson 1997; Dunleavy 2009). Robert J. Thomson describes the proliferation of quality programming on U.S. television with an ambiguous but simultaneously clear definition: "these shows were generic mongrels, often scrambling and recombining traditional TV formulas in unexpected ways; they had literary and cinematic ambitions beyond what we had seen before, and they employed complex and sophisticated serialized narratives and inter-series 'mythologies'" (Thompson 2007, xix).

British television culture has an intricate relationship with U.S. content, and consequently with the development of U.S. quality programming. U.S. content has long featured on British screens. Paul Rixon argues that "American programs have always, for me, been both part of British television whilst also appearing different; they were often faster paced and more colorful, while infused with different narrative rhythms" (Rixon 2006, 1). In addition, the BBC has continued to concretize its position within the television market outside of the UK, a process that began in the 1940s (see Johnson 2010). The growth of BBC Worldwide as a co-production deal broker, such as the one it negotiated with Masterpiece Theater for *Sherlock*, and the development of BBC America has positioned the BBC directly within the home market of U.S. quality content. Robin Nelson argues that the UK broadcasters cannot escape the influence of the U.S. quality tradition: "Where HBO Premium and Fox television have led, the American networks — and, in a slightly different context, the UK terrestrial channels — are bound in a competitive, global marketplace to follow" (Nelson 2007, 161).

British-produced content has responded to this competition by emulating

U.S. quality television, with a number of programs such as *Spooks* (2002–2011) adopting the aesthetic of U.S. quality television (Nelson 2007; Evans 2011, 11–13). In its 2010 *Strategy Review*, the BBC acknowledged that "the popularity of imported U.S. drama is creating higher quality benchmarks" (BBC Trust 2010; downloads.bbc.co.uk) that its own content must reach. *Sherlock* can be seen within attempts to reach this benchmark, with the series featuring prominently in BBC Worldwide corporate literature (www.bbcworldwide.com). Shot in high definition, the series certainly looks like a quality production in the U.S. tradition. The narrative involves several layers of plot and subplot, with the mysterious Moriarty mentioned throughout the series until his final reveal in TGG. Both Sherlock and John are well rounded and given individual quirks, as discussed above. The series also fits into industrial characteristics assigned to quality drama such as the presence of established auteurs (see Hilmes 2002, 312; Messenger Davies 2007) in the form of Steven Moffat and Mark Gatiss, both of whom had quality credentials through *Doctor Who* (1963–) and *The League of Gentlemen* (1999–2002), tentpole status in BBC documentation as "exemplifying our creative ambition" (BBC 2011, Annual Report and Accounts; www.bbc.co.uk), and critical recognition in its multiple BAFTA, Royal Television Society, and Peabody awards.

However, in each of the above accounts of quality television, apart from Nelson's, UK-produced programs are rarely mentioned; the overwhelming majority of texts held up in this manner emerge from the U.S. industry. Whilst the U.S. tradition of quality is apparent within British television culture, if quality television is defined as being elevated above the mundane (Thompson 1996, 13), alternative meanings of quality emerge within British television history. Whilst programs such as *Spooks* are certainly held up as tentpole productions, with the BBC using them to advertise the high standard of its drama department, critical discourses within Britain have also privileged specific *genres*, a tendency that stretches back to the 1960s and what is called by some the "golden age" of British television (Shubik, 2000, xiv). One is social realist drama, found in programs such as *Cathy Come Home* (1966) or, more recently, *The Street* (2006–2009) (see Nelson 2007, 180). Of particular relevance to the BBC's *Sherlock*, however, are the discourses of quality attached to heritage programming and literary adaptations, what could be termed "prestige" drama.

Robin Nelson argues how contemporary-set literary adaptations such as *Inspector Morse* were packaged by ITV as "Quality Popular Drama" (2007, 175). Literary series such as *Brideshead Revisited* (1981), *The Jewel in the Crown* (1984) or, more recently, *Bleak House* (2005) and *Cranford* (2007–2009) are elevated above mundane television content such as reality shows and soap operas, regularly winning awards and critical recognition, inviting effusive descriptions such as "exemplary" (Davis, 2009). Programs that directly engage with Britain's cultural past, either though literary adaptations, a period setting or both, are core components of British broadcasters' annual programming and the 2010 Christmas television schedule was a timely reminder of such privileging. Many of the most prominent programs, in terms of scheduling and marketing, fell into the literary/heritage category, including the *Doctor Who* Christmas special (a loose adaptation of Charles Dickens' *A Christmas Carol*), ITV's much-publicized broadcast of *Agatha Christie's Murder on the Orient Express* at 9P.M. on Christmas Day, three new *Miss Marple* episodes, and the BBC's resurrection of *Upstairs Downstairs*. The BBC, in fact, featured at least one literary adaptation or period-set piece in prime time (6P.M.-10P.M.) everyday from Christmas Day until December 30.

Such programming shares characteristics with U.S.-style quality programs, with high production values, complex, layered narratives and psychologically rich characters. Indeed, U.S. broadcasters have also recently begun producing period set drama series such as *Mad Men* (AMC, 2007–) and *Boardwalk Empire* (HBO, 2010–), demonstrating the two traditions' potential for convergence. However, it is the particular generic specificities of such programs and the way that they consciously work through contemporary British culture's relationship to its past that distinguishes it from the U.S. tradition. Sarah Cardwell raises the association between literary adaptations and notions of distinction in her examination of the critical discourses that emerge around such programs, arguing that "critics are surprisingly complimentary about the television genre of classic-novel adaptation" (Cardwell 2002, 32–33). She goes on to write that "the best television is, it appears, television which tries to be 'non-televisual'" (34). Cardwell's analysis indicates the strong association in critical discourses between distinction and programming that calls on Britain's literary heritage. Where proponents of U.S. quality television elevate it through emulative associations with non-televisual forms (see Mittell 2011; Smith 2011), in British television culture direct adaptation of a literary source, and the subsequent association with Britain's political, social and cultural past, provides nationally-specific distinction. Just as *Sherlock* contains many of the characteristics of U.S. quality drama, it equally represents this tradition of British prestige drama. It is, obviously, an adaptation of one of a revered novelist's work. Furthermore, the character of Sherlock himself embodies this tradition in the casting of Cumberbatch, the retention of antique elements in the mise-en-scène surrounding him, and his detachment from the world around him. The character, and by extension the series, emphasizes and gains distinction from his roots in British literary culture.

The BBC's version of Sherlock Holmes therefore encapsulates a combination of the U.S. quality tradition and the UK prestige tradition of television drama. This combination can be seen as a direct response to the BBC's need to act as a British public service broadcaster whilst simultaneously competing in a global television market. Although literary adaptations have long been a staple of BBC content, in their 2004 *Building Public Value: Renewing the BBC for a Digital World,* the corporation emphasized its role in "creating cultural and creative value" by "celebrat[ing] our cultural heritage" (BBC 2004; downloads.bbc.co.uk), something that became a key strategy shortly after *Sherlock*'s first season in the Corporation's "Year of Books 2011" (BBC Press Office 2011; www.bbc.co.uk). The way in which *Sherlock* maintains the character's literary origins fits into this task and what Mark Bell in his "Speech to the Book Industry Conference" calls the BBC's ability to bring "new life to books and a new generation of readers to the books" (2011; www.bbc.co.uk). At the same time, the corporation has also been given the task of "showcasing the best of British culture to a global audience"(BBC 2004; downloads.bbc.co.uk), bringing them explicitly into competition with U.S. broadcasters. Alongside other prestige/quality programs such as *Doctor Who* (2005–), *Life on Mars* (2006–2007) and *Ashes to Ashes* (2008–2010) that similarly combine quality aesthetics with a working through of Britain's past, *Sherlock* allows the BBC to respond to both of these public service priorities. Unlike these other examples, however, is it the character of Sherlock himself that particularly achieves this heritage/contemporary balance. The series may recreate the aesthetic and narrative characteristics of highly-praised U.S. quality drama, but the deliberate emphasis on the character's literary provenance and Victorian origins allows it to call on the literary pedigree of Holmes and so maintain a clear place within British cultural history.

Conclusion

Whilst the presence of an original literary version of Holmes suggests the potential for consistency amongst screen Holmeses to emerge, very different versions actually appear. As demonstrated by the extreme differences between Warner Bros.' and The Asylum's versions of Holmes, institutional practice and policy plays a key role in how Conan Doyle's template is adapted for each screen iteration. A large Hollywood studio's Holmes is very different from a Holmes that emerges from a niche science-fiction production house. By creating a character that acts as an echo of Victoriana in the 21st century the BBC's version of Sherlock Holmes reflects his source in a modern public service broadcaster negotiating both its position within a global television market and its own cultural past. The combination of quality and prestige drama that he encapsulates echoes both the BBC's response to the growing global popularity of U.S. drama and how it continues to negotiate its place within a long history of British heritage and literary productions that pre-dates television. *Sherlock*'s Sherlock ultimately demonstrates how a single component of narrative, a character, is shaped by not only issues such as historical context or narrative form, but also the institutional policy and practice of its source.

Works Cited

Bennett, Tony, and Janet Wollacott. 1987. *Bond and beyond: The political career of a popular hero*. London: Macmillan Education.

Cardwell, Sarah. 2002. *Adaptation revisited: Television and the classic novel*. Manchester: Manchester University Press.

Davis, Serena. 2009. Cranford, BBC One, review. *The Telegraph* December 18, www.telegraph.co.uk.

Dunleavy, Trisha. 2009. *Television drama: Form, agency, innovation*. Basingstoke: Palgrave Macmillan.

Evans, Elizabeth Jane. 2011. *Transmedia television: Audiences, new media and daily life*. London: Routledge.

Feuer, Jane. 1984. *MTM quality television*. London: BFI.

Hilmes, Michelle, 2002. *Connections: A broadcasting history reader*. Belmont, CA: Wadsworth Press.

Hunter, I.Q. 2009. Exploitation as adaptation. In *Cultural Borrowing: Appropriation, Reworking, Transformation,* ed. Iain Robert Smith. Special issue of *Scope: An Online Journal of Film and Television Studies* 14, www.scope.nottingham.ac.uk.

Jankovich, Mark, and James Lyons, ed. 2003. *Quality popular television*. London: BFI.

Johnson, Catherine. 2010. Trading Auntie: the exploitation and protection of intellectual property rights during the BBC's monopoly years. *New Review of Film and Television* 7: 441–458.

Margolin, Uri. 2007. Character. In *The Cambridge Companion to Narrative,* ed. David Herman, 66–79. Cambridge: Cambridge University Press.

Messenger Davies, Máire. 2007. Quality and creativity in TV: The work of television storytellers. In *Quality TV: Contemporary American Television and Beyond*, ed. Janet McCabe and Kim Akass, 171–184. London: I.B. Tauris.

Mittell, Jason. 2011. All in the game: *The Wire*, serial storytelling, and procedural logic. www.electronicbookreview.com.

Nelson, Robin. 2007. *State of play: Contemporary 'high-end' TV drama*. Manchester: Manchester University Press.

Pearson, Roberta. 2007. Anatomizing Gilbert Grissom: The structure and functions of the televisual character. In *Reading CSI: Television Under the Microscope,* ed. Michael Allen, 39–56. London: I.B. Tauris.

_____. 2009. Chain of events: Regimes of evaluation and *Lost*'s construction of the televisual character. In *Reading Lost: Perspectives on a hit TV show,* ed. Roberta Pearson, 139–58. London: I.B. Tauris.

Shubik, Irene. 2000. *Play for today: The evolution of television drama*. Manchester: Manchester University Press.

Smith, Anthony. 2010. Decompressed Storytelling and the specificity of institutional configuration in the contemporary U.S. mainstream comic-book industry. Paper presented at Theory and Practice: A Conference on Comics, Comics Forum. Leeds, November 19.

_____. 2011. TV or Not TV? *The Sopranos* and contemporary episode architecture in U.S. network and premium cable drama. *Critical Studies in Television* 6:1.

Thompson, R. J. 1997. *Television's second golden age: From* Hill Street Blues *to* ER. Syracuse: Syracuse University Press.

_____. 2007. Preface. In *Quality TV: Contemporary American Television and Beyond,* ed. Janet McCabe and Kim Akass, xvii-xx. London: I.B. Tauris.

Sherlock's Webs

What the Detective Remembered from the Doctor About Transmediality

CB HARVEY

Abstract — One of the more prominent examples of transmediality associated with the *Sherlock* television program is the transmedial storytelling exhibited by the official tie-in web sites that complement and expand the series. In this regard *Sherlock* is emulating the approach of another long-running franchise, that of the science fiction and fantasy series *Doctor Who*, also produced by the BBC, and which similarly utilizes tie-in web sites to help deepen the story experience. As I will show in this essay, Sherlock Holmes and *Doctor Who*'s relationship is enduring, and often transmedial in myriad, unexpected ways. This relationship has often been manifested in the Sherlockian archetypes and iconography encountered by *Doctor Who*'s eponymous adventurer, even extending to storytelling strands that stretch from the Detective's world to the Doctor's universe, especially evident in terms of spinoff material. *Sherlock* is meanwhile replete with connections to *Doctor Who*'s past and present that operate on the levels of the intermedial and transmedial. Additionally, there exist structural similarities with regard to the two franchises' formal approach to the implementation of transmedial content and in terms of production processes and personnel. Employing theoretical conceptions from the diverse field of memory studies and transmedial theory, I will examine these ongoing dynamics, specifically in terms of *Sherlock*'s web sites but also with regard to the manifold other transmedial exchanges that characterize the relationship between Holmes and Who. The resulting discussion should offer some broader, significant insights into the nature of contemporary transmedial relationships and the role memory plays in attenuating those relationships.

Introduction

Sherlock Holmes has long exerted an influence on the BBC's science fiction series *Doctor Who*. With the advent of *Sherlock*, the Doctor in his turn exerts an influence on the Great Detective. This extends from the archetypes and aesthetics populating both series to comparable relationships with the news and entertainment media seeking to report on or otherwise publicize the shows. It is evident in *Sherlock*'s emulation of the transmedia storytelling techniques successfully employed by the makers of the revived, post–2005 *Doctor Who* and apparent in commonalities in the production teams working on both franchises, commonalities that extend from the programs themselves to supporting transmedial material. A key recurring feature is, of course, Steven Moffat, who acts as the chief creative force driving the two programs.

Central to the ways in which Moffat's *Sherlock* echoes Moffat's *Doctor Who* are the acts of remembering, misremembering, and forgetting. As well as existing in relationship to each other, both programs exist in relation to the wider mediascape, in which their histories are necessarily implicated. In this essay I will go in search of the transmedial links, intertextual references, intramedial connections and production contexts through which the world's only consulting detective remembers the last of the Time Lords. In my quest for evidence, I will utilize perspectives from the burgeoning field of memory studies in an analysis of the official *Sherlock* web sites written by Joseph Lidster, who also authored many comparable *Doctor Who* web sites. Through these discussions I will seek clues as to how contemporary media franchises transmedially remember their own history and also the past and present of other media.

Transmedial Storytelling, Intertextual Referencing, and Kinds of Remembering

Sherlock Holmes and *Doctor Who* can be understood in terms of transmedia storytelling, both having engaged in the activity long before the term was coined. The descriptor "transmedia" is used by Marsha Kinder in her wide-ranging study of children's consumption of media, in which she identifies their active and cognizant participation in the processes involved in negotiating meaning across media platforms. Kinder suggests that the "fairly consistent form of transmedia intertextuality" these young consumers engage in is promulgated by media producers (1993). According to Kinder, children are encouraged to identify, differentiate, and merge iconography from popular genres, often working across media.

Henry Jenkins identifies transmedia storytelling as a specific kind of storytelling in which narratives sharing a storyworld are told across different media platforms (Jenkins 2008). For this process to work, consumers — in this case not just children — are encouraged to become "hunters and gatherers," tracking the narratives across disparate media platforms and sharing their experiences with other such consumers (Jenkins 2008). The associated branding and promotion of transmedia products relies on the assumption that the consumer is "a more active spectator who can and will follow these media flows" than is ordinarily the case (Jenkins 2006). Jonathan Gray observes a key component for some — media producers and fans alike — is that transmedial storyworlds need to be "*inhabitable*," in other words the fictional world offers rich enough experiences that the consumer feels he or she wants to repeatedly immerse themselves in the environment (2010,187).

As Jon Dovey has observed, for the term transmedia storytelling to possess any legitimacy, it must be a distinct process from that of adaptation and/or dramatization, enlarging the fictional universe rather than merely translating a particular story from one medium to another (2011). This is a point echoed by Joseph Lidster, author of the various *Sherlock* tie-in web sites, who argues that "the web sites can't just regurgitate what we see on the screen; otherwise, there's no point to them" (Lidster 2011).

Transmedia intertextuality provides a framework to discuss the ways in which the first series of *Sherlock* is informed by the fifth series of the revived *Doctor Who*, outside of specific diegetic connections between the storyworlds of the two franchises. As I will explore, such story connections are inherited from previous iterations of both franchises across a variety of media forms, and are not explicitly articulated within either of the contemporary series. However, the trace memories of such linkages can be understood as informing the dynamics between the two shows, and between the shows and their audiences.

Intertextual references suggest conscious or unconscious allusions on the part of the creators of the media artifact to other media or cultural artifact(s). Intertextual references within the same medium, for example, television, utilizing its specific audiovisual language, can be understood as intramedial (Rajewsky 2005). Intertextual references that cross the boundaries from one media platform to another can be understood as transmedial or intermedial. Since *Sherlock*'s source material is constituted in the main by the original Sir Arthur Conan Doyle prose stories, it is primarily engaged in transmedial activity. As I will demonstrate, however, there is a palimpsestic quality to this, whereby other iterations of Sherlock Holmes adapted for media such as television and film also influence the *Sherlock* series, in terms of both remembering and deliberate forgetting: crucially, *Sherlock* is a memory but it is also a *memory of a memory*.

Clearly, transmedial storytelling and intertextual references (the latter constituted as transmedial and intramedial activity) rely for their success on the provocation of appropriate memories possessed by the audience. Whether consciously or subconsciously, both transmedial storytelling and intertextual referencing call upon the consumer of the media artifact to recall some aspect of another artifact or series of artifacts. Without such recall, the impact of the transmedial and intertextual is lost. In the case of transmedial storytelling, this involves recalling points of diegesis from the original artifact or artifacts that are then picked up again by the destination story. An intertextual reference, by contrast, might consist of an image or archetype which is referred to by the newer narrative but which does not necessarily directly tie to the diegesis of the earlier story. Crucially, as with intertexual references, while a process of remembering is central to the enterprise of transmedia storytelling, a process of forgetting or non-remembering — and sometimes of deliberate mis-remembering — is also important. What is not referred to is at least as important as what is referred to.

Evidently, then, ideas of remembering, mis-remembering and forgetting ought to be central to this discussion, and an appropriate academic framework is required. The emergent field of memory studies offers useful mechanisms for framing such a discussion. For instance, a continuing important debate within the field is the interrelationship between subjective and collective memory, helpful for contextualizing forthcoming discussions of continuity and canonicity with regard to *Sherlock* and its relationship to *Doctor Who*. Indeed, the sociologist Barbara Misztal makes understanding the interrelationship between subjective and collective remembering central to the understanding of memory more broadly (Misztal 2003), while Jenny Kidd builds on the view that although memory is psychologically located, it is articulated through culture and through language (Kidd 2009).

As I will show, *Sherlock* remembers Doctor Who, just as *Doctor Who* has in the past frequently remembered Sherlock Holmes. Disentangling where one kind of remembering ends and where another begins is a complex task, however, rendered all the more complicated by the frequent overlaps between instances of the transmedial, the intermedial, the intramedial, and the intertextual, not to mention the production contexts of the two programs.

Holmes and Doctor Who in History

From its inception, Sir Arthur Conan Doyle's creations of Sherlock Holmes and Dr. John Watson proved very successful at the time and attracted many fans and imitators.

This popularity meant that Conan Doyle's Sherlock Holmes stories, characters and motifs transported to film, theatre, radio, comic books, and video games, adapted with varying degrees of fidelity to the source material. In addition to straightforward adaptations, the figure of Holmes — and also Watson, as well as other characters and elements of the stories — have been repurposed in a wide variety of contexts. This suggests Conan Doyle's creations possess a seemingly contradictory blend of distinctiveness but also sufficient mutability to enable them to traverse specific media artifacts and also to cross from one medium to another.

The same might be said of *Doctor Who*, and might similarly account for its longevity relative to other television programs. The series first appeared on the BBC in 1963, continuing until 1989 when it was effectively cancelled. It returned fleetingly in 1996 for a television movie co-produced by the BBC and Amblin Entertainment, but for the most part survived for nearly two decades in the form of tie-in and fan products. In 2005, BBC Cardiff launched a new iteration of the series, under the auspices of Russell T. Davies.

As with the Sherlock Holmes stories, as well as lending itself to straight-forward adaptations — novels, two feature films, stage plays — over the years *Doctor Who* has spawned new stories across multiple spinoff media. Early examples of such spinoffs tended to offer only marginal fidelity with the television series, sometimes flatly contradicting events on screen. Later merchandizing tended toward greater faithfulness, reflecting the BBC's current construction of *Doctor Who* as a transmedia brand.

If the early series of *Doctor Who* borrowed most obviously from H.G. Wells and the idea of the Victorian explorer, by the time of Jon Pertwee (1970–1974) the Holmesian influences are altogether clearer. The character of the Master was introduced by then producer Barry Letts as a "Moriarty" to the Doctor's Holmes, and Roger Delgado's portrayal assiduously obeyed that template. During the so-called gothic era of *Doctor Who*, when Phillip Hinchcliffe was producer and Robert Holmes script editor, Sherlockian iconography is recurrent. It is most obvious in the 1976 serial *The Talons of Weng Chiang*, in which Tom Baker's Doctor dons deerstalker and cape in a deliberate trans-medial echo of Basil Rathbone's cinematic version of Holmes. Indeed, Baker himself makes the point that this particular story led to him being cast as Holmes in the later film version of *The Hound of the Baskervilles* (Baker 1997), a further example of the palimpsistic character of some transmedial activity.

Fittingly for this discussion, conceptions of what constitutes canon in *Doctor Who* have drawn upon precedents established by Sherlock Holmes fandom. As Lance Parkin observes, the definition of the term canon with regard to *Doctor Who* is informed both by F.R. Leavis' "Grand Tradition" and also by the Biblical conception of "canon" (Parkin 2007). An additional "third meaning of the word 'canon' is used by fans of the Sherlock Holmes stories" to describe the fifty-six short stories and four novels authored by Conan Doyle but excluding an additional range of Sherlock Holmes material which we might (at least in some cases) identify as transmedial — a plot outline, self-parodies, and stage plays — also written by Conan Doyle (Parkin 2007, 246–262).

According to Parkin, *Doctor Who* fans negotiate those aspects of the spinoff media they consider canon leading to the oxymoronic idea of personal canon: arguably a canon is only canon if it is agreed upon collectively by a mass of participants. This in turn recalls the complexity involved in accounting for the subjective and collective with regard to memory (Kidd 2009; Misztal 2003).

For some fans, *Doctor Who* can be understood as one continuing story across multiple media platforms, taking in the television series but also associated audio adventures, novels, short stories, comic strips, graphic novels, video games, stage plays, and web sites (Wood 2007).

Those fans engaging with both Moffat's *Sherlock* and Moffat's *Doctor Who* might therefore perceive diegetic links between the two series in addition to the transmedial intertextual links through which *Doctor Who* has remembered Sherlock Holmes. Two *Doctor Who* spinoff novels published by Virgin — Andy Lane's *All-Consuming Fire* (1994) and Paul Cornell's *Happy Endings* (1996) — *in fact* feature Sherlock Holmes and Dr. Watson as characters. The Faction Paradox range, itself a spinoff from the *Doctor Who* spinoff books, features Kelly Hale's *Erasing Sherlock* (2006), in which a young doctoral candidate travels back in time to observe Holmes' early career. *Jago and Litefoot* is an ongoing series of audio adventures produced by Big Finish and featuring two characters who originally appeared in the *Doctor Who* television serial *The Talons of Weng Chiang*, in which the echoes of Holmes and Watson remain resonant. Though explicitly connecting the classic rather than "Nu" era of *Doctor Who* to Sherlock Holmes, such spinoff media can be seen as part of a wider tapestry, of which *Sherlock* and the new *Doctor Who* are necessarily also a part.

Within the diegesis of the new *Doctor Who* television there exist a number of junctures at which "facts" about the Whoniverse are utilized from spinoff media, thus arguably legitimizing such media in its entirety. On this basis there is therefore a transmedial flow moving from the original Sherlock stories and their adaptations via the classic television series of *Doctor Who* and its spinoff media, which in their turn inform post–2005 *Doctor Who* and, by extension, the *Sherlock* series. Clearly such memories are little more than traces, evident to few but hidden to many, again recalling the tension between subjective and collective memory.

Production Links

The production contexts in which *Sherlock* and *Doctor Who* are produced add an additional layer of complexity to discussions of the transmedial and intertextual. Steven Moffat is the most obvious point of commonality, producing and acting as lead writer on both series, having previously written a number of critically well-regarded episodes for the first four series of the revived *Doctor Who* when it was produced by Russell T. Davies. *Sherlock*, like the new *Doctor Who*, is made at the BBC's base in Cardiff, Wales. Euros Lyn, a frequent director on the new *Doctor Who*, directed the second episode of *Sherlock*, entitled "The Blind Banker." Mark Gatiss, Moffat's co-creator and author of *Sherlock*'s third episode "The Great Game," also plays the recurring character of Mycroft in *Sherlock*; Gatiss wrote for the first, second, third and fifth series of the new *Doctor Who*, as well as appearing in several episodes. Gatiss' involvement in Big Finish-produced *Doctor Who* audio productions as writer and performer constitutes a way by which *Doctor Who* spinoff media is sutured with the "official" iteration of the show and linked by extension to *Sherlock*.

These myriad intersections between textual and production crossovers are further exemplified in the way the separation between on-screen intertextuality and off-screen production context is easily elided. The July 27, 2010 edition of the British tabloid newspaper *The Sun* carried a story headlined "Holmes: I turned down Dr Who job" (www.thesun.co.uk). The article contends that Benedict Cumberbatch refused the role of Doctor Who, having been offered it at the conclusion of David Tennant's tenure. The reason Cumberbatch gives in the article is the worry of typecasting, saying "I didn't really like the whole package — being on school lunchboxes." Again, this suggests the tension between subjective and collective conceptions of remembering, except that this time it is anticipatory, itself built on Cumberbatch's perception — and therefore memory — of how past actors have had to subjectively cope with the experience of being remembered in a collective fashion by an adoring fanbase.

The article further maintains that Cumberbatch might yet be offered the role once Matt Smith, the incumbent Doctor, chooses to give it up. This particular association — and the fact that both shows were nominated for BAFTAS in 2011, with *Sherlock* winning — further reinforces the links between the two shows, potentially re-inscribing any future performances by Cumberbatch in the role of Holmes with this intertextual trace; or at least enhancing this trace for those audience members who have already made the association. Additionally, should Cumberbatch eventually take up the role of the Doctor, this will carry intramedial intertextual associations of *Sherlock* for subsequent viewers of *Doctor Who*.

Transmedial Techniques

Since 2005 the BBC have sought to exploit the transmedia potential of the new series of *Doctor Who* in a more considered fashion than ever happened with regard to the "classic" iteration of the show. The success of this strategy is reflected in the BBC's belief that *Doctor Who* now constitutes the paradigm for transmedia storytelling to the extent that other properties owned by the Corporation should emulate this approach (Perryman 2008), although as Elizabeth Jane Evans demonstrates the BBC's *Spooks* had previously utilized web games for the purposes of transmedial storytelling (2008). In the case of post–2005 *Doctor Who* this transmedial storytelling extends from the television shows to novels, comic serials in the officially licensed *Doctor Who Magazine* published by Panini, to graphic novels, a role-playing game, video games, and a toy range produced by Character Options (Richards 2005).

An important aspect of the wider transmedia storytelling process are the web sites tied to the new series of *Doctor Who*. These range from largely prose-based 'fake' web sites 'updated' by characters or organizations mentioned in the diegesis of the show, to short stories and web comics written by authors responsible for other spinoff artifacts, such as officially licensed audio dramas, novels and comics. *Doctor Who*'s two BBC produced spinoff shows, the adult-oriented *Torchwood* (BBC 2006–) and child-oriented *The Sarah Jane Adventures* (BBC 2007–2010) both utilize similar transmedial techniques.

Perryman identifies the *Doctor Who* metatextual web sites in terms of what Will Brooker has characterized as "television overflow," in which media producers use the Internet to enhance the television program and afford interaction with it (2008, 29). In encouraging audience interaction with the ur-text, the *Sherlock* tie-in web sites might be seen as borrowing an approach trialed with other BBC programs but exemplified by *Doctor Who*. The transmedia intertextuality promoted by producers of children's media and identified by Kinder has conceivably spread to adult consumers, perhaps aging with them as they have themselves aged (1993).

As with the links between the *Sherlock* program itself and the wider *Doctor Who* franchise, connections between the transmedial storytelling aspects of the two franchises are evidenced in the production processes governing the *Sherlock* web sites. The *Sherlock* tie-in web sites were all written by Joseph Lidster, well-known in *Doctor Who* fandom for authoring many BBC-licensed audio dramas produced by Big Finish. More recently, Lidster has written for both *The Sarah Jane Adventures* and *Torchwood* television programs, and has also authored *Torchwood* radio plays. Most significantly in this context, Lidster additionally wrote tie-in metatextual web sites for *Doctor Who*, including the MySpace page for Martha Jones (played by Freema Agyeman), the Doctor's main companion in Series Three of the revived program. My discussion of the *Sherlock* web sites is augmented throughout by insights offered by Lidster during an interview conducted in February 2011.

For the most part, the *Sherlock* web sites constitute an example of what Jason Mittell has described as "centrifugal transmedial storytelling," radiating outward from the ur-text of the television program (2011). Each site borrows thematic concerns, plot points and characters from the *Sherlock* program which Lidster then extemporizes around, largely limiting himself to material derived from the television show rather than the Conan Doyle source material (Lidster 2011).

One of the *Sherlock* web sites, "The Science of Deduction," purports to be written by Sherlock Holmes himself (www.thescienceofdeduction.co.uk). The title is set against a stripped backwash which serves to frame the web site's written material, displaying an image of central London — the view from the South Bank, including the Thames and St. Paul's Cathedral — remembering aspects of the credit sequence from the *Sherlock* program and associated branding of the program. A series of buttons runs across the top of the main section, entitled Home, Forum, Hidden messages, and Case files. An image of blue lights causing lens flare also evokes the program's content, the haziness of the picture suggesting an ambiguous, fuzzy attitude toward law and order.

The accompanying text, written in first person, tells us that Sherlock Holmes is "the world's only consulting detective," rearticulating a central premise from the original stories. Here, though, the phrase is elevated to become the franchise's "high concept," uniting the different iterations of the *Sherlock* transmedial product. The approach is comparable to that employed in the post–2005 *Doctor Who*, in which the eponymous hero is constructed as "The Last of the Time Lords." In both cases such slogans connect the urtext of the television program to the web site in question but they are clearly chosen because they represent something essential about the premise, in both instances associated with the significance of the central character's individuality. In these instances the importance of storyworlds being seen as "*inhabitable*" in terms outlined by Gray may owe much to the quirky allure of the central character and the idea that the fans would want to spend time with the character, or indeed *be* the character (2010, 187).

The prose element of the site goes on to explain that the author will not go "into detail about how I do what I do because chances are you wouldn't understand," invoking Sherlock's aloof attitude from the series but also remembering a key characteristic from both the original stories and other iterations. The author goes on to tell us that he can be contacted about "Interesting cases," before explaining his criteria for investigating criminal cases:

> This is what I do:
> 1. I observe everything.
> 2. From what I observe, I deduce everything.
> 3. When I've eliminated the impossible, whatever remains, no matter how mad it might seem, must be the truth [www.thescienceofdeduction. co.uk].

This list clearly reinvents the archetypal Sherlockian conceit from Conan Doyle's stories: "When you eliminate the impossible whatever remains — however improbable — must be the truth." In so doing, the web site's prose remains consistent with the *Sherlock* series' transformation of key aspects of the original stories. The approach to remembering the source material remains the same, because the transmedia product dictates it should. Lidster admits that he was not able to use the Conan Doyle source material as much as he would have liked, "because you never know what Steven [Moffat] and Mark [Gatiss] will want to use in the TV series" (2011).

Clearly, those concerned in the creation of the *Sherlock* program maintain strong links with those involved in the creation of the complementary web sites. Lidster's close ties with the *Sherlock* program's chief architects recall Gray's contention that some media producers 'see the creation of [the] paratext as part of the act of creating the text in general' (2010:214). Interestingly this is a departure from Lidster's experience of working on the *Doctor Who* web sites, where he had less direct contact with Russell T. Davies or any of the television writers; Lidster suggests that this might be because the *Sherlock* team is considerably smaller (2011).

Sherlock's particular, studiously selective approach to remembering or discounting its own history is consistent with the post–2005 *Doctor Who* franchise in terms of *its* attitude to its past as manifested in the series proper and the associated spinoff media. In the *Sherlock* television program a "three pipe problem" transforms into a "three patch problem," alluding to Holmes' attempts to give up smoking and securing a transformation of the character from the Basil Rathbone archetype — deerstalker, cape, pipe — to a suitably contemporary reinvention. A comparable process is evident with regard to the setting of both the series and the web sites in contemporary London as opposed to the source material's then contemporary setting in the late Victorian/early Edwardian period. This recalls the point about the fixedness of the Sherlock character and the character's seemingly contradictory mutability but also suggests a comparable tension between the rigidity and fluidity of the wider *Sherlock Holmes* format: while aspects of the character and his milieu are retained and entrenched, other aspects can be satisfactorily discarded by drawing attention to their absence. Our prior knowledge means that we are aware of what we are being asked to forget.

While retaining fidelity with both the *Sherlock* series and refracting elements of the original stories, the official *Sherlock* web sites must simultaneously intramedially evoke the approach of specific kinds of web site. In the case of "The Science of Deduction," this takes the form of a kind of help site for individuals wanting assistance. According to Lidster, "Some of the 'archived case files' are variations of Conan Doyle titles" (2011). The intention, clearly, is that these references are offered up to fans in possession of suitable prior knowledge of Sherlock Holmes: in other words they are fragments of memory designed for Jenkins' "hunters and gatherers" to seek out.

Scrolling down the homepage reveals the title "Latest Forum Activity" with "Found. The Bruce-Partington Plans. Please collect. The Pool. Midnight — SH." Referencing the content of the show directly, this fractured approach is consistent with the series and its thoroughly engaged attitude to new media, whereby Conan Doyle's source material is reimagined in terms of new technologies. As Lamerichs observes elsewhere in this volume, the deployment of technology in the context of *Sherlock* is presented unobtrusively, as a "perfect fit" (2011, 6).

Lidster in fact suggests that there are clues and jokes embedded in each of the web sites and indeed "Characters crossover from one web site to another and have little storylines of their own" (2011). Again, for such techniques to succeed, the consumer of Kinder's transmedia (Kinder 1993) and Jenkins' transmedia storytelling (Jenkins 2006) must be suitably active. Such techniques also recall Misztal's conception of "culture's active meaning-making" whereby individuals' personal experience has to be actively transfigured to become part of the collective memory (Hamilton 2010).

Dr. John Watson's blog supplies a series of entries commenting on the events of the television series as they transpired (2010; www.johnwatsonblog.co.uk). In the right hand corner of the screen, adjacent to a picture of Martin Freeman portraying Watson, is a description of the character headed "About me" and consistent with the approach of this kind of blog. Watson describes himself as "an experienced medical doctor recently returned from Afghanistan." These character details are remembered from Conan Doyle's original version of *A Study in Scarlet*, though clearly attenuated for the contemporary context of the *Sherlock* series and the supporting transmedial framework.

Watson's entries begin with fairly nonsensical notes of the kind made by someone trying to grapple with new technology, again consistent with Freeman's portrayal of Watson in *Sherlock*. As the entries progress further details about Watson's personal life are revealed: in one entry Watson talks of going drinking with his rugby club friends, consistent with a figure heralding from a military background. Other entries concentrate on adumbrating the character of Holmes as perceived by Watson. The entry for February 7, entitled "A Study in Pink," voices Watson's surprise that while Sherlock is able to deduce facts from limited details he knows nothing of more commonplace details.

> This morning, for example, he asked me who the Prime Minister was. Last week he seemed to genuinely not know the Earth goes round the Sun. Seriously. He didn't know. He didn't think the Sun went round the Earth or anything. He just

didn't care. I still can't quite believe it. In so many ways, he's the cleverest person I've ever met but there are these blank spots that are almost terrifying [2010; www.johnwatsonblog.co.uk].

As with the details about Watson's military and medical experience, the sentiments of this passage are remembered from *A Study in Scarlet* via the *Sherlock* program. Such memories are both constituted by a process of adaptation and transmedial extension, a process which might again be seen as palimpsistic in its remembering of a memory. Once again, similar strategies are employed here as have come to characterize post–2005 *Doctor Who*: a biography for the character of Sarah Jane Smith contains some memories but omits others, in an attempt to finesse the character's insertion into the franchise's contemporary transmedial diegesis. Watson's blog is in its turn alluded to in the third episode of the *Sherlock* television series, with Sherlock angry at Watson for revealing his lack of basic knowledge concerning astronomy.

Arguably, however, this particular instance constitutes an inversion of the dominant centrifugal mode of transmedia storytelling that otherwise constitutes the relationship between the television series and the web sites (Mittell 2011). The appearance of Dr. Watson's blog prior to the airing of the third episode in the first series arguably renders this particular example a kind of "centripetal transmedial storytelling," informing the program rather than vice versa. This perhaps suggests that temporality is liable to disrupt the spatial parameters by which centrifugal or centripetal definitions of transmedia storytelling are otherwise determined.

Other of the web sites authored by Lidster deal with supporting characters from the *Sherlock* program. "Molly Hooper" is constructed as a blog-cum-diary for the character of the same name from the first episode of *Sherlock*, "A Study in Pink" (2010; www.mollyhooper.co.uk). A garish wallpaper backwash surrounds text written in pink; three kittens adorn the perimeter of the frame. A series of dates travels vertically down the right hand side of the web page, offering links to entries supplied by Molly Hooper. The entry marked April 1 sits at the top center of the page and is followed by this prose:

> Jim, are you reading this? I'm sorry we argued and I don't mind if you're gay or not but where are you? Please, I miss you and I'm worried about you! Why aren't you answering your phone? And why aren't you at work? Your manager's going mental! Please!! Just get in touch!! Let me know you're okay!! [2010; www.molly hooper.co.uk].

Again, the web site must simultaneously echo the *Sherlock* series and its refracted idea of the Conan Doyle original, whilst also intramedially deploying tropes and techniques familiar from a particular, popular genre of web site. Necessarily the idiom is contemporary and suited both to the character as established in the corresponding episode from the television series and to the particular instance of the online blog. Clearly the web site is not intended to be an entirely realist rendering of comparable web sites: just as the series itself plays with the audience's prior knowledge of the Sherlock Holmes stories to ironic effect, the Molly Hooper web site utilizes our existing appreciation of the blog genre of web site.

Lidster makes the point that "it's often easier to use the more secondary characters such as Mickey Smith in *Doctor Who* or Molly Hooper in *Sherlock* as I can have more fun with them without disrupting the television episodes' narrative" (2011). Once again, the interplay between subjective experience and a communal experience is brought to the fore: Lidster stresses the importance for himself— as a writer — of telling a story personal to him, while at the same time remaining consistent with the storyworld established by the *Sherlock* television program. Evidently — unsurprisingly — the creators of *Sherlock* are as subject to competing memories as the audience of the program Lamerichs identifies (2011).

According to Lidster, the processes governing the production of material for the *Sherlock* web sites echoed that of the processes by which the *Doctor Who* web sites he worked on were produced (2011). In both cases he was given access to scripts and rough edits of the episode in question. Lidster was then able to discuss those fertile elements in the scripts he thought could be tied to online content with the producer of both the relevant television episode and those responsible for producing the online content. Once agreed, he would work on the material before handing it over for online development. Again this illustrates the symmetries guiding the transmedial development of *Sherlock* with the post–2005 *Doctor Who*, as well as reinforcing Hoskins' point that collective memory is not just "directed and made visible through new media technologies" but simultaneously formed by media cultures and through the practices of those media professionals constituting those media cultures (Hoskins 2009).

Conclusions

The transmedial and intertextual linkages between *Sherlock* and *Doctor Who* are manifold and complex. In part this arises from the longevity of Sherlock Holmes as a popular fiction figure and the relative longevity of *Doctor Who* in televisual terms. That the two icons remain so linked in the popular imagination may owe much to the influence of the original Sherlock Holmes stories, their formal characteristics and subsequent media adaptations on both the format and diegesis of *Doctor Who*; and the influence of both icons on the current generation of producers, writers and performers in relation to both *Sherlock* and *Doctor Who*, an influence that is often palimpsestically realized.

The diegetic links between the storyworlds of the first series of *Sherlock* and the fifth series of *Doctor Who*, inherited from the "classic" era of *Doctor Who*, are a matter of negotiation on the part of fandom and subject to conceptions of continuity and canonicity. More broadly, arguably digitality — DVDs, web sites, mobile technology — abets fandom's ability to check "facts" and immerse themselves in the object of their fascination, so that contemporary transmedia storytelling strives for consistency where spinoff merchandizing in the past was content with only broad fidelity to the style of the show. In addition, digitality facilitates "peer-produced relationships" (Hoskins 2009), rendering easier and more immediate the ability of fans to discuss with one another specific memories concerning the piece of transmedia storytelling. Digitality also, of course, allows the fanbase to access medium-specific material that expands the storyworld of the program, such as the web sites authored by Joseph Lidster for both *Sherlock* and *Doctor Who*. For at least a proportion of the fan base of *Sherlock* and *Doctor Who*, the multiple, enduring relationships connecting the two franchises are a subject for explicit discussion, informed as much by a knowledge of commonalities in production personnel and processes as by textual links.

Just as fans of both programs struggle to reconcile their subjective memory of either program with collective ideas of canon — some fans engaging with the web sites, others choosing not to participate in such transmedial storytelling, others perhaps ignorant of the web sites' existence, despite the BBC's marketing — so do the production crews. In creating the transmedial landscape of *Sherlock*, Moffat, Gatiss, Lidster, and other individuals are negotiating their own subjective experiences — of Conan Doyle's stories, of other iterations of Sherlock Holmes, of authoring *Doctor Who* in a wide variety of production contexts — with a shared, transmedial memory of what Sherlock Holmes is.

Indeed, the transmedial, intramedial, and intertextual aspects linking *Sherlock* to *Doctor Who* are further complicated by the production contexts of both shows and the production contexts of the transmedia storytelling supporting the two shows. These associations are palpable and extensive, and are reflected in the media reportage of the two series. In some cases individuals working on both shows also serve to link *Doctor Who*'s transmedial past with its transmedial present, and in doing so link *Sherlock* with its own past and that of *Doctor Who*.

Importantly, while the *Sherlock* tie-in web sites articulate the memory of the *Sherlock* series through transmedia storytelling and transmedial intertextual references, they are also tasked with emulating the web site as a medium. Not only that, they must also remember specific *kinds* of web site: the help site, the blog, the diary. Transmediality and intertextuality suggest a merging and a convergence of form; but in order for the transmedial to function, a specificity of medium — and of genre — must evidently remain distinct. In its blend of distinctiveness and flexibility of format, the Sherlock Holmes storyworld has lent itself to transmedia storytelling and intertextual borrowing while simultaneously retaining its beguiling identity. In an era in which transmedia storytelling has become considerably more formalized, the case of the detective offers manifold clues as to a future that will assuredly become more transmedial.

Works Cited

Baker, Tom. 1997. *Who on earth is Tom Baker? An autobiography.* London: HarperCollins.
Brooker, Will. 2003. Overflow and audience. In *The audience studies reader*, ed. Will Brooker and Deborah Jermyn, 322–335. London: Routledge
Cohen, Gillian. 1996. *Memory in the real world.* East Sussex: Psychology Press.
Cornell, Paul. 1996. *Happy endings (New Doctor Who adventures).* London: Virgin.
Dovey, Jon. 2011. "Web drama? Designing transmedial narrative." Technologies of Transmediality Conference. Bristol, January, 8.
Gray, Jonathan. 2010. *Show sold separately: Promos, spoilers, and other media paratexts.* New York: New York University Press
Hamilton, Paula. 2010. A long war: Public memory and the popular media. In *Memory: Histories, theories, debates*, ed. Susannah Radstone and Bill Schwartz, 299–311. New York: Fordham University Press.
Harvey, CB. 2010. Canon, myth, and memory in Doctor Who. In *The mythological dimensions of* Doctor Who, ed. Anthony Burdge, Jessica Burke, and Kristine Larsen, 22–36. Crawfordville: Kitsune Books.
Hoskins, Andrew. 2009. The mediatisation of memory. In *Save as: Digital memories*, ed. Joanne Garde-Hansen, Andrew Hoskins, and Anna Reading, 27–43. London: Palgrave.
Jenkins, Henry. 2006. *Fans, bloggers, and gamers: Essays on participatory culture.* New York: New York University Press.
_____. 2008. *Convergence culture: Where old and new media collide.* New York: New York University Press.
Kidd, Jenny. 2009. Digital storytelling and the performance of memory. In *Save as: Digital memories*, ed. Joanne Garde-Hansen, Andrew Hoskins, and Anna Reading, 167–183. London: Palgrave.
Kinder, Marsha. 1993. *Playing with power in movies, television, and video games.* London: University of California Press.
Lane, Andy. 1994. *All-consuming fire (New Doctor Who adventures).* London: Virgin.
Lidster, Joseph. 2011. Interview by CB Harvey. February 28.
Misztal, Barbara. 2003. *Theories of social remembering.* Maidenhead: Open University Press.
Mittell, Jason. 2011. Strategies of storytelling on transmedia television. Storyworlds Across Media conference. Mainz, June 30.
Parkin, Lance. 2007. Canonicity matters: defining the *Doctor Who* canon. In *Time and relative dissertations in space: Critical perspectives on* Doctor Who, ed. David Butler, 246–262. Manchester: Manchester University Press.
Perryman, Neil. 2008. *Doctor Who* and the convergence of media: A case study in transmedia storytelling. *Convergence* 14: 21–39.
Rajewsky, Irina O. 2005. Intermediality, intertextuality, and remediation: A literary perspective on intermediality. *Intermedialities* 6: 43–64.
Wood, Tat. 2007. *About time: The unauthorized guide to* Doctor Who *1985–1989, Seasons 22 to 26, the TV Movie.* Des Moines: Mad Norwegian Press.

Holmes in the Small Screen

The Television Contexts of Sherlock

TOM STEWARD

Abstract —*Sherlock* engages with a history of adapting Conan Doyle's Sherlock Holmes stories for television as old as the medium itself. As a 90-minute Sunday night detective drama, the program taps into institutionalized conventions of TV scheduling, format, ecology, and genre. The involvement of established writer/producers Steven Moffat and Mark Gatiss and interconnections with other TV shows embed the series within a number of past and present program and industrial discourses. As such, *Sherlock* feeds off and into a multitude of television contexts. The series responds to and reappropriates many tendencies established across the history of Sherlock Holmes TV adaptations. Its scheduling, format, reception context, and use of genre derive from and re-mediate contemporary and historical trends within international TV institutional policies and program aesthetics. The writer/producers negotiate the work of previous TV dramatists and challengingly intervene into contemporary drama adaptation production cultures. This essay unravels the relationship between *Sherlock* and these myriad television contexts and argues that *Sherlock* should be understood as an invention and product of television and its history rather than simply contemporary media. I observe how *Sherlock*'s contemporaneity responds to the burden of relevance in previous period adaptations of Holmes stories. I examine the TV-fan authorship of Moffat and Gatiss and its impact on the program's production and aesthetics. I consider prestige and populist connotations of the 90-minute format and Sunday night slot and the program's interventions into crime and heritage television. The essay also uses *Sherlock* as a site to explore the specificity of television as a medium, particularly its programming and production cultures, and issues of adaptation and authorship in contemporary media, such as fan fiction. I find that *Sherlock* speaks to and plays with its television contexts and legacy and illuminates our historical, industrial and aesthetic understanding of the medium of television.

Introduction

Sherlock (BBC, 2010–) aggressively foregrounds new technologies and media devices and adopts a visual style based on new media aesthetics, such as iPhone screens. It makes insistent references to social issues in the UK post–2008 (for example, the banking crisis) and to contemporaneous media cultures and products, such as blogging and recent TV programs. In this way, *Sherlock* dares us not to contextualize or historicize it beyond a commonly known frame of immediate reference. Given its pointing away from television towards new media platforms and an ongoing adaptation tradition of Conan Doyle's Sherlock Holmes stories in other media (some of which are more established than television), it is possible to lose sight of how *Sherlock* is specific to the medium and its history. This essay contends that *Sherlock* is better understood when located within the international history and contexts of TV: the adaptation of Sherlock Holmes stories, production and authorship conditions, and ritualized conventions of TV programming. Through this, we can see *Sherlock* as having significant implications and interventions in contemporary and historical practices as well as in the patterns and policies of TV adaptation, production, scheduling, format, and genre. This is not to devalue the difference or originality of *Sherlock* but to re-connect the program with its TV heritage in order to show that its innovations come from distinctive re-mediations of medium-specific historical tendencies. Brendan Riley argues that recent TV detectives embodying cultural shifts to digital media ("the hero for electrate culture" 2009, 915) often conceal an old-fashioned defense of literacy and rationality. So too *Sherlock*, with its new media surface and contemporary fetishes, disguises older TV contexts that contribute to the programs' meanings and significances.

Previous scholarly and/or historical analyses of adaptations of Sherlock Holmes characters and stories tended to combine different media, such as film, television, literature, theater in their readings, though there were notable exceptions (see Haining 1994). This essay examines what is distinctive about the television adaptations. It is self-evident that there is a media tradition of adaptations of and allusions to Holmes stories and characters which stretches back much further than television and I comment on how previous media adaptations pre-figure many of the TV programs and practices I discuss. However, unlike other essays in this collection that emphasize the transmedial nature of Holmes adaptation, I focus on the place of the Sherlock Holmes franchise within the myriad contexts of a single medium. I begin by examining *Sherlock* as a response to previous TV adaptations of Holmes stories and characters and then look to the industrial significance of its authorship and production contexts. I move on to how *Sherlock* fits with routinized TV scheduling, formats, conventions, and genre. I argue for close historical and ontological links between the Holmes canon and television, which are negotiated by *Sherlock* and clearly identifiable in its content, form, production, and reception. On a broader scale, the study of *Sherlock* within the contexts of television helps illuminate the specificity of television by analyzing how the program both reflects and contributes to the industrial, institutional, and aesthetic development of the medium. It also addresses larger questions of transmedia adaptation and authorship by examining *Sherlock* within the context of the wider franchise and movement in the production of literary adaptations between media industry formulas and fan-oriented discourse.

Sherlock *and Television Adaptations*

Television adaptations of Conan Doyle's Sherlock Holmes canon and its characters have a history as old as the medium itself. As Peter Haining reports in *The Television Sherlock Holmes*, Holmes was used as a "character in trial broadcasts" of television in the U.S., and the first adaptation was an NBC production of the short story "The Three Garridebs" as early as 1937 (1994, 43). Investigating reasons for the affinity between Holmes adaptation and television would be a project in its own right, but I will briefly speculate on some possible factors. Riley notes links between the detection methods used by Holmes in the original stories and the new medium of photography (2009, 911–912), so it is perhaps not surprising that there is a connection between the Holmes stories and film and television, moving image media which succeeded photography. Holmes adaptations had also been a staple of media that pre-empted and occasionally interrelated with television, such as theater and radio. But what makes Holmes adaptation *specifically* suitable for television? A great deal of the stories' action is confined to domestic settings, typically 221B Baker Street or clients' residences, and Holmes is often described as a creature of domestic comfort and as having "homely ways"(76). Such descriptions speak directly to a medium that is intended for domestic reception contexts, with the majority of programs set in or referring to the home. This parallel is acknowledged in the credit sequence of Granada television's *Sherlock Holmes* adaptations (1984–1994) where Holmes (Jeremy Brett) is pictured watching life on Baker Street from the restricted view of his flat window in a claustrophobic and cluttered close-up that sees him confined to the domestic.

Speaking industrially, Holmes adaptations seem to fulfill many of the varied aims of TV program makers. They are attractive to commercial TV producers as the continuing popularity and fandom of Conan Doyle's stories gives any adaptation a built-in audience base. For public service or mixed model broadcasters, the literary source and period setting serves their remit for quality television and producing programs with cultural and artistic value. Discussing Holmes adaptation in all media, Thomas Leitch in "Film Adaptation and Its Discontent" argues that Holmes adaptations tend to reference the franchise rather than the original source material, so that one adaptation will follow the example of a previous one and miss out the founding text (2007, 213). Such "quasi-canonical sources" (Leitch 2007, 214) create shared references, such as Sidney Paget's illustrations for *The Strand* with Holmes in a deerstalker hat that has become all but synonymous with Holmes in popular culture. Television adaptations are certainly no exception to this rule and *Sherlock* coming in after 70 years of Holmes on television is particularly prone to inter-reference with this history. The program can, therefore, often be read as a response to and reappropriation of many of the established tendencies of TV adaptations. It reacts to and reinflects trends in the TV adaptations, and contributes to key issues and debates in previous TV versions, often trying to resolve several problems that have beset bringing Holmes to the small screen.

TV adaptations of Sherlock Holmes stories have traditionally tended to produce the most youthful and vigorous versions of the characters of Holmes and Watson. Many producers have presented this as proof of their fidelity to the source material, claiming to be introducing the characters at the same stage of their fictional lives that Conan Doyle first gave them to his readers. Sheldon Reynolds, producer of the U.S. telefilm series *Sherlock Holmes* (1954), spoke of how in *A Study in Scarlet* "Holmes was a young man ... subject to ... overeagerness and lack of experience" (Haining 1994, 57). *Sherlock* likewise presents the youth of its leads as a commitment to the source material, using it as a means of restoring the original chronology of the stories by reinserting the scene of the two meeting at St. Bart's hospital in "A Study in Pink," which has rarely been televised in the last seventy years. The exception to this rule is the casting of middle-aged Jeremy Brett as Holmes in the Granada *Sherlock Holmes* series, who became the actor most associated with playing the character on television. Even in this case, the original series *The Adventures of Sherlock Holmes* (1984–1985) takes pains to emphasize Holmes's physical prowess, such as the boxing match in "The Solitary Cyclist." Making Holmes and Watson youthful and vigorous clearly also speaks to the demographic priorities of producers and the requirements of television companies to attract young audiences, both by cornering the market for family and teenage viewing and enticing the 16–35 demographic with their spending and cultural power to watch. The address to viewers in their twenties and thirties is explored later in this essay when considering how Conan Doyle's stories have been adapted as quality television, which Jane Feuer argues in regards to U.S. commercial TV demographics (1984, 3–4) is a mode representing educated middle and upper-class tastes which TV companies target at young adult viewers of these ages who regularly consume and spend more when then do. Here I comment on the marketing to child and teenage viewers.

Many UK TV adaptations have hovered on the precipice between adult and children's drama, making the lead characters children as in *Young Sherlock* (1982) or changing the interest for family audiences, for example, *The Baker Street Boys* (1983). *Sherlock* is marketed towards young TV audiences, with its repeat on BBC Three, a channel aimed at teenagers and viewers in their early twenties, and co-publicization alongside Moffat's *Doctor Who* (1963–), a BBC drama program with a historically family audience. Yet the program counters this with a post-watershed darkening of content through a preponderance of adult subjects, including serial killing, terrorism, and sociopaths, and occasional explicit violence or gore. Scenes referring to Sherlock's childhood, such as his first case as a teenager in "The Great Game," suggest an implied or potential family-friendly spin-off, as the BBC has done with the gothic drama *Being Human* (2008–). However, the episodes also question the possibility of representing their version of Sherlock as a child. John speaks of his inability to imagine Sherlock "as a child" and the utterances of "Mummy" between Sherlock and brother Mycroft are employed incongruously, perhaps even parodically.

Television adaptations of Sherlock Holmes stories are often channeled into comedic forms distinctive to the medium and its national contexts. There is a longstanding literary and filmic tradition of lampooning Conan Doyle's stories. Leitch (2007, 211), for example, refers to literary parodies by Mark Twain and Bret Harte, and both *The Private Life of Sherlock Holmes* (1970) and *Without a Clue* (1988) have elements of spoof and farce. Comical Sherlock Holmes TV adaptations helped to develop and reinforce television's functions as comedy and entertainment. This demonstrates that Sherlock Holmes adaptations were not simply engaging with television's quality and youth remits, but also its connections to popular culture and entertainment. Recent TV scholarship, such as Su Holmes' *Entertaining Television* (2008, 2), has reconsidered this engagement as a characteristic of the medium *throughout* its history rather than a fall-away from the cultural credibility of earlier periods. In the U.S. during the formative period of television, Sherlock Holmes stories and characters featured in the popular domain of TV vaudeville. Comedian Milton Berle starred in a farce featuring the character for NBC's *Texaco Star Theater* in 1949 and the character of Holmes appeared in variety show skits and advertisements throughout the 1950s (Haining 1994, 49). In the UK, Holmes adaptations have been re-interpreted as television genre pieces that are parts of national cultural traditions; situation comedy and political satire. *Elementary, My Dear Watson* (1972) and *The Strange Case of the End of Civilization as We Know It* (1977) were two updated comedy adaptations featuring the former *Frost Report* (1966–1967) and future *Fawlty Towers* (1975–1979) actor John Cleese as Holmes. The former was a situation comedy Pilot for BBC Comedy Playhouse and the latter a political comedy featuring Richard Nixon and

Henry Kissinger as characters. *Sherlock*'s interpretation of this comic mode is, therefore, a peculiarly British one. Showrunners Steven Moffat and Mark Gatiss, both former situation comedy writers, re-envision Sherlock and John's shared flat as a "domestic difficulty" comedy along the lines of *Peep Show* (2003–) and *Steptoe and Son* (1962–1974). Several scenes make light of the difficulties and hostilities of co-habitation between an oddly matched couple, particularly when Watson is attempting to cope with Sherlock's eccentric domestic habits, as in "The Great Game" when John discovering a decapitated head in his fridge when looking for food. It is played as an example of Holmes' bizarre and disgusting behavior of irritating a flatmate, one of the staple set pieces of the house-share situation comedy. The program's throwaway jokes about Britain's failures in wars in the Middle East ("Stupider than invading Afghanistan?") and the reliability of British bankers ("I thought they were heartless bastards") locates it firmly in a British televisual tradition of political satire about contemporary events in the vein of *Have I Got News for You* (1990–) or *That Was the Week That Was* (1962–1963).

A notable tendency in TV adaptations is the injection (sometimes literally) of contemporaneous relevance into the dramas set in the original Victorian and Edwardian periods of the original stories. This is typically done by introducing notes of presumed contemporary interest into the dramas; the BBC's *The Hound of the Baskervilles* (2002) discussing drug abuse through drawing out Holmes' recreational use of cocaine into a full-blown discourse on addiction, for example. Many adaptations have been shot in modern media styles that jar with the period setting, such as the use of comic book-style graphics in the Canadian TV movie *Sherlock: Case of Evil* (2002) (Davies 2007, 186–187). The main problem in these instances is how such additions upset the historical specificity of the drama, aptly demonstrated by the BBC's *The Case of the Silk Stocking* (2004) in which Holmes is seen using methods of psychoanalysis in lieu of contemporaneously popular TV pathologists (such as Fitz in *Cracker* [1993–1996] whose criminal detection methods reference Holmes' preoccupation with forensics and add psychological speculations) but in a time period long before there was widespread awareness of the new science (Davies 2007, 192–193). This ahistorical affect was frequently held up as the main reason for the critical and viewer derision for this adaptation, and critics have always identified the lack of fit with contemporary thinking in previous versions, like this *Times* review of Goddard's *Sherlock Holmes*: "a period character ... not at all easy to adapt to our current conceptions of crime and retribution" (Haining 1994, 63).

Sherlock can then be seen as an attempt to ease the burden of relevance that weighed heavily on the shoulders of period-set adaptations and contributed to their failures. The updating of the Holmes mythology to 2010

London naturalizes the flow of contemporary references, discussions of burning social issues and recent shooting styles (for example, time-delay cinematography) that were so artificially forced upon the period pieces. However, there remains a desire to hold a contemporary/classical dichotomy in place from the other side. There are many overlaps between 2010 and the original time of writing (for example, wars in Afghanistan), contrasts between new and classical aesthetics and narrative processes (for example, Internet research set against book searches in "The Blind Banker") and anachronisms in the publicity for the program as with the BBC continuity announcer speaking before "A Study in Pink": "A classic detective who's a man for our times." The split historical focus of program marketing has also been noted in other essays in this collection, namely Elizabeth Jane Evans' "Shaping Sherlocks" on DVD packaging. This suggests *Sherlock* has successfully resolved the problems of historical accuracy and atmosphere present in previous adaptations whilst maintaining the dualities of context also prevalent in previous Sherlock dramas.

Sherlock *and Television Production*

Sherlock can be put in TV contexts by evaluating its production circumstances against past and present TV production cultures and modes of authorship, particularly those of TV adaptation, in order to examine *Sherlock* in light of industrial issues in TV drama. The influence of models of TV authorship and production cultures from the U.S. since the 1980s is strongly present in *Sherlock*, both onscreen and off. Moffat and Gatiss are the co-creators of the series, write key episodes and produce the program. Roberta Pearson identifies the "hyphenate" model of authorship that appeared in U.S. network television in the 1980s and throughout the 1990s whereby a single artist combined roles of creator, director, writer, and producer, such as David Lynch and Joss Whedon (Pearson 2005, 11–26). The co-creator model is also typical of U.S. TV drama production since the 1980s (for example, Steven Bochco's series). Setting up the production culture in this fashion for *Sherlock* reflects how the U.S. hyphenates/creator model has infiltrated UK television drama. The showrunner model was previously evident during Russell T Davies' tenure as executive producer of *Doctor Who* (2005–2010), a role which Moffat himself inherited, as well as in the anthology series of Jimmy McGovern such as *The Street* (2006–) and serials of Paul Abbott like *Shameless* (2004–). The production situation on *Sherlock* also impacts on television form. The hyphenate model is concomitant with a flexi-narrative format where storytelling oscillates between discrete episodes and ongoing story lines, which best suited this mode of production and authorship. In the flexi-narrative format, showrunners maintain larger, framing narrative arcs while writers work on stand-alone episodes, as was certainly the case with Sherlock's first season, as Gatiss and Moffat wrote the first and last episode, while the second episode was written by staff writer Steve Thompson.

As Robin Nelson has observed, flexi-narrative is also linked to the narrative form of soap opera which makes it consonant with less culturally valid examples of television than Abbott and McGovern's quality drama (1997, 30–31). The fact that Sherlock's narrative combines one-off dramas (cases opened and shut within the episode) and serial narration (the continuing threat of Moriarty over the three episodes) suggests that the influence of the production culture bleeds into the text. The cultural fluidity of flexi-narrative demonstrates the oscillation of value in the format chosen for Sherlock, which I discuss later in the essay. The interplay of serial and episodic storytelling in Sherlock also reflects a symbiotic relationship between the two present not only in contemporary production culture, but also structurally throughout the history of television narrative. Examples of this include what Christopher Anderson calls the "disguised anthology series" of U.S. TV in the late 1950s (1994, 208) where a continuing character would encounter new situations and supporting characters each week, for example, The Fugitive (1963–1967) or BBC 1970s UK crime series Law & Order (1978) which narrated a criminal case from start to finish through distinct anthology plays.

It is also important to recognize that Steven Moffat and Mark Gatiss come from a tradition of fan authorship both inside and outside television. Both men have done fan writing on Doctor Who, Gatiss for the New Doctor Who Adventure Series and Big Finish Radio Productions and Moffat a Comic Relief Special based on the program. They have written literary pastiches, Gatiss on authors such as Dennis Wheatley and Ian Fleming in his Lucifer Box novels and Moffat with Robert Louis Stevenson in Jekyll (2007). Both have written episodes for the official Doctor Who canon that revel in references to details from canonical episodes and its fan communities: Gatiss' "Victory of the Daleks" references Dalek toy merchandise and Moffat's 'A Christmas Carol' reprises fan debates about the TARDIS "isomorphic controls." In an article on cult television, Matt Hills observes that fan knowledge of and activities around a TV program can build a market for a show after it ends and can also create future opportunities for authorship and publishing (2004, 519). Moffat and Gatiss are implicated in both these enterprises, having built careers as TV authors out of fan fiction on television and literature, and then, as I demonstrate below, transferring their fan authorship into TV adaptation with Sherlock.

Sherlock contains many of the tendencies of TV fan writing identified by Henry Jenkins in Textual Poachers (1992). Jenkins notes that fan fiction typically involves a *recontextualization* of the original text often achieved by *expanding the series timeline* (1992, 162–165). The program's shifting of time period to contemporaneous London fits this category. He also observes a predilection for the *eroticization* of established characters, typically represented through slash fiction where the subtextual homosocial relationships between male characters threatens to explode into a dominant focus on homoerotic sex and romance (1992, 175–190). The way in which Sherlock and John are frequently mistaken for lovers throughout the first series of *Sherlock* (for example by a restaurateur who brings them a candle for their supposedly romantic dinner) clearly acknowledges the potential for slash in their relationship, addressing the program to fan communities who appreciate slash, and referencing the swathe of prior slash fiction which features Holmes and Watson. However, the references to a romance between the couple are often played for comic effect with many in the form of farcical misunderstandings, suggesting an ambivalence towards the eroticization of the characters that is simultaneously skeptical of and respectful to the slash conventions of fan fiction. The resultant ambiguity and potential for multiple interpretations of Sherlock and John's relationship resists the perceived fannish extremes of slash fiction but nods to and plays with fan discourses of a homosexual subtext in the fiction's central partnership.

Leitch argues that authorship of Holmes adaptations bypasses the authority of Conan Doyle in favor of subsequent dramatists of his writing (2007, 209). This remains true in television, and therefore we need to acknowledge how Moffat and Gatiss' approach to *Sherlock* fits within and differs from previous television dramatists of Holmes stories. The conceptual aims of the producers of previous TV adaptations influence how Moffat and Gatiss dramatize the Sherlock Holmes stories. The production issue of fan authorship remains important here. Leitch argues that adaptations of Holmes stories feed off fan-authored works within the franchise more than the original stories (2007, 213). In TV adaptations, however, fan authorship and consciousness of Sherlock Holmes fandom has been variable. UK TV adaptations of the 1960s were criticized by fans (who were often cast members) for producers' lack of detailed knowledge of the Conan Doyle stories. Peter Cushing, for instance, castigated his producers' expediencies with the original text in the BBC's *Sherlock Holmes* adaptations in 1968 (Barnes 2002, 186). As Louisa Ellen Stein has argued, TV fan authorship, for all its experimentation, tends to be constrained by the original source material (2008, 241) and further to this point that this constraint is an inspiration to creativity, limitations that fan-authors see as pleasurable and productive rather than inhibiting. Likewise, Sherlockians have found different ways to engage with canon constraints in their fan activities as Ashley D. Polasek explores in her "Winning 'The Grand Game'" in this collection.

In turn, there have been Sherlock Holmes TV adaptations that demonstrated fan knowledge of and commitment to the original stories and these tended to pleasurably reproduce the plot and incidental details of the source texts to the point of pure pastiche. A notable example of this is *The Adventures of Sherlock Holmes* (1984–1985) in which the authors not only mimicked the stories to the letter but went further, basing images on the Sidney Paget illustrations of the stories drawn for *The Strand Magazine* and giving personnel a document called "The Baker Street File" which indexed all possible available knowledge featured in the stories including notes on characterization, locations and objects used by the characters (Haining 1994, 123–135). The Granada cycle of Holmes adaptations was not all done in a pastiche mode and the replacement of Conan Doyle purist Michael Cox with heritage drama stalwart June Wyndham-Davies as producer brought about a change in approach where the details of the stories were interpreted more flexibly according to the demands of narrative television.

Sherlock oscillates between the fan-conscious and impartial TV adaptations of Holmes stories. The first two episodes both demonstrate a close affinity with the narratives, characters, and (often minor) details of the Conan Doyle canon. "The Blind Banker," while incorporating elements of the canon (cipher plot devices from "The Dancing Men," for example), privileges the series' generic and institutional affiliations with the episodic police procedural formula. This is linked to authorship with writer Steve Thompson schooled in BBC drama genre formulas (with episodes of medical and legal drama *Doctors* [2000–] and *Silk* [2010–] in his corpus). "The Blind Banker" also bears the mark of the interrelations between the episode and other BBC products. Indeed, the story in this episode had been tested out in an episode of retirement police drama *New Tricks* [2003–]), and its action set-pieces wouldn't look out of place in an episode of a BBC One police series such as *Luther* (2010–). As such, this episode may well have been given over to Thompson and BBC drama conventions to extend the audience beyond Sherlockians and suggest to BBC executives the longer-term potential of *Sherlock* as a flagship detective drama. This alternation between canon and genre, therefore, speaks not just to authorship and production cultures but also issues of scheduling and programming discussed in the next section.

Sherlock *and Television Conventions*

The televisual familiarity of *Sherlock* comes predominantly from its fit with institutionalized conventions of international TV drama scheduling, program formats, ecologies, and genre typicalities. In *Television After TV,*

Charlotte Brunsdon argues that "taking a scheduling period ... can produce an object of study that is specific to the broadcast medium" (2004, 86), suggesting that we can better understand television in its broadcasting contexts this way rather than just focusing on programs. Holmes TV adaptations have traditionally been scheduled in quality television slots in both the U.S. and the UK, such as the BBC's Classic Serial Sunday teatime opening or PBS' Masterpiece Theatre strand, which has featured the BBC's Holmes adaptations since 2002. The 9 P.M. Sunday slot in which *Sherlock* is broadcast is one typically reserved in UK television for period drama and literary adaptation, especially on the BBC, but is also open for mystery dramas (*Midsomer Murders,* 1997–) and police procedurals (*Waking the Dead,* 2000–), many of which also fulfill the period and literary remit, such as *Agatha Christie's Poirot* (1989–). The U.S. scheduling of *Sherlock* has the same genre hybridity, because the Masterpiece Theatre strand features numerous period dramas and literary adaptations from British television while more recent genre offshoot Masterpiece Mystery has incorporated contemporaneously set, police-based programs, such as *Lewis* (2006–) and *Zen* (2011).

In these scheduling contexts, *Sherlock* treads a fine line generically between period literary adaptation and the police-detective program as well as straddling the categories of quality television and popular culture. The program arguably foregrounds its relationship to the police drama (hunts for serial killers and police press conferences in ASiP) and the mystery drama (the self-contained puzzles and ciphers of TBB and TGG) over its period and literary connotations, especially as those are partially effaced by the updated setting and array of new media on display. However, there is still a historical flexibility about the program's aesthetic and narrative clash of classic and contemporary tropes, for instance in the technologized laboratory where Sherlock beats a corpse with a riding crop. The written word and literary culture also play a considerable part in the narratives: the solution to "The Blind Banker" lies in ciphers contained within shared books and gives an insight into contemporary British reading habits. While *Sherlock* affects a surface of artistic and cultural legitimacy (visits to museums, galleries, and art events) it continually offsets this by re-locating to the realms of popular culture (graffiti art, daytime television). *Sherlock*, therefore, juggles the myriad generic and cultural rituals of its slot and scheduling period.

The 90-minute format in which *Sherlock* is produced and shown (often referred to anachronistically as feature-length) is synonymous with prestige television. This format has housed flagship period/literary dramas, critically acclaimed mystery dramas, and carries a cinematic cachet of greater aesthetic and narrative sophistication and complexity than 30- or 60-minute television. However, it also suggests TV at its most populist; the cable made-for-TV movie or the blockbuster film shown on TV. It is also significant that *Sherlock* was originally conceived as an hour-long drama (with an unaired Pilot this length) as this suggests the program was thought of more as popular genre television (for example, the hour-long police drama) rather than prestige product. Previous TV Holmes adaptations have also alternated between the 60- and 90-minute format. In fact, the Granada cycle of Sherlock Holmes adaptations switches between the two formats depending on ITV's programming requirements, such as. whether the channel needed seasonal TV movies or period serials. *Sherlock* interprets its format more in terms of the populism of TV movies than the quality drama, indicated by the frequency and amount of action set-pieces throughout the series (chase sequences, shootings, fights). There is a definite tension between the prestige and populist dimensions of the format that speaks to the uncertainty of its design. In particular, the drawing out of episodes into ninety minutes using multiple murders and kidnappings connected by a single perpetrator through the series relates the program to the serial killer sub-strand of police drama (*Wire in the Blood* [2002–]) and the lurking supervillain (or terrorist) of TV and film action and adventure fare such as *24* (2001–2010) and *Speed* (1994).

In terms of crime television, *Sherlock* adopts the aesthetics and narrative style of contemporaneous U.S. police/detective series which foreground new technologies intra-diegetically and in the production process (*CSI: Crime Scene Investigation* [2000–], *Numb3rs* [2005–2010]). The program overlaps particularly with *CSI* in terms of technology being made part of the visual style, for instance the Internet text on screen in *Sherlock* mirrors *CSI*'s graphic representations of forensic databases. It also dictates the way shots are composed and edited: laboratory poses and montages in *Sherlock* eerily resemble those in *CSI*, as does the mode of narration, for example. The centrality of technology in the detection process and the use of flashback in an alternate visual style. However, *Sherlock* also has elements of the UK mystery drama (*Inspector Morse*, 1987–2000; *Midsomer Murders*) with corresponding formats (the 90-minute drama), literary sources (mystery novels) and some form of anachronism, be that older periods or contemporary settings which refer to the past. *Sherlock* shares many qualities with *Inspector Morse*, particularly in its juxtaposition of classical tropes and a contemporaneous setting and the self-conscious design of episodes around a puzzle or game. Morse solves his mysteries like crosswords just as Sherlock resolves cases by interpreting ciphers and riddles. It is the negotiation of these two manifestations of the TV crime genre that makes *Sherlock* distinctive. The contemporary aesthetic styles and intra-diegetic uses of new technology in the program characteristic of the techno-crime series offset nostalgia normally associated with mystery dramas. However, the literacy and anachronism synonymous with the mystery drama calls some of the contemporaneity of the program into question, revealing a classical tradition behind the new media surface and technological immediacy of the narrative.

Sherlock and its predecessors are heavily implicated in heritage television. This mode of television is characterized by UK historical drama with exquisite period detail, uses of British heritage sites (halls, stately homes, etc.) and classic literature, and, as argued by Charlotte Brunsdon, an export of national identity based on Britain's imperial past (1997, 143). The TV form is often seen as playing a key role in Britain's heritage industry in the 1980s and is synonymous with a set of contemporaneous ITV period and literary adaptations like *Brideshead Revisited* (1981) and *Jewel in the Crown* (1984). The Granada cycle of Sherlock Holmes adaptations were very much the successors to the heritage niche on ITV. Moreover, Holmes adaptations have often been made by producers of heritage television, such as June Wyndham-Davies in the later Granada series. TV adaptations have also interacted with the UK heritage industry. For instance, as reported by Alan Barnes in *Sherlock Holmes on Screen*, the BBC 1951 *Mr. Sherlock Holmes* was considered an offshoot of the Sherlock Holmes exhibition at the Festival of Britain (2002, 222).

Sherlock's format and scheduling tends to identify it as a heritage production, and its display of 21st century London landmarks (the Gherkin, the Millennium Wheel) and city skylines clearly function as promotion of UK tourism, with an image of UK global business dominance and technological advancement surrogating for imperialism. Its heritage contexts are felt in the focus on the history of culture and art in the episodes (Sherlock is often seen in museums and galleries) but there are tensions here as the program usually locates this history within contemporary buildings and spaces, such as the independent modern art gallery in TGG, or marginalizes it to focus on contemporary culture and art, as with the teenage graffiti artist tagging behind the National Gallery in TBB. Brunsdon also argues that one of the characteristics of heritage television is that it is "uncontroversial" in its formally unchallenging style and restrained and tasteful deployment of high production values (1997, 143). *Sherlock* breaks from heritage production values by emphasizing formal stylization, with visual uses of onscreen text (text messages, Internet tabs) and a cacophonic synasthesia of audio-visual elements, most evident in the fight with The Golem in TGG in a planetarium suffering a technical breakdown with narration, music, color and shadows re-mixed and accelerated at the same time. The program mobilizes its high production values not towards restrained visuals, nor even for culturally legitimate purposes of aesthetic experimentation, but for flashy spectacle. The master shots of London and its landmark features are full of excessive and garish uses of light and color and stylized editing. We have spectacular special effects (the explosion through Sherlock's window) and slick, speeded-up montages designed to dazzle the viewer. *Sherlock*, therefore, challenges the conservative aesthetics and nostalgia discourses of heritage television while fulfilling certain other heritage remits.

Sherlock's medium-specificity can be traced out by studying its television contexts, which I have selected as adaptation, authorship, production, and programming conventions. In order to recognize the true significance of *Sherlock* as a TV adaptation of Sherlock Holmes stories and product of the television industry and ecology, we need awareness of its reception and historical contexts. *Sherlock* is a culmination of and testament to the history of Holmes on TV, established TV programming practices, issues in authorship and genre intertextuality. Conversely, *Sherlock* tells us a great deal about contemporary trends in adaptation, authorship, programming, and production in TV (and other media) whilst simultaneously shedding light on the history and specificity of the medium. Just as *Sherlock* negotiates past and present in its transposition of a period detective to contemporary society, it illuminates television practice now in relation to how it has been. While the characteristics of *Sherlock* have evidently been rehearsed throughout television history, the program engages these contexts to re-inflect, challenge, or innovate with established TV histories, forms and styles. It has experimented with and resolved tensions in prior methods of TV adaptation, played with discourses of fan authorship and production models, and made compelling interventions into programming conventions of format, scheduling and genre. In the introduction, I suggested that it was possible to be blinded to the television contexts of *Sherlock* by the fetishization of new media and technology in its updated setting and the transmedia legacy of Sherlock Holmes adaptations. The emphasis on contemporary television in the program and its production discourses can also conceal *Sherlock's* relevance to television history. In contrast, this essay has demonstrated that *Sherlock* is primarily an invention of television and a product of its history.

Works Cited

Anderson, Christopher. 1994. *Hollywood TV: The studio system in the fifties*. Austin: University of Texas Press.
Barnes, Alan. 2002. *Sherlock Holmes on screen: The complete film and TV history*. London: Reynolds and Hearn.
Brunsdon, Charlotte. 1997. *Screen tastes: Soap opera to satellite dishes*. London: Routledge.
_____. 2004. Lifestyling Britain: The 8–9 slot on British television. In *Television after TV: Essays on a medium in transition*, ed. Lynn Spigel and Jan Olsson, 75–93. Durham: Duke University Press.
Davies, David Stuart. 2007. *Starring Sherlock Holmes*. London: Titan Books.

Feuer, Jane, Tise Vahimagi, and Paul Kerr, ed. 1984. *MTM: Quality television.* London: BFI.

Haining, Peter. 1994. *The television Sherlock Holmes.* London: Virgin Books.

Hills, Matt. 2004. Defining cult TV: Texts, inter-texts and fan audiences. In *The television Studies Reader,* ed. Robert C. Allen and Annette Hill, 509–524. London: Routledge.

Holmes, Su. 2008. *Entertaining television: The BBC and popular television culture in the 1950s.* Manchester: Manchester University Press.

Jenkins, Henry. 1992. *Textual poachers.* London: Routledge.

Leitch, Thomas. 2007. *Film adaptation and its discontents: From* Gone with the Wind *to* The Passion of the Christ. Baltimore: John Hopkins University Press.

Nelson, Robin. 1997. *TV drama in transition: Forms, values and cultural change.* London: Macmillan.

Pearson, Roberta. 2005. The writer/producer in American television. In *The contemporary television series,* ed. Michael Hammond and Lucy Mazdon, 11–26. Edinburgh: Edinburgh University Press.

Riley, Brendan. 2009. From Sherlock to Angel: The twenty-first century detective. *The Journal of Popular Culture* 42: 908–922.

Stein, Louisa Ellen. 2008. Pushing at the margins: Teenage angst in teen TV and audience response. In *Teen television: Essays on programming and fandom,* ed. Sharon Marie Ross and Louisa Ellen Stein, 224–243. Jefferson, N.C.: McFarland.

PART FOUR

Interpreting *Sherlock*

"Good Old Index"

Or, The Mystery of the Infinite Archive

ROBERTA PEARSON

Abstract — This essay outlines the challenges posed to traditional scholarly research by the infinite archive's infinite data. It identifies the most probable sites for *Sherlock* related data in order further to illustrate the methodological dilemma and to suggest a solution. It then discusses the interpretive frameworks and practices of the inhabitants of the many and varied sites in which *Sherlock* related data appear, distinguishing between "affirmational" and "transformational" fandoms and the protocols that govern their productivity. It concludes that fan studies should shift from studying individual web page contents to studying the protocols that govern them.

"Good Old Index" (The Adventure of the Sussex Vampire)

In 1901 Sherlock Holmes received an inquiry concerning vampires. Turning to his faithful biographer, Holmes said, "Make a long arm, Watson, and see what V has to say" (II:1556). Watson reached for Holmes' "great index volume," a "record of old cases, mixed with the accumulated information of a lifetime" (II:1556). Perusing nearby entries for voyage of the Gloria Scott, Victor Lynch the forger, venomous lizard, Vittoria, the circus belle, Vanderbilt and the Yeggman, vipers and Vigor, the Hammersmith wonder, Holmes exclaimed, "Good old index. You can't beat it" (II:1556). In 1996, I began an essay on Sherlock Holmes in cyberspace by remarking that "were Holmes still in practice today, one warrants that a high powered PC, a collection of CD-ROMs and a modem would beat the good old index hands down" (Pearson 1997, 143). In 2010, Steven Moffat and Mark Gattiss took the hint about updating the great detective, their 21st century Holmes swapping the good old index for the Internet's infinite archive. Said Moffat, "He was born for the Internet and for the chat room and for forums.... It would finally be the speed and the intensity of information that that demented man craves" (October 15, 2010; www.wgbh.org). But do the speed and intensity of the infinite archive beat the painstakingly amassed hard copy of the good old index? In 1996, my answer would have been a resounding yes, but now I share the doubts of many of my colleagues in the arts and humanities who face the digital transformation of their research. The massive expansion of the Internet in the years since 1996 made my writing of this essay much harder than anticipated. What had initially seemed reasonably self-contained (gauge fan response to a mere three episodes of a television show) turned unmanageable, as I frantically clicked from site to site, copying and pasting into a massive document that made increasingly little sense. Realizing that my customary sense-making procedures no longer applied, I decided to begin this essay by reflecting upon scholarly methods in the age of the infinite archive.

First, however a brief caveat concerning the "infinite archive." The term gives the illusion of completeness but censorship and copyright militate against comprehensiveness, whilst search engine protocols structure the retrieval of data. Nonetheless, the Internet archive's vast data store challenges the relevance of traditional methodological values and procedures, posing intractable problems with regard to reliability, provenance, generalizability, replicability, and expertise. My first encounter with a virtual rather than real world archive occurred in the Web 1.0 days when I sought evidence for my Holmes in cyberspace essay. In the mid-nineties it was still possible to identify a key site and conduct a rough systematic analysis of the accumulated data. The data for my essay came from the Hounds of the Internet, an email mailing list dating from 1992 which describes itself as "the longest established online group for the discussion of Sherlock Holmes" and which is described as attracting "many of the leading lights among Sherlockians" (www.sherlockiannet/hounds). The essay used these data to investigate the ways in which posters produced "very different appropriations of the same popular hero at the same historical moment" with particular reference to gender (Pearson 1997, 148). I was able to report that the Hounds had 475 users, the majority, 401, having U.S. Internet addresses. There were 284 men, 124 women and 67 posters whose gender could not be identified (150–151). In a footnote I discussed the reliability of this breakdown, noting, "some posters use initials and some pseudonyms. Some foreign names are not readily assignable to a gender.... And some posters may be using partners' or friends' accounts" (160–161). The limited data harvested from the Hounds enabled a traditionally scholarly discussion of its own limitations. I had established provenance to the extent my research question required; gender and nationality could be assigned to most posters, most of whom were, judging from the content of the posts, fairly knowledgeable long-term fans. Established provenance in turn permitted generalizing my conclusions to the larger Sherlockian community. Anyone wishing to replicate my procedures to test the validity of those conclusions needed simply to turn to the Hounds web site.

My scholarly expertise remained fairly intact in the face of the emergence of an entirely new medium of communications; Web 1.0 posed methodological problems, but the existing boundaries of an Internet still under construction enabled me to use my customary sense making procedures. But when I returned to the topic of Sherlockian fandom in the vastly expanded and interactive Web 2.0, I encountered a cyberspace of infinite links and infinite data in which one can no longer judge provenance, draw generalizable conclusions nor expect other scholars to replicate one's procedures. How then to solve the three pipe/patch problem of the mystery of the infinite archive? This essay first identifies the most probable sites for *Sherlock* related data in order further to illustrate the methodological dilemma and to suggest a solution. It then discusses the interpretive frameworks and practices of the inhabitants of the many and varied sites in which *Sherlock* related data appear. I draw on obsession_inc's terminology of "affirmational" and "transformational" fandoms (June 1, 2009; www.dreamwidth.org) and articulate these specific fannish differences and the protocols that govern their productivity.

"That web has a thousand radiations" (The Final Problem)

Holmes deduced the thousand radiations composing Professor Moriarty's criminal web by working backwards from outward tremors to the evil genius sitting motionless like a spider at its center. The absence of a fixed center negates tracing the infinite radiations of the infinite archive, but as Allison Cavanagh argues, there is a discernible architecture to the web: "The shape of the web ... is highly fragmented overall but exhibits clustering around centers of gravity formed by the pull of brands and portals" (Cavanagh 2007, 153). A rough taxonomy of the Sherlockian brand's centers of gravity initially guided my research.

1. producers/distributors: Hartswood Films, the BBC, WGBH (U.S. broadcaster), Amazon (DVD distributor).
2. general reception: newspapers and magazines (e.g., *The Guardian*, *SFX*); fan or former fan sites (e.g., Ain't It Cool News, IMDB, TV Without Pity, Den of Geek); "prosumer" sites such as YouTube.
3. Sherlockian specific sites

But my early optimism proved unfounded as I soon found myself lost among the potentially infinite radiations of the BBC's *Sherlock* site, which constructs what my colleague Paul Grainge refers to as the "promotional surround" through embedded links, ancillary content and the exploitation of fan activities (Grainge 2009, 97). Links point users to three review and opinion sites (the Internet Movie Database, tv.com, and *The Guardian*) as well as web pages for Benedict Cumberbatch, Martin Freeman, the BBC press pack, and Sir Arthur Conan Doyle. Ancillary content produced by the BBC web team includes Sherlock's site, "Science of Deduction," and Dr. John Watson's blog. The links to review and opinion sites as well as the ancillary content are now standard practice amongst media producers as is the exploitation of fan activities, as many media producers now seek to take advantage of the productive capacity of their fans in the interactive Web 2.0 environment. But it was here that the methodological problem of infinite radiations became glaringly apparent.

The *Sherlock* site has a section labeled "Buzz about this programme," further divided into "discussion on blogs" and "discussion elsewhere on the web." The "discussion on blogs" section has three links: BBC iPlayer: *Sherlock* Episode 3, "The Great Game," connects to Faded Glamour, "a collaborative British music and film blog" (www.fadedglamour.co.uk); "*Sherlock* Update: What Moriarty Did Next" connects to the "Culture and the City" blog (cultureandthecity.blogspot.com); and "Codes and Ciphers" connects to the "Stories from the Laughing Lemon" blog (hyperploid.blogspot.com). All of these blogs include comments and/or links to other sites. The "discussion elsewhere on the web" section includes the Internet Movie Database, tv.com, and *The Guardian* links as well as another link labeled "see all buzz for Sherlock" which again connects to various blogs, such as The Philosophy of Lists (philosophyoflists.blogspot.com) and The Innocent Flower (theinnocentflower.blogspot.com), which yet again abound with comments and/or further links. The web designers augmented my increasing confusion by ensuring the constant multiplication of the radiations. The "buzz about this programme" page asks, "Seen a site discussing Sherlock? Tell us about it." Clicking on "tell us about it" brings up the following text. "Links to blog posts are found automatically and you can find out here [clickable link] how to get your blog picked up." It also tells users that "if you run or know about a web site where people are discussing a BBC programme then let us know here [clickable link]." Tracing the radiations leading outward from just one of my previously designated relevant sites would take vast amounts of time and generate vast amounts of data. It was at this point that I concluded that this essay required not an analysis of web site contents but a fundamental reassessment of my sense-making procedures.

Beginning my reassessment with Lisa Gitelman's theoretically informed history of recording technologies and the Internet, *Always Already New: Media, History, and the Data of Culture*, I discovered that the author shares my methodological concerns:

> Selecting singular examples from the World Wide Web in order to support claims about the Web or digital culture as a whole is a lot like manufacturing one's own evidence, minting one's own coin.... One hedge ... is to take a longer view, to focus on tools, methods, and protocols rather than the dubious exemplarity of Web pages themselves [2006, 130].

Gitelman substantiated my intuitive conclusion that web site contents should not be the primary focus of my argument and the concept of media protocols offered a way to address the methodological conundrum. Gitelman never gives a precise definition of the term but it would seem that protocols are all the factors that structure users' interactions with a specific medium, including technological requirements, hardware, software and social/cultural norms.

> If media include what I am calling protocols, they include a vast clutter of normative rules and default conditions.... Email includes all the elaborately layered technical protocols and interconnected service providers that constitute the Internet, but it also includes both the QWERTY keyboards on which email gets 'typed' and the shared sense people have of what the email genre is [2006, 7–8].

Gitelman observes that "media become transparent when ... society at large forget[s] many of the norms and standards they are heeding, and then forget that they are heeding norms and standards at all" (2006, 7). It's at this point that users pay attention to content rather than protocols:

> the success of all media depends at some level on inattention or 'blindness' to the media technologies themselves (and all of their supporting protocols) in favor of attention to the phenomena, 'the content,' that they represent for users' edification or enjoyment [2006, 6].

The Internet medium has become transparent for many fan studies scholars; taking for granted the protocols of Internet fandom leads to a focus on the analysis of content, with all the attendant methodological pitfalls. One notable exception is Louisa Ellen Stein and Kristina Busse's "Limit Play," in which they argue "The constraints of fan textual artistry come in many forms, from the constraints of the source text to those of community expectations, from the broader cultural expectations of genre to the limitations of technological interfaces" (2009, 195). Nevertheless, this rarity is noteworthy given Gitelman's (and my) argument that content-based deductions are limited at best.

The infinite archive's contents may be limitless, but the relatively limited number of protocols, at least within specifically defined sites of interest and activity such as television fandom, constitutes a manageable object for scholarly analysis. I suggest that the field of fan studies should pay less attention to content and more attention to protocols; here I focus upon the most proximate social/cultural protocols that structure the reception of *Sherlock* on the Internet. These are the interpretive frameworks and practices brought to bear on the text, which encompass factors such as the author function, canonical fidelity, specialized language and the norms governing user interaction on a web site or web site host such as livejournal.com.

"The inhabitants of this great city" (A Study in Scarlet)

Louisa Ellen Stein, co-editor of this volume, and Sean Duncan, the co-founder of the first *Sherlock* web site, suggest that *Sherlock*'s success stemmed from the text's deliberately engineered appeal to fannish sensibilities and networks. In her blog post, *"Mad Men* vs. *Sherlock*: What Makes a Fandom," Stein notes that "with two episodes aired at the time of writing, [*Sherlock*] already has a full host of communities, fan fiction, vids, and fan art" resulting from "the ready to go networks of community that we've seen launch and deploy for *Sherlock* at record speed these past weeks" (August 10, 2010, blog.commarts.wisc.edu). In comments, Duncan agrees, pointing to several factors that ensured *Sherlock*'s rapid take-up in Internet fandom: Moffat and Gatiss' Whovian credentials; Cumberbatch's allure; the gay not-so subtext and "snappy writing, clever direction, a century's worth of fans [and] rich source materials to revisit." Duncan concludes that, compared to quality programs such as *Mad Men*, "*Sherlock* fandom seems much less complex and much more easily identifiable as, uh, 'standard issue fannish,'" by which he means that it's "easy to translate into common internetty fan practices (slash, 'squeeing,' fan vids, etc.)." Duncan correctly asserts that *Sherlock* perfectly suits some "internetty fan practices"; standard issue fannish behaviors, governed by standard issue fannish protocols, indeed dominate certain neighborhoods of the Internet's vast city such as LiveJournal, but different interpretive frameworks and practices govern the behavior of other neighborhoods' inhabitants. *Sherlock* elicited no slashing or squeeing on the Sherlock Holmes Society of London or Adventuresses of Sherlock Holmes web sites nor, I warrant, would any of those web sites' inhabitants either know the meaning of the terms or wish to engage in the practices if they did. These affiliated Sherlockians, proud members of that "century's worth of fans" which Duncan acknowledges, greeted *Sherlock* just as eagerly as anyone with a LiveJournal account but their own long-established real world and virtual protocols resulted in site-specific receptions different from that in LiveJournal sites. Contra reception theories that completely dissolve the text in favor of the reader, I hypothesize an interaction between text and protocols: specific textual and paratextual attributes encourage the application of specific protocols and specific protocols encourage engagement with specific textual and paratextual attributes. This requires first looking at textual and paratextual attributes, which might broadly be termed the producer discourse, before considering their interaction with specific protocols on specific sites.

Much of *Sherlock*'s producer discourse foregrounded the author function (in its Foucauldian sense) and canonical fidelity, interpretive frameworks that play a key role in fandom and therefore in franchise extensions or reboots that must cater to the core fans in addition to other audiences. Indeed, Matt Hills (this volume) discusses this specific concern, which he calls canonical fidelity, as it relates to *Sherlock*. One of the most widely circulated of *Sherlock*'s paratexts was the forty-two second trailer, elements of which directly addressed the existing core Sherlockian fandom. Two updated paraphrases of well-known (at least among knowledgeable Sherlockians) Holmes quotes feature prominently. At the beginning, John asks Sherlock, "Who are you? What do you do?" Sherlock explains that he is a private detective: "when the police are out of their depth they consult me" (ASiP). In *The Sign of the Four*, Holmes tells Watson, "When Gregson or Lestrade or Athelney Jones are out of their depths — which, by the way, is their normal state — the matter is laid before me" (III:217). Hurriedly leaving the Baker Street rooms, Sherlock calls out, "The game, Mrs. Hudson, is on" (ASiP). In "The Adventure of the Abbey Grange," Holmes rouses his flatmate from his bed with an excited cry of "Come, Watson, come! The game is afoot" (II:1158). In the trailer's penultimate shot the eponymous character says, "The name's Sherlock Holmes and the address is 221 B Baker Street." That bold declaration would send a frisson of excitement through any Sherlockian, even one harboring suspicions about the updating (such as the author of this essay).

The three episodes deliver on the trailer's implicit promise to Sherlockians with a myriad of canonical references (Watson first meets Holmes at Bart's, Watson's brother's pocket watch morphs into his sister's smart phone, and pipes and cigarettes turn into nicotine patches) as well as plot points (for example, the murderous cabbie in "A Study in Pink") lifted directly from Conan Doyle. Many paratexts foregrounded the Moffat/Gatiss author function, presumably as an appeal to Whovians, but in interviews the showrunners repeatedly stressed their shared Sherlockian fandom and respect for Conan Doyle. For example, the BBC press release quoted Moffat: "On our many train journeys from London to Cardiff, we talked about our love for Sherlock Holmes, how brilliantly modern Conan Doyle's writing was and how someone should do a contemporary version." Gatiss said, "Arthur Conan Doyle was a writer of genius and it's worth trumpeting that point." The release also noted canonical fidelity: "The first episode, A Study In Pink, is partly an homage to Conan Doyle's first story to feature the fictional detective, A Study In Scarlet, written in 1887" (July 7, 2010; bbc.co.uk).

The following examines the protocols that structured the reception of *Sherlock* in two different Internet neighborhoods that broadly represent affirmational (interpretation and evaluation) versus transformational (reworking the text) fandoms: (1) general audience/fan sites and established Sherlockian sites and (2) newer Sherlockian and new *Sherlock* sites, such as those on Live-Journal. My first Internet neighborhood consists of Amazon UK, the Internet Movie database, and older Sherlockian and general fan sites, which are governed by a primary protocol of interpretation and evaluation, together with subsidiary protocols regarding the relevant interpretive frameworks. For example, Amazon, which predicates its business model upon customer feedback, encourages interpretation and evaluation through several strategies: the rating of recently acquired items to improve recommendations; customer reviews of all items; Listmania, for which customers compile lists of favorite this and top that as well as the discussion forums that I explore here.

The following compares the interpretive frameworks in play in these sites, particularly with regard to the conformance with those elements of *Sherlock*'s producer discourse outlined above. Sherlockians' real and virtual protocols encourage consonance with producer discourse concerning the author function; this is a feedback loop since foregrounding Conan Doyle constitutes part of the deliberate appeal to the core fandom. Anticipating the arrival of *Sherlock* on U.S. television, a poster to alt.fan.holmes said, "ACD was a unique and talented author. The atmosphere he established in the original canons has never been matched...." (R. Lombardo, October 24, 2010; groups.google.com). A comment on the Sherlock Holmes Society of London site fretted that *Sherlock*'s second episode had strayed off-author. "After an unexpected — indeed inexplicable — side track into the world of Sax Rohmer in 'The Blind Banker' I was delighted to return to that of Sir Arthur Conan Doyle in 'The Great Game'" (J. McCafferty, August 24, 2010; Sherlock-holmes.org.uk). The author function featured as prominently in Amazon posts as in Sherlockian ones, some Amazonians writing as if Moffat and Gatiss were directly channeling Sir Arthur: "a great contemporary reworking of a classic; just as Conan Doyle would have written it himself if he were here now" (J. Raines, February 11, 2011; amazon.co.uk) and "the three stories of this first series definitely have the Conan Doyle DNA running through them" (Theater Addict, November 25, 2010; amazon.co.uk). The author function also framed negative evaluations: "Conan Doyle would of hung his head in shame at the travesty of what his 'great detective' has become" (W. Nicholls, August 10, 2010; amazon.co.uk). For another Amazonian, Moffat's and Gatiss' Sherlockian credentials boost their own authorial authority: "Stephen Moffat and Mark Gatiss ... clearly know their Sherlock Holmes and borrow selectively from the original short stories and novels" (K. Leadbetter, August 15, 2010; amazon.co.uk). Sherlockian protocols also encourage deploying canonical fidelity as an interpretive framework, as seen in comments posted to The Sherlock Holmes Society of London site: "The essence of why we love the Sherlock Holmes canon was all present" (R. Graham, August 16, 2010; Sherlock-holmes.org.uk), and "There's so much canonic ... reference ... I can see an excellent game of shout the reference being played" (A. Kurlis, August 22, 2010; www.sherlock-holmes.org.uk). Amazonians too delight in the series' hat tips to the originals: "Devotees of ACD canon will delight in spotting the references" (528491, February 3, 2010; amazon.co.uk); "The show is literally littered with references, names, places and lines and conversations from Conan Doyle's stories" (G. Christoffersen, December 30, 2010; amazon.co.uk); and "I love how the authors used those tiny details from the original Doyle stories" (Alies, December 12, 2010; amazon.co.uk).

The similarity between the interpretive frameworks in play on established Sherlockian sites and Amazon not surprisingly results in similar adherence to the author function and to canonical fidelity and therefore to consonance with producer discourse. However, posters to the Internet Movie database exhibit the same allegiance to canonical fidelity as Sherlockians and Amazonians, perhaps a testament to the prevalence of this interpretive framework among those drawn to review and opinion sites or, indeed, in the culture generally. An IMDB thread concerning a specific *Sherlock* paratext reveals intimate knowledge of the Holmes canon. When the BBC commissioned three more episodes, Moffat teased the audience with hints about the next series: "Adler, Hound, Reichenbach. Those are your clues" (January 3, 2011; www.guardian.co.uk). IMDB.com posters thought it too early for Reichenbach (the location of Holmes' supposed death in "The Final Problem") and too obvious to sex up Irene Adler ("the woman" who appears in "A Scandal in Bohemia") but welcomed an updated version of the *Hound of the Baskervilles*. Other posters simply provided lists of stories they'd like to see with some elaborating upon the reasons for their choices. All these posts revealed wide and detailed knowledge of the originals that, by some definitions of fandom, would make these posters fans. Yet no transformational fannish protocols were suggested — no hurt/comfort, no slash, no crossovers, no shipping. One poster proposed the germ of an AU (alternative universe) story, "a Sherlock-gone-bad episode," but wanted a real world motivation: "it must turn out to be for some other reason (undercover)" (S. Holmes, January 18, 2011; www.imdb.com). *Sherlock* fandom in Sherlockian sites, Amazon and IMDB does not exhibit what Duncan terms standard issue fannish behavior. But, indicating perhaps the restrictiveness of Duncan's conception of fan behavior, the Sherlockians implicitly acknowledge their fandom through their posts to Sherlockian sites and many of the Amazonians proudly proclaim their fandom: "I have always been a massive Sherlock Holmes fan" (J. Raines, Feb. 11, 2011; amazon.co.uk); "us Holmes 'purists'" (EFD, December 22, 2010; amazon.co.uk); "I am a Sherlock Holmes addict" (J. Van Limpt, November 4, 2010; amazon.co.uk); "a confessed Holmes nerd" (Dani, August 11, 2010; amazon.co.uk); and many more.

If the fans on Amazon and IMDB don't behave like fan studies fans, at least within Duncan's narrow definition of the term, might the protocols of review and opinion sites directly aimed at "cult" media fandom elicit Duncan-like fannish behavior? Den of Geek describes itself as "one of the UK's fastest growing entertainment web sites"; Moffat's and Gatiss' granting interviews signals the site's centrality to UK media fandom. More importantly the site seems intended for a distinct demographic. Editor Simon Brew offers a playfully knowing self-description: "Bald, overweight, don't shave enough, bit smelly. Love movies, games, TV and cake. Likes writing things. There's no fitting of clichés going on here. Oh no" (May 2, 2007; denofgeek.com). Brew deliberately portrays himself as the stereotypical fanboy, British cousin to *The Simpson*'s Comic Book Guy, or, in other words, a geek. Geeks, like Sherlockians and Amazonians, display consonance with producer discourse. A "lifelong fan of the Conan Doyle stories" thought "A Study in Pink" an "excellent start to this ... series" (SpeakerToAnimals, July 26, 2010; denofgeek.com). Said another, "Conan Doyle fans will have recognized the fobwatch scene straight off and marveled at the modern take" (Eryndil, July 31, 2010; denofgeek.com). But the geeks show an awareness of fannish protocols absent from the other review and opinion web sites. The Moffat and Gatiss interview inspired talk of a *Sherlock/Doctor Who* crossover: "And was there a whiff of a DW/Sherlock crossover down the line should things take off?" (Omniaural, July 1, 2010; denofgeek.com). Displaying knowledge of the *Who* canon, another poster responded, "If there's gonna be a crossover, it would never be with Sherlock Holmes, it'd be Arthur Conan Doyle, like Agatha Christie from Season 4" (FonceFalooda, July 21, 2010; denofgeek.com). Brixe responded to the interview by saying, "I wish they would just use the words 'fan fiction'! Because that's what it is! Brilliant! I love fan fiction!" (July 21, 2010; denofgeek.com).

The geeks do indeed look more stereotypically fannish than their Sherlockian and Amazonian counterparts; while they place comparable value upon the author function and canonical fidelity, they augment their interpretive frameworks with knowledge of such typically fannish protocols as crossovers and fanfic. But we're still looking for squeeing or slashing or fanvidding; the search begins by returning to the producer discourse for specific textual and paratextual attributes that might elicit engagement different from that of the review and opinion sites. As we have seen, the trailer's canonical fidelity directly targets the core fans we've seen in the Internet's older neighborhoods. But a sly reference to the "real" nature of the Holmes/Watson relationship would have appealed to the slashers, squee-ers, and vidders who gather in the Internet's newer neighborhoods of LiveJournal, Wordpress, Dreamwidth, and the like. In the trailer, Holmes is seen introducing Watson to a client. "This is my friend, John Watson." Close-up of client smiling, cut to close-up of Watson who says, "colleague," as if to set the record straight. The straight or gay question serves as a running joke throughout the series. At one point, when John inadvertently sends the wrong signals, Sherlock says, "I think you should know I consider myself married to my work and while I am flattered by your interest, I am really not looking for anyone" (ASiP). Just as the author function and canonical fidelity resonated with the protocols of review and opinion sites, this "slashiness" resonated with the protocols of newer fan sites already engaging in slashy practices — fanfic, vids, art, photos, and so forth.

The queer but not slashy site Queering-holmes (www.dreamwidth.org) sits on the boundary between the Internet's older and newer Sherlockian neighborhoods, aligning itself with neither. It describes itself as "a community for research/discussion of Sherlock Holmes and queerness" to address the "lack of serious discussion of queerness wrt the Sherlock Holmes canon (especially in academia or old-school Sherlockian circles)." But it stipulates that "this is obviously a fan-friendly community, but it's not a slash community. While many of us here are probably H/W slashers, this community is not the place to post your slash fiction/art/etc or general slashy squee." The site's founders establish their protocols partly through the explicit rejection of the protocols of both the older and newer neighborhoods. A discussion thread initiated by one of the founders explicitly explores these different protocols. Damned Colonial said that she was

> interested in hearing from anyone who was involved with Holmes fandom in its earlier/older incarnations — any of the Sherlockian societies, or zine-based slash fandom, or mailing lists, or even LJ/DW fandom prior to the 2009 movie — about your experiences and the changes you've seen. As for fic-writing fandom, I know when I read older H/W slash online I find it has a different aesthetic and different tropes than modern LJ/DW-centered slash fandom commonly uses [May 14, 2010].

My Daroga responded at length.

> I started in Holmes fandom through Prodigy before the WWW, around 1993. The group there seemed to be transitional, mostly older, many involved in zines, amateur press associations, and local scion societies.... "Fandom" as it currently exists in an ever-changing but loosely codified set of expectations, activities, and inter-

actions was either outside my purview or didn't exist in the form it does today. By which I mean to say that internet Fandom today looks similar (in a general sense) from fandom to fandom across the internet, and skills or interests gained/learned/developed in one can be transferred easily to the next thing that pings your fannish radar. It's my guess, and it's unfounded, that current H/W and Holmes fandom is going to look a lot more like other internet fandoms and a lot less like old Holmes fandom. I think that's because moving between fandoms is so much easier, media is so much more easily distributed, and internet fans are often on the same page (broadly defined) rather than somewhat insular groups or individuals connected by mail [May 14, 2010].

My Daroga's unfounded guess in regard to similarities amongst Internet fandoms echoes Stein's argument that "ready to go networks of community" accounted for *Sherlock*'s rapid uptake in Internet fandom. Easily moving between fandoms and ready to go networks both result from the common protocols governing the Internet's newer neighborhoods; knowledge of these protocols, the skills to which My Daroga refers, facilitates mobility across the fandoms represented in LiveJournal and elsewhere.

A shared language protocol enables fans to move easily between neighborhoods and fandoms, as seen in the responses to two *Sherlock* paratexts posted to YouTube, a site where the lingua fannish enables communication among multiple fandoms. In the best tradition of fan vidding, two trailers produced by Korean cable network OCN (Orion Cinema Network) transformed *Sherlock*'s gay-friendly subtext into overt text, a romantic song accompanying cut-together shots of meaningful looks between Sherlock and John. The trailers' resemblance to fan practices provoked YouTubers to express their astonishment in the lingua fannish.

> Either they let some slash fangirls into the editing room ... or other people are starting to realize how cannon [*sic*] and obvious their relationship is.
> This promo inceptioned slash goggles to viewers! lol I know this is SUB TRAILER BUT THIS IS CANON, NOT FANON, IT'S THE TRUTH
> Not gonna need any slash goggles AT ALL
> My shipper heart is racing [in response to allufuslos February 1, 2011; youtube.com].

Terms such as slash, slash goggles, canon versus fanon and shipper are readily comprehensible to initiates but not to outsiders; fans have to learn a new language to move into the Internet's newer neighborhoods. Indeed, the sherlockbbc site Fanworks FAQ includes a helpful lingua fannish glossary for newbies that explains some of the YouTubers' terminology.

While review and opinion site protocols remain largely implicit, Live-Journal and the other newer neighborhoods that so quickly responded to *Sherlock* routinely foreground protocols, as the glossary attests. As well as introducing newbies to the lingua fannish, sherlockbbc's Fanwork FAQ also instructs them in the protocols governing the sites' productive practices: "Any fic which is directly centered on *Sherlock* is acceptable — whether the overall theme is gen, slash, het or even a crossover with another fandom, provided the *Sherlock* aspect is central to the story." Authors must however post a warning about themes that "may trigger personal emotional sensitivity — such as self-harm, drug use, eating disorders, abuse or rape." Such warnings feature in the information in the "fanfic header," which may include: "the title of your story; the names of any betas ...; *the rating (mandatory)*; pairing(s) featured in the story; an approximate wordcount; *warnings about content which people may prefer not to read for personal reasons (mandatory)*; a disclaimer, to make it clear you are not profiting from the work you are sharing" (September 5, 2010; www.livejournal.com).

Productive practices such as fanfic predate the Internet, although Internet fan communities have vastly elaborated the governing protocols. But the Internet's newer neighborhoods have generated many original productive practices and protocols to which the new *Sherlock* sites conform. Sherlock_flashfic, "inspired by the new BBC Sherlock," is a Dreamwidth community for Sherlock Flashfiction, with rules based on those of "previous communities like ds_flashfiction and sga_flashfic." The administrators and the members issue "challenges" in the form of "The Case of ... [fill in the blank]" to which others respond with short fan fics of one hundred to one thousand words. The Sherlock Holmes kink meme site on Tumblr derives its productive practice from LiveJournal sites. Members post a pairing and a kink and other members respond with art or fanfic. The site offers a full description of the subsidiary protocols; administrators must be notified of forthcoming "fills" to the "prompt," ratings and warning must be included, submissions cannot be anonymous and so forth. Shared productive practices and the protocols governing them such as those seen in these two sites and many others enabled the rapid uptake of *Sherlock* among newer Internet fan communities. But *Sherlock* would not have appealed to these communities without the fit between text and protocols that I have hypothesized above and illustrated with regard to the text's gay-friendly textual and paratextual attributes.

"The impressions of a woman may be more valuable than the conclusion of an analytical reasoner" (The Man with the Twisted Lip)

This essay began by reflecting upon scholarly methods in the age of the infinite archive; it concludes with the suggestion that analytical reasoning may still prevail, followed by a couple of impressions. I have applied Gitelman's injunction to focus "on tools, methods, and protocols rather than the dubious exemplarity of Web pages themselves" (2006, 130) to address the methodological conundrum of potentially infinite data. The individual web pages and even the individual contents thereof discussed above are not representative of the reception of *Sherlock* within fan communities; they do not in any way constitute a "representative sample" of all those on the Internet or indeed of all Sherlockians who responded to the program in some form. Rather, they are representative of the dominant interpretive frameworks, practices and protocols structuring reception in two different Internet neighborhoods, the older ones exemplifying an "affirmational" fandom that engages in interpretation and evaluation and the newer ones a "transformational" fandom that reworks the primary text. Shifting from the level of individual web page contents to the level of protocols permits compliance with the scholarly practice of drawing generalizable conclusions as well as with the scholarly practice of replicability should other researchers feel inclined to adopt my method.

The impressions result from tugging on two themes threaded throughout the essay, but which space constraints preclude fully unraveling. I've tried to comply with Gitelman's warning to pay attention to protocols' historical specificity; in terms of the Internet, for example, Gitelman says that we might consider the ways in which the Web can "work as evidence of its own past" (127). We cannot now recapture the fan Internet of the 1990s, except through essays such as my original Holmes in cyberspace chapter and similar contemporaneous documentation, but we can investigate the ways in which the different protocols that structure the reception of *Sherlock* on different sites may reflect their formation at different periods of both fandom's and the Internet's history. This essay may offer an historical snapshot of fan Internet protocols in transition in the second decade of the 21st century, as the older "affirmational" sites give way to the newer "transformational" sites. I suspect however that these two different modes of reception and the protocols governing them will both continue to flourish, since the different sites attract very different kinds of fans.

This point relates to another of the essay's implicit threads, my accepting the distinction between affirmational and transformational fandom. Fanlore wiki (www.fanlore.org) attributes the term's coinage to a 2009 essay by obsession_inc (June 1, www.dreamwidth.org). In it she argues that the industry sanctions affirmational fans who re-state the source material and respect the creators and does not sanction transformational fans who lay "hands upon the source" and twist it to their own purposes. This formulation returns us to an early fan studies that celebrated the resistance of "productive" fans while ignoring those who limit their activities to evaluation and interpretation. While my research confirms the distinction between fans who interpret and evaluate and fans who rework the text, I would resist privileging the latter over the former, together with the implication that creators necessarily dislike the latter. As I've shown above, *Sherlock*'s producer discourse contains appeals to both affirmational and transformational fandoms. The newer Internet neighborhoods abound with transformational fans who readily responded to the producer discourse. These fans may just as readily respond to other producer discourses, since their knowledge of fannish protocols facilitates their moving from site to site and fandom to fandom. Are those who engage in practices such as fanfic fans of the productive form rather than of specific texts and might this be not only a transformational fandom but a transformation of the concept of the fan? These questions concerning fandom deserve further inquiry but for now I close the book on the mystery of the infinite archive.

Works Cited

Cavanagh, Allison. 2007. *Sociology in the age of the internet*. Maidenhead: Open University Press.

Gitelman, Lisa. 2006. *Always already new: Media, history, and the data of culture*. Cambridge: MIT Press.

Grainge, Paul. 2009. Lost logos: Channel 4 and the branding of American event television. In *Reading* Lost*: Perspectives on a hit television show*, ed. Roberta Pearson, 95–118. London. I.B. Tauris.

Pearson, Roberta. 1997. "It's always 1985": Sherlock Holmes in cyberspace. In *Trash aesthetics: Popular culture and its audience*, ed. Deborah Cartmell, Heidi Kaye, Imelda Whelehan, and I.Q. Hunter, 143–161. London: Pluto Press.

Stein, Louisa Ellen, and Kristina Busse. 2009. Limit play: Fan authorship between source text, intertext, and context. *Popular Communication* 7: 192–207.

Sherlock

Critical Reception by the Media

PAUL RIXON

Abstract — When *Sherlock* was broadcast on British television there was almost universal praise from the television critics working for the national press. This was a program that, seemingly, had brought Sherlock Holmes into the modern age. Steven Moffat and Mark Gatiss, two of the producers behind the production, had taken the fictional Victorian detective and applied, as some saw it, a *Doctor Who* makeover. It was no longer about a Victorian London but a contemporary one: Sherlock Holmes had come of age. In this essay, I will analyze the critical reception of *Sherlock* by the British national press and the resulting media image that appeared. I will do this by first analyzing the publicity material provided by the broadcasters, as they sought to create a pre-image of the series, and the subsequent reception by the television critics. As I explore the image of the program that appeared in the press I will identify certain underlying values, themes, and tensions that ran throughout the coverage. Such analysis suggests that *Sherlock*, in its new updated form, mirrored wider concerns and tensions relating to British identity and Britain's past at a time of change; indeed, it could be argued that the critical and popular success of *Sherlock* was partly linked to how it dealt with these issues in a non-threatening way.

Introduction

In the summer of 2010 a rare thing occurred: almost all the major television critics writing for the British national press came to laud the new BBC series *Sherlock* (BBC/Hartswood Films 2010–). Here was a program that simultaneously excited the critics writing for the quality press and those working for the tabloids. This essay explores the coverage these writers and reviewers gave to this series. I suggest that their critical discourse is important, and moreover that it is a discourse in which broadcasters also play a role: together, media critics and broadcasters help to provide a shared framework for viewers through which to view programs and, at another level, they shape and guide wider debates about the nature of television and popular culture. As I explore the discourse of broadcasters and critics around *Sherlock,* I identify reoccurring themes and tensions, themes and tensions that are important in understanding the development of a shared cultural and social understanding of *Sherlock.* While interpretative discussions do take place beyond the sphere of professional media critics, I will argue that professional critical reception is important because of the high media profile of these writers and critics.

The Role of Television Critics

Critics are not just cultural judges, as in a way we can all be, but are also public arbiters of taste (MacDonald 2007, 54). They play a role in shaping public debates around what constitutes good or bad television, and assisting in maintaining or changing the cultural consensus. However, they do not stand above or outside of society; indeed, media critics operate within a cultural field where certain values are dominant. Depending on their social and cultural background, media critics will tend to be positioned differently within this field. Some with more cultural capital will align themselves with the dominant cultural values; others, with less, might take on a more subservient position while a few will take up more radical positions (Bourdieu 1984, 234–235). For Mike Poole, most British television critics have tended to align themselves with dominant literary values, focusing on television as a form of text created by particular authors or artists, rather than viewing it as a collective enterprise that requires a more contextual approach (1984). This has meant that these critics, or taste leaders, have come to create and maintain a particular discourse of how, collectively, television is spoken of and valued.

Therefore the mediated discourse of such critics tells us something of the cultural debates that dominate about television and popular culture at any particular time; it also tells us something of the discursive interaction between the newspaper and broadcasting industries and the wider culture. By analyzing television reviews and associated critical articles, we can gain an insight into how a society values, reflects on, and struggles over the meaning of television as a cultural medium, and how this relates to wider ideological, cultural, and social questions. As part of this discursive struggle over meaning and value, we must also take account of the attempts by broadcasters and other capitalist concerns, such as program producers, to shape the image of programs through the use of press releases and previews which, until now, have primarily been used to engage with media critics. Through this interaction between various parties such as advertisers, broadcasters, and critics, images or meaning frameworks for programs and series develop in the public arena. While these images or frameworks are not always accepted and taken up by viewers, the critics do play an important role in how they are formed and mediated. This essay will explore the development of the public mediated discourse around *Sherlock,* focusing on the role of the broadcasters and their press releases and the discourse of the critics. As I do this I will delineate and highlight some of the main issues, themes, and tensions around which these debates occur, which include that of British identity and questions of modernity.

The BBC's Pre-Image

All industries seek to protect their product, not just in terms of illicit copies, but also in relation to the brand, how it is spoken of, reported on, and written about. Businesses know that in this modern world we live in, it is not need that most drives sales but desire which is created through the discourse around a product. In a similar way, when any new program is produced, broadcasters seek to engender and engage with the media debate around their program. By creating a press release they seek to shape the pre-image that will appear in the media (Rixon 2006, 126). The *Sherlock* press pack (SPP) was originally released on the web on July 12, 2010 (www.bbc.co.uk).

Throughout the five linked web pages that make up this press pack, and the trailer provided with it, a number of key themes are established and repeated. This suggests that there are a number of perspectives that the broadcaster feel are important for the image of the series which they highlight for the press, and especially for the television critics. For example, there is constant linkage of the writers, creators, and actors to past series and programs they have worked on or been in; a form of intertextuality is being used here, making connections for the critics between different texts. Steven Moffat and Mark Gatiss are linked to another BBC success, *Doctor Who* (BBC 1963–), as well as, for Moffat, *Coupling* (BBC 2000–04), and Gatiss, *The League of Gentlemen* (BBC 1999–2002). While Benedict Cumberbatch is linked to *Small Island* (BBC 2009) and *Starter for Ten* (BBC Films/ HBO Films/ Neal Street Productions 2006) and Martin Freeman to *The Office* (BBC 2001–03) and *Hitchhiker's Guide to the Galaxy* (Touchstone Pictures/ Spyglass Entertainment/ Everyman Pictures 2005). The press pack emphasizes that *Sherlock*'s production draws on a team of writers and actors that have pedigree and have worked for the BBC before.

The press pack also touches on the original stories by Conan Doyle and how this series, while trying to be faithful in some respects to his characters, has updated them. Although this version is set in modern day London, all the interviews and background pieces talk about the classic nature of the original books and how the essence of the original is maintained. As Gatiss notes:

> Arthur Conan Doyle was a writer of genius and it's worth trumpeting that point.... His short stories, particularly, are thrilling, funny, lurid, silly, strange, wonderful pieces of exciting adventure which lend themselves incredibly well to a modern setting [SPP].

Sherlock even plays homage to Conan Doyle, as Moffat notes, with the first episode, "A Study in Pink," playing on the original story, *A Study in Scarlet.* Throughout the press pack there are numerous mentions of the fans and the Sherlock Holmes Society, an important group of viewers the broadcasters want to attract and please. The press release appears to be trying to balance the idea that this is a Sherlock Holmes series, one that has a linkage to the original, which, at the same time, has been updated; it is now modern à la *Doctor Who.* This is a world where the old fashioned forms of detection and technology are replaced by new ones, such as the mobile phone, the Internet, and GPS, all of which Sherlock uses. In so doing, the series creates what Coppa calls in her chapter in this volume a cyborg styled character, one that escapes the confines of the body by linking his mind up to the web. Gone is the dirty Victorian city, replaced, as Cumberbatch states in the BBC press release, by a London made up of "iconic locations such as Soho, Chinatown, Piccadilly Circus, Westminster Bridge and everything that modern London life involves — London cabs, the River Thames, traffic jams, mobile phones and computers" (SPP).

The press pack also links this particular series not just with Conan Doyle's original stories, but also with some of the later incarnations of Sherlock Holmes in film and on television. Moffat talks of Guy Ritchie's film, *Sherlock Holmes* (Warner Bros. 2009), and of having watched the 1940s films starring Basil Rathbone and Nigel Bruce as Holmes and Dr. Watson. Benedict Cumberbatch and Martin Freeman both mention Basil Rathbone and also Jeremy Brett, who played Holmes in ITV's series in the 1980s-90s. The press release situates this new production in relation to the huge number of adaptations, and especially in relation to the two important ones noted above, but at the same time suggests that this one stands out as it has contemporized Sherlock Holmes, bringing it up-to-date while still maintaining its integrity and linkage to the essence of the original stories. But, as I will argued, there is something of a tension here: this white, middle-class gentlemen detective who once typified a particular view of Britishness is now living and working in a modern, multicultural city where the old notions of Britishness are changing. The broadcasters through their PR suggest that the new series manages to redefine the old image of Sherlock Holmes for this new age, for the modern London, but, as Basu in her chapter argues, *Sherlock* in many ways seems tied to the past and it is not fully able to present a modern view of London or Sherlock Holmes. As the press release emphasizes, Sherlock, though living in the modern city, is still linked to his fictional roots in the Victorian period and by being shown as such he cannot but help bring the old identity of Britishness into this new era. In this way, the modernization of *Sherlock* both in the series and in surrounding critical and broadcasting discourse, comes to problematize the question of British identity: should such an identity be defined by its linkage to the past or should it lose the baggage of an earlier time, of the Empire and the Victorian gentlemen, to be defined by the here and now?

The Meaning Framework: What the Critics Wrote

The coverage in the national press of *Sherlock* was fairly high profile and lasted for a number of weeks, starting before the airing of the first episode, "A Study in Pink" (July 25, 2010), and continued past the last episode, "The Great Game" (August 8, 2010). This critical coverage, engaging TV critics and broadcasters, created a certain image in which a number of dominant themes and tension can be identified. I will now explore these under a number of relevant headings.

LINKAGE TO THE LITERARY SHERLOCK HOLMES

As Sherlock Holmes is a fictional character from the literary work by Conan Doyle, it would seem obvious that much of the coverage by TV critics would mention or at least utilize this as a way of talking or assessing *Sherlock*. After all, BBC's publicity package itself foregrounded this literary connection. It could be assumed that some critics took note of this publicity as well as using their own knowledge of the literary work when assessing this new adaptation. As Victoria Segal notes, writing for the *Sunday Times*, "[s]tick a deerstalker on a melon and it is instantly recognizable as Sherlock Holmes" (2010, 60). Although the BBC's Sherlock does not wear a deerstalker, it would appear that, however much this character and stories are adapted or changed for the modern era, this is still Sherlock Holmes and is recognizable as such. If it were changed too much, one would assume it would not be identifiable as an adaptation of the Victorian novels.

Indeed, in some reviews, critics wondered whether this was "[a] Holmes that Conan Doyle would possibly approve of" (2010, 25), as Sam Wollaston wrote. Or, as David Stephenson asks, "is he [the new Sherlock] better than the original Sherlock, given that he also has forensics and technology at this disposal. Well, no he's not. The original Sherlock was at the cutting edge of science" (2010, 60–61). As a number of critics suggested, *Sherlock* takes from, and adapts elements of the original stories but, as we shall see, with a modern twist. Where Conan Doyle's Holmes in *A Study in Scarlet* deduces various observations from scratches on Watson's watch, for example, Sherlock performs his feat of insight on John's mobile phone (Grant 2010, 29).

Even though comparisons of the literary work and the new *Sherlock* would be an obvious angle, it could be argued that some of this has been framed by the information given out by the BBC. The publicity is an attempt to feed into, to seed, and to shape the discussions around the program. Such publicity can be useful for the critics, providing some background and initial thoughts about a series they might not yet have seen fully, as they write a preview or review, often in some haste. It provides a ready built framework, an easy short hand, for the critics (Himmelstein 1981, 30). However, sometimes the critics will focus on particular tensions within the program, those the broadcasters often try to ignore or paper over: the fact that, unlike the literary Holmes, the new Sherlock no longer stands at the forefront of forensics developments is one such example that critics pick up on even though the press package bypasses this issue.

A CONTEMPORARY TWIST

In the publicity produced by the BBC, it would seem that one of the most important points of the series was the updating of Sherlock Holmes. Yes, it is connected to the original stories, it is about a detective called Sherlock Holmes, who lives in London, but the London, at first glance, is now a contemporary city with all the modern things that come with it. The critics are able to read such publicity material and to deduce these points from watching the series. As Euan Ferguson for the *Observer* states, "Cumberbatch's fabulous Sherlock may look a little Victorian, admittedly, but there's no easy time shift device: he is utterly 21st-century man, just with a very fat brain" (2010, 27). And as Richard Arnold noted in the *People*, Cumberbatch is "a souped-up 21st century Sherlock Holmes" (2010, 35). Most critics thought this twist, this modernization of the stories and character, worked. "The idea of modernising it, bringing him up to date, was clever, and Benedict Cumberbatch is a darkly interesting Sherlock" (Gill 2010, 14–15). The critics touch on the way this modern London is depicted, the shiny glass buildings and slick black taxis, as well as the new technologies that have, in some ways, changed the world we live in, and the one Holmes originally inhabited; though some of the critics mention that some elements of London are seemingly hidden from view in the program, such as its housing estates, tower blocks, and homeless people. This is a world where Sherlock has "abandoned the fabled pile and deerstalker for nicotine patches, a mobile phone and a web site called The Science of Deduction" (Hoyle and Foster 2010, 10).

One could take up these discussions, to suggest these various reviews reveal a tension around this modernization of Sherlock. He is of another time, but is now living in modern London. This is no longer the London once easily recognizable from earlier Sherlock Holmes outings. This is London inhabited by modern people, a shiny city with skyscrapers, trendy cafés and bars. The London of *Sherlock* provides a particular vision of Britain, one where what it is to be British is changing, but what is on offer is not a multicultural vision of the city, but more an attempt to reconcile the past with the future in an unthreatening way. *Sherlock* offers nostalgia, a detective with a Victorian heritage, mixed with a view of London as a modern metropolis. This provides a constructive tension in the program, which keeps attracting the interest of the critics as they try to fathom how successful the program is in situating a fictional detective from an earlier age in a modern setting.

THE CANON OF ADAPTATIONS

A number of the reviews, in a similar way to the press release and its attempts to provide intertextual reference points, highlighted some of the other Sherlock Holmes productions that have appeared over time, on stage, film, and television. Indeed, many noted a then current stage production and the recently released film by Guy Ritchie. Any work of fiction that has been produced many times and has become an iconic part of British culture consists not only of the original written stories but also of the wide range of adaptations and other forms of media development (see Redman 2009). And it is to this "canon" that critics, in different ways, compare this new production. How does it stand up against the, so identified, greatest versions of Sherlock Holmes? Also, how does it compare to contemporary versions, such as the concurrent stage production and the latest film?

Throughout the reviews, a number make reference to what are described as two of the best known adaptations of Sherlock Holmes, those starring Basil Rathbone (1940s) and Jeremy Brett (1980s-90s): "Gone are the deerstalker hat and the Meerschaum pipe favored by his gentlemanly predecessors, Basil Rathbone and Jeremy Brett" (*Sunday Times* 2010, 19). Seemingly, attempts are made to compare like with like, to use a familiar and relevant touchstone offered by other adaptations of Sherlock Holmes. While a few go back to the original literary work, most tend to focus on the way the majority of readers would have experienced Sherlock Holmes, through television series or films.

The Creative Talent Behind Sherlock: Producers and Writers

The BBC's publicity package highlights the creative team behind *Sherlock*, with one web page put over to a discussion between two of the producers, Steven Moffat and Mark Gatiss (SPP). Indeed, on the main page where their names appear, reference is made to some of the other programs they have been involved with. Reviews and related pieces on the series mention these two writers and producers, often linking to their past record of successful productions. For example, they are both mentioned in relation to *Doctor Who*, though Steven Moffat more so. For some of the critics the linkages between the characters of Sherlock and Doctor Who go beyond these writers, as noted by others, such as Harrington and Basu in their essays in this book. Both characters are closely linked to popular British culture; they are idiosyncratic figures, much loved and, in their own way, unique. Indeed, some make the link rather obvious: "It [*Sherlock*] was created by the Doctor Who team and, if I'm not mistaken, that's why Sir Arthur Conan Doyle's formerly Victorian hero is a carbon copy of the guy in the Tardis" (O'Sullivan 2010, 23). As Jim Shelley writing for the *Mirror* suggests, *Sherlock* "is somewhere between Guy Richie's super-slick blockbuster and Steven Moffat's new Doctor Who, Sherlock was good fun" (2010, 21).

Part of the media discussion focuses on the way the creative team has reenergized Sherlock Holmes to create a new exciting series, which succeeds on television. "Somehow Moffat and Gatiss have sewn old and new into a very modern, very human drama, and what fun they must have had doing so" (Ferguson 2010, 27). These are writers who have already proved themselves elsewhere; these are writers who have shown themselves able to produce modern popular programs that seemingly are in tune with the *zeitgeist*:

> The character of Holmes as reworked by writers Mark Gatiss (the multitalented *League of Gentlemen* comic) and Steven Moffat (*Doctor Who*'s new supremo) is a conceited, sociopathic ass whose genius ranges somewhere on the autistic spectrum, but who nevertheless possesses a sense of humor [Davies 2010, 27].

Critics, in this way, focus on the oeuvre of the creative talent behind a program, using this to assess whether this has continued into a new production; they use it to help make linkages the public would understand, from programs they have already seen. As these critics often note, this is Steven Moffat's *Sherlock*, not the BBC's or even Benedict Cumberbatch's. It would seem that behind an artistic endeavor such as *Sherlock*, there must be a creative agent or author. Moffat as auteur thus takes over or at least stands in for all other talents, all the crafts people that shape and make such a collective cultural enterprise as television. In this way, the television critics continue to uphold a traditional way of viewing and judging art, by focusing on the artist behind the production rather than exploring new ways of understanding television. This, of course, is a critical approach to television which some have argued needs to change if it is to become one more able to treat television as television (McArthur 1982; Poole 1984; Rixon 2011).

THE TALENT IN SHERLOCK: ACTORS

In a similar way to how the BBC highlights the creative talent behind the series, it also focuses on the main actors appearing in *Sherlock*. While they clearly focus in particular on Benedict Cumberbatch as Sherlock and Martin Freeman as John, they also mention a number of others, including Rupert Graves as Detective Inspector Lestrade, and Una Stubbs as the old housekeeper. For each actor they mention some of the main programs and films that they have been in and, in this way, try to show some type of pedigree that might attract the interest of the reviewers or critics. Critics, in their turn, focus heavily on the main actors appearing in the production, as well as the characters they play.

For example, a number of critics are interested in the choice of Martin Freeman to play John, partly because he is an actor who is usually associated with more comic roles.

> One of the surprises is Martin Freeman, as John Watson: crippled not, as so boringly usually, by a light weight intelligence but by an actual limp, psychosomatic though it may largely be, and by Afghanistan trauma ... and Freeman caught this whole subtle new persona with magnificence, and this part might deservedly free him, finally, from *The Office* [Ferguson 2010, 27].

Though others saw it differently. "Martin Freeman, as Watson, was indecipherable as a piece of casting.... Freeman had a limp that was supposed to be combat stress psychosomatic, but was really just bad acting" (Gill 2010, 14–15). Almost all critics used their assessment of Freeman's past roles to weigh up how successful he was at being cast as John in the series rather than taking his performance at its face value.

In a similar way many of the reviews focused on Cumberbatch as Sherlock, often, conflating his on-screen and off-screen existence. Many saw Cumberbatch "born to the role of Holmes" (*Sunday Times* 2010, 19). Seemingly he is "perfect for the role" (Heal 2010, 60). How he is perfect is less clear. For some it seems to be his looks, the way he interprets the part or his background. As one critic wrote, "[h]e looks amazing — as odd as you'd expect The Cleverest Man in the World to look. Eyes white, skin like china clay and a voice like someone smoking a cigar inside a grand piano" (Moran 2010, 14). It would seem that "Cumberbatch had the makings of a rather good Holmes" (Preston 2010, 35) and that "Benedict is a darkly interesting Sherlock ... the new crop of leading young men are all sort of emo, pale and interesting, androgynous, with a lick of gothic" (Gill 2010, 14–15). For Coppa, writing elsewhere in this book, he appears as a kind of Byronic figure. The critics in their reviews compared Benedict's casting as Sherlock to their own views of what made a good Sherlock. For most, it seems, he brought the necessary quirkiness that such a character required.

Sherlock *as* Must-See Television

Because of the comparison critics always make between programs and the wish to highlight those that are worth seeing and those that are not, *Sherlock* gets positioned in a wider debate about program quality. Many of the reviews enthused about the production, seeing and writing about it in a similar way to what some have called "must-see" programs such as *Doctor Who* and *The Office*. This standing in the eyes of the critics is in some ways reinforced by knowledge of the creative team behind the program and actors involved, which was also highlighted in the press pack. Critics and broadcasters alike seem to share a view and wish to write about these programs as part of a new or on-going British wave of quality "must-see" programs, ones that depict and show Britain in a new light. This is a development in television that critics wants to be associated with, as it is one that can do nothing but help their professional standing.

So, for Richard Arnold, writing for *The People*, "the scene is set for what promises to be the best drama this summer — unsurprisingly given the scribe is Stephen Moffat, the Dr Who supremo who has turned Cumberbatch into the crime solving doppelganger of Doc, Matt Smith" (2010, 35). Many pointed to the dark edge of the program: "[t]his fantastic new drama series created by *Doctor Who* supremo Steven Moffat and *The League of Gentlemen*'s Mark Gatiss gives us a dark and glittering Holmes" (Harvey 2010, 37). Seemingly, for these writers, this production is "a must-see for Sunday nights, and it is a long time since we've had one of those" (Mount 2010, 18). Indeed, Mark Lawson, critic of the *Guardian*, suggested that with "[t]he overwhelmingly positive response to Steven Moffat and Mark Gatiss's drama Sherlock ... it will be a strong contender when it comes to this year's TV prizes" (2010, 19). And, it is interesting to note, *Sherlock* duly did come to win the BAFTA for the best television series in 2011.

Others, however, were less taken with the production: "[T]he London in *Sherlock* didn't look remotely like the city Londoners know or live in ... the show must be a co-production with Americans" (Gill 2010, 14–15). Indeed, it was co-produced with WGBH Boston for its Masterpiece anthology series, though it is doubtful that the American broadcasters had that much direct input into the series. This London is not one we in London know, it is not one that really exists. This "modern" London is one created by the producers to provide a contemporary setting for the series that, it is hoped, will provide the right kind of background for this updated Victorian detective. As the above-quoted view suggests, it also creates a view of London that would appeal to international audiences, one that blends an image of London as a modern exciting city with a hidden Victorian past, playing with a nostalgic and contemporary view of London. For many of those taking this more critical view of the series, it was the first episode's case that let the otherwise excellent production down (Heal 2010, 60). As Kevin O'Sullivan wrote, "while this film-length crime drama succeeds in characterization and atmosphere, I conclude it is badly let down by a silly serial suicide saga that makes no sense" (2010, 23). Others felt that the chemistry between the characters did not work on screen, the stories were a little slow and the adaptations did not work well and this iconic character should have been left alone. It would seem that not all critics felt that the updating of Sherlock completely worked and that some would have preferred for it to have been left alone.

AUDIENCES / FANS

Whether or not the BBC knew it had a hit on its hands, it did try, in the publicity material, to take note of the existence of the fans. And while it focused on Sherlock Holmes fans, one could also suggest that it was also aware of those of Moffat and Gatiss, fans of programs such as *Doctor Who*. If it could link this series to the original stories and to these other programs it might attract the support and interest of these important readers and viewers. Many of the critics, in a similar way, also make reference to the fans and the viewers. For example, Harry Mount, writing for the *Daily Telegraph*, notes that fans will get pleasure from the adaptation "in spotting how that modern molding is done" (2010, 18).

After the first episode many of the critics mentioned the popularity of the program, noting that its initial outing attracted 7.7 million viewers, thus drawing clearly not just the die hard Sherlock Holmes fans but also viewers attracted by the publicity of this new and interesting television series (Hoyle and Foster 2010, 10). Seemingly the old view of millions of viewers watching the same drama still happens, even in the summer when many people are on holiday. This was news. Indeed, it was reported that a BBC worker had noted that "the top brass are made up by the Holmes ratings.... They really want to do more so the question is not really if, but how and when can we do them" (Robertson 2010, 1).

Some go further, reflecting on which viewers the program attracted and why. So, for example, Euan Ferguson of the *Observer*, suggested, "men love it because of the clevers, and the clues, and the chases. Children, even, will get echoes of that bloody boy-wizard thing.... Women will love it because of the clues ... and more possibly, because of Cumberbatch" (2010, 27). Indeed, the special attraction of Sherlock, and similar characters that exhibit particular intellectual abilities and repressed emotions, to women is something explored further by Coppa, in another chapter in this book, who suggests that the attraction lies in the mind-body conjunction. For Ally Ross, "[i]t's also one of the few dramas the Beeb hasn't aimed purely at women and could turn out to be one of the best things Auntie 1's done since Occupation" (2010, 13). The reviews show that some of the critics were interested in who was attracted to the series, what pleasures they received and why it was one of the few programs aimed at such an audience.

While the critics are often reflecting on their own experience of the series there is some attempt to engage with and to think about who the program is aimed at and who might be watching it. Part of this debate is linked to the nature of Sherlock Holmes and his typical appeal, the types of programs Gatiss and Moffat are associated with, in particular *Doctor Who*, and the attraction of Cumberbatch. However, with Holmes' large fan base, there is also some attempt to identify what his fans might like, or not, about this modern version of their hero.

Conclusion

The critical mediated debate about *Sherlock* is an area where a number of discourses overlap. The broadcasters, keen for the media to focus on their programs, rather than on any wider failings, provide publicity material about the program directed at the reviewers and critics. They hope that such material will help them shape the pre-image of a program, to provide background material that all journalists, and critics, will use. The broadcasters do not invent material and background stories, but they can select what they focus on and provide. They try to point out connections and linkages. Also, as cost and time pressures increase in journalism, many journalists, including television reviewers, increasingly rely on PR releases or publicity material for their copy (Manning 2008, 262–271).

As shown above, the critical and popular debate about *Sherlock* echoed the themes presented by the press release while adding some topics and indeed tensions of their own. As Poole argues, the broadcasters and critics share the same values, and therefore often view television in a similar way, and it is often only the worth of the program, of what is good or bad, where they might differ (1984). For example, one of the themes that appeared in such a debate was focused around the pedigree of those making the program, the talent and creative forces behind it. Debates also focused on the relationship of this series to others, to the canon of Sherlock Holmes, and the modern form the adaptation took. For some of the reviewers, this modernization was a risk, and for a couple it did not work, but for most it helped bring Sherlock Holmes into the modern age. Many saw this as successfully bringing of the character of Sherlock and John up-to-date. By modernizing Sherlock Holmes in this way, the series was able to explore concerns of changing British identity within an increasingly multicultural London from a safe white middle-class viewpoint. While reviews did not overtly suggest such an interpretation, their predominant celebration of the series suggests its ideological safety.

Running throughout the mediated discourse around the updating of Sherlock Holmes, a tension is thus visible. On one hand, Sherlock has a traditional linkage to a certain type of Britishness, but on the other he is now living in 21st century London. While he is still quirky and strange, appearing as a quasi–British gentlemen with a certain education and upbringing, he is now modern and technologically savvy. The reaction of many critics to this re-envisioning of Sherlock was, initially, that the premise of a modern Sherlock Holmes seemed strange, but that in the end it seemed to work. Indeed, for many the "genius" of the series lies "in the willingness to adapt Sherlock to modernity" (Ferguson 2010, 27). This updating is something that the critics in their reviews focus on and develop in relation to questions of identity. In a way, *Sherlock* seems to highlight the problematic nature of British identity at this cultural moment, when traditional white, English centric view of being British jostle with more modern view of British identity as the center of a global media complex. However, while critics' reviews implicitly echo this tension, their responses also help deflect and dissipate it. This is a series that critics and the public celebrate. Thus, in its reception, we see evidence that *Sherlock* does not present a threatening image of London, but one in which the modern comes to be known through a more traditional and accepted viewpoint.

Works Cited

Arnold, Richard. 2010. Fab Baker Boys. *People.* August 1: 35.

Bourdieu, Pierre. 2005. *Distinction: A social critique of the judgement of taste.* Trans. Richard Nice. Cambridge: Harvard University Press.

Davies, Serena. 2010. Meet the new Sherlock: an electrifying sociopath. *Daily Telegraph, Features.* July 26: 26.

Ferguson, Euan. 2010. Hi honey, I'm Holmes.... *Observer: Review.* August 1: 27.

Gill, Adrian Anthony. 2010. More join-the-dots than the art of deduction. *Sunday Times.* August 1: 14–15.

Grant, Olly. 2010. 21st-century Sherlock. *Daily Telegraph: Review.* July 24: 29.

Harvey, Chris. 2010. What to watch. *Daily Telegraph: Review.* July 31: 37.

Heal, Clare. 2010. Case of a new Holmes cracked. *Sunday Express.* August 1: 60.

Himmelstein, Hal. 1981. *On the small screen: New approaches in television and video criticism.* New York: Praeger.

Hoyle, Ben, and Patrick Foster. 2010. Sherlock's TV creator hails it as reason to save licence fee. *The Times.* July 31: 10.

Lawson, Mark, 2010. Running on empty: Sherlock got rave reviews this week, and looks set to win awards. So why is it going out in the dog days of summer? *Guardian, G2 Arts.* July 29: 19.

MacDonald, Ronan. 2007. *The death of the critic.* London: Continuum.

Manning, Paul. 2008. The Press Association and news agency sources. In *Pulling newspapers apart: Analysing print journalism*, ed. Bob Franklin, 262–271. London: Routledge.

McArthur, Colin. 1982. Point of review: Television criticism in the press. *Screen Education* 35 (summer): 59–61.

Moran, Caitlin. 2010. Sherlock is so good, if BBC funding is ever called into question, I'll pay for it myself. *The Times: Saturday Review.* July 31: 14.

Mount, Harry. 2010. The riveting riddle of the enduring detective The timeless appeal of Sherlock Holmes is due to Conan Doyle's powers of observation. *Daily Telegraph.* July 27: 18.

O'Sullivan, Kevin. 2010. The sleuth truth. *Sunday Star.* August 1: 23.

Poole, Mike. 1984. The cult of the generalist: British television criticism 1936–83. *Screen* 25: 2: 41–61.

Preston, John. 2010. Sherlock's elementary failings. *Sunday Telegraph, Section Seven.* August 1: 35.

Redman, Christopher. 2009. *Sherlock Holmes handbook.* Toronto: Dundurn Press.

Rixon, Paul. 2006. *American television on British screens: A story of cultural interaction.* Basingstoke, Hampshire: Palgrave Macmillan.

_____. 2011. *TV critics and popular culture: A history of British television criticism.* London: I.B. Tauris.

Robertson, Colin. 2010. Holmes: I turned down Dr Who job; 7.5m See sherlock tvbiz exclusive. *Sun.* July 27: 1.

Ross, Ally. 2010. Random TV irritations: The BBC. *Sun.* July 27: 13.

Routledge, Paul. 2010. Who gives a tinker's cuss. *Daily Mirror.* July 30: 33.

Segal, Victoria. 2010. Critic's choice *Sunday Times, Culture.* August 1: 60.

Shelley, Jim. 2010. Masterchef's celebs overcook the drama. *Daily Mirror.* July 26: 21.

Stephenson, David. 2010. The fab Baker St. boys. *Sunday Express.* July 25: 60–61.

Sunday Times. 2010. What fun, Watson, whipping a corpse. August 1: 19.

Wollaston, Sam. 2010. The weekend's TV: Sherlock has a great new take on the characters — but what happened to the plot? *Guardian, G2.* July 26: 25.

Holmes Abroad

Dutch Fans Interpret the Famous Detective

NICOLLE LAMERICHS

Abstract — Discussing the interpretations of Dutch fans of *Sherlock*, I seek to understand how viewers make sense of the series in relation to other texts and what kind of literary competence they display in their reception. The study is based on seven in-depth interviews with Dutch fans of the series. Through this data, I explore how a local audience makes sense of the transmedial elements in the series. I elaborate upon the interviewees' understanding of the modern aspects of *Sherlock*, its characters, and its Englishness. Contemporary texts increasingly make use of transmediality to develop their narratives across various media platforms. This is often hailed as a strategy that companies use to construct a more active reader base that is prone to discuss its scattered fictional content. I add to this by showing how readers understand the narrative by "naturalizing" it through other texts and genres they are familiar with, aiming to shed light on individual ways of reading in an increasingly complex media landscape. Rather than explicitly relating the series to additional texts and instalments related to *Sherlock*, I argue that viewers explore the text through their implicit understanding of related genres, local and global popular texts, as well as their own experiences of what constitutes plausible character behavior.

Introduction

For international readers, Sherlock Holmes has always been considered the epitome of English culture. We picture him riding in a hansom cab through London, investigating dark alleys and tracing clues at a crime scene near the Thames. Throughout the years, pastiche writers have reworked the *Sherlock Holmes* stories by relating its main character to the cultural history of Britain and Europe, to other fictional texts such as gothic novels, or by introducing him to local detectives such as Arsène Lupin and scientists such as Freud (Den Boef 2005). The staff of the BBC series *Sherlock* (2010) explicitly revises this characterization and chooses to portray Holmes in a contemporary setting. Writer Mark Gattis stresses in the documentary *Unlocking Sherlock* (2010) that the idea of Sherlock Holmes "has become so much about the trappings, about the hansom cabs, about the costumes, the fog, Jack the Ripper will creep in here. It's become a strange maelstrom of stuff." In contrast, Mark Gattis and Steven Moffat give a fresh spin in a new time and setting.

Sherlock deconstructs some of the recognizable Sherlock Holmes features while at the same time echoing an awareness of the stories and the history of their reception. Reworking a character like Holmes, who is widely recognizable, is not an easy task. International readers often have their own ideas of Holmes as a figure that are not influenced by the novels but by popular and local culture. This contribution focuses on Dutch fans specifically and how they understand a foreign series as *Sherlock* and interpret its transmediality in practice. Dutch broadcasting and literature is influenced by Anglo-American media and, as a result, the image of Sherlock Holmes is constituted in relation to derivative works such as *House M.D.* (2004–). At the same time, local adaptations shape the image of the famous detective. Dutch television or movie versions of *Sherlock Holmes* are non-existent but the stories have been mediated into stage adaptations and pastiches (Den Boef 2005, 97–98). In the theater play *Hond van de Baskervilles* (2011), for instance, a few English actors gather in a mansion to re-enact *The Hound of the Baskervilles*. By depicting these actors as English, rather than the well-known Dutch actors they are, the play explicitly categorizes Sherlock Holmes as the terrain of England's cultural heritage.

Dutch culture is a good example of how international viewers make sense of *Sherlock* because it has a different literary canon than Anglo-American countries and, at the same time, a local culture of detectives that influence the reading process. *Sherlock* has been broadcasted in Belgium (Canvas) and in the Netherlands (KRO) as part of their KRO detective evening. Unlike Germany and France, the Dutch networks showed the original version of the series with subtitles. Fans of *Sherlock* focus on this broadcasted version, on a downloaded version, or on the local or imported DVDs. Despite the accessibility of the series, there are no local fan communities of BBC's *Sherlock* for Dutch-speaking fans. Smaller discussion threads can be found on the forums of broadcasting communities. Fans also communicate about *Sherlock* in English-speaking fan communities. The drawback of this is that the audience is spread globally. Dutch fans find each other haphazardly by meeting other local fans on larger online boards (for example, Bakerstreet Supperclub, baker-street.org.uk) through each other's profiles, or on specific national threads. Some stumble upon fans in real life or recruit them by recommending the show.

This means that the Dutch fan culture of *Sherlock* is not one interpretive community (Fish 1980) but rather a label that helps analyze how a heterogeneous group of people, who identify themselves as fans, makes sense of the series. The interviewees' interpretations of *Sherlock* are substantiated by reader-response theories that underline how each singular reading is derived from the experiences of the individual reader. I argue that although Dutch culture is influenced by Anglo-American media texts, the Dutch fans still understand *Sherlock* as foreign content that fits in a particular popular culture. My findings show that fans explore a transmedia text not just by relating it to its source texts but also through their implicit understanding of related genres and local and global imagery.

Transmediality and Active Readers

Nowadays watching a television series is not just limited to a box set but increasingly takes place online and on other media as well. This phenomenon is discussed in this book as transmediality (Stein and Busse, this volume). Henry Jenkins (2006; see also December 12, 2006; henryjenkins.org) describes the trend in *transmedia storytelling* as the spread and extension of narratives across various media platforms, including comics, movies, animations, and games. Corporations increasingly rework existing narratives and provide additional content that together create a larger story world or franchise. They substantiate existing story worlds by providing new plot lines, background information, or characters. Transmediality demands a particular kind of active viewership, because audiences who are familiar with all the texts of a franchise will understand the story better or feel motivated to discuss it amongst each other. When analyzing *Sherlock*, we can thus wonder how viewers understand and contextualize a text that is so deeply entrenched within networks of other texts.

I discuss transmediality in *Sherlock* in two ways. First, I relate *Sherlock* to other texts and the source text, Conan Doyle's *Sherlock Holmes* stories; and second, I pay attention to the migration of form, namely the mimicking of aesthetic content of other texts. As an adaptation, *Sherlock* provides meaning to existing narratives by remediating the content and form of earlier texts, a process that is never a direct translation. As a modernization, it also has original qualities because it remediates the existing versions of *Sherlock Holmes* more liberally. Specifically, I aim to find out whether explicit transmedial elements in *Sherlock* enable a more active reading as Jenkins (2006) implies when he argues that these function as cues that guide readers to related texts.

I draw from *reader-response theory* to analyze the role of the reader. This type of criticism focuses on how the interpretation of the reader constructs the text into a coherent whole: Hans Robert Jauss (1984) and Wolfgang Iser

(1974) highlight how readers *actualize* texts; in other words, they give full meaning based on his expectations and experiences; responding to formalism, Stanley Fish (1980) develops ideas on how readers' interpretive strategies are developed within interpretive communities; and Jonathan Culler draws from French structuralism to nuance reader activity. In literary and media studies, reader-response theories have been the groundwork for many studies that analyze how (local) groups of readers and viewers are affected by texts (Radway 1987; Ang 1985).

To analyze fan reception, I use Culler's *Structuralist Poetics* (1975), in which he coins the concept *naturalization* to explain how readers make sense of the text, a strange and alien construct that has to be decoded. A reader actively gives meaning to a text in order to understand it at all. Each reading, in a sense, is singular and new, because a reader will interpret the text differently based on his or her expectations, which in turn are based on his or her cultural repertoire. Readers, for instance, naturalize a text by relating it to their own experiences, shared cultural knowledge, conventions of the medium or narrative, genres, and references to other texts (1975, 131–161).

Culler explains this interpretation process or naturalization through the idea of *literary competence*. This means that the ability with which we interpret texts depends not only on our reading skills, but also on connecting the reading to meaningful discourses, such as the critical institute of literary studies (1975, 113–130). As a result, Culler sometimes refers to a reader who is especially competent, such as the critic, who is seen as more en par with these discourses and thus more knowledgeable. And yet, the concept is not limited to literary studies and the privileged critic: literary competence can be a fruitful way to understand the competences that fans display which are shaped by diverse repertoires and associations.

Here, literary competence implies that fans are also affected by their fan (and thus interpretive) communities. Different communities tend to privilege particular concepts and genres, which have emerged throughout the years. Importantly, fans have specific ways to read characters and plot lines (Pugh 2004). Often, characters are judged as if they were real, and fans describe them as "in character" or "out of character," depending on whether they believe them to behave as they would in the source text or not. In Monika Fludernik's reading of Culler's naturalization, she helpfully adds her own term *experientiality*, which she defines as "the quasi-mimetic evocation of 'real-life experience'" (1996, 12).

A narrative should not only be understood in a spacio-temporal sense but also as a construction of plausible characters and events. Fludernik argues that characters or *actants* have "consciousness," meaning that they behave in a certain manner with which readers can empathize. Experientiality relates to transmediality in two ways. On the one hand, transmedial elements complicate characterization, because characters are also understood in the light of previous texts. On the other hand, transmedia texts assure that certain readings of characters will become more dominant because, as interpretations of these characters, they solidify certain readings.

Dutch Sherlock *Fans*

In order to explore the specific ways Dutch Sherlock Holmes fans responded to *Sherlock*, I recruited interviewees by posting at fan communities or SNS sites. All of the informants are in their twenties or thirties. I met two interviewees at a *Sherlock* board that I subscribed to for this study: *The Bakerstreet Supper Club*. Before submitting this article, I asked interviewees whether they wanted to be anonymous, published with their nicknames, with their actual first names or a variation thereof. Though some had no strong opinion about this, others showed a strong preference for getting credit with their first name, especially since the information was not deemed sensitive. In the end, I decided to use first names in order to provide some anonymity, yet remain faithful to the interviewees' expressed wishes. In general, the interviews took at least an hour and were conducted either in real life or, because of logistics, through Skype or phone calls.

The selected fans all have different repertoires concerning *Sherlock* and *Sherlock Holmes*. One of the moderators, Sanne, is mostly interested in the series rather than the books, while another regular visitor, Margriet, emphasized her long-lasting passion for the books since she was a teenager. Astrid is passionate about the Holmes' stories and detective series in general but not active in fan communities. The others are not, or barely, familiar with the original books. Iris is active at some of the *Sherlock* fan communities and interested in BBC productions as such. Marissa, Shanna and Roderick are all active in fan communities but not those of *Sherlock*. Nonetheless, all three of them are enthusiastic about the series and familiar with different television and movie versions of *Sherlock Holmes*.

The selected set of interviewees thus reflects a strategic sampling of diverse audience members (Gray 2003, 100–101). The sample has a small scale, and while using small sets is not uncommon in ethnographical audience studies (see also Thomas 2002; Hermes 2004), the drawback is that the data is difficult to generalize and cannot be seen as fully representative for Dutch *Sherlock* fans. Still, the sample suffices for my purpose, which is to highlight the singularity of reading processes rather to make general claims about the local fandom of *Sherlock*.

A Modern Spin

When the interviewees are asked at the start of the interviews to generally describe what they like about the series, they independently mention its modernity as its most entertaining aspect. This is not so much as an emotional judgment as a statement that emphasizes the series' most apparent feature. Perhaps my occupation as a scholar or the educational setting influenced them to justify their pleasure in watching *Sherlock* through a more formal response. When pressed for more details regarding their investment in *Sherlock*'s modernity, the interviewees often elaborate the series' use of modern media such as iPhones and Internet sites. Roderick tells: "*Sherlock*'s most apparent feature is that it wants to be very modern. Examples of that are the camera tricks, the introduction as well as the texts that are being visualized."

The interviewees stress the importance of these digitally influenced visual features in their viewing pleasure. Both Astrid and Sanne describe that they were drawn to the series during an early shot in the first episode when all of the phones at the police station go off simultaneously during a presentation. We see Sherlock's text message hovering above them, stating, "Wrong." "At that moment," Sanne tells me, "I was sold." In a comparison with the movie *Sherlock Holmes* (2009) and *House M.D.* (2004–), Roderick describes how *Sherlock*'s visualization stands out yet fits within a larger detective tradition: "Modern means are used very well here to show what happens in the minds of these characters. That is entertaining but it is certainly not a must. In the past you could express this just as well in an explanation scene in which everyone is locked in the same room and the killer is revealed." Here, Roderick naturalizes *Sherlock*'s visuals by placing the series in a wider tradition and pointing out the explanatory function of *Sherlock*'s stylistic flourishes.

The use of technology is not seen as obtrusive but as a perfect fit with the Holmes format. Astrid and Roderick mention how technology makes the surveillance of all the parties, such as criminals and the police, more feasible. Others state that technology contributes to the investigation itself. Iris describes: "With Google at your disposal on your cell phone it is much more credible that you can find out all of these obscure facts you did not know ten minutes ago. It is much easier now to collect information that the older Sherlock Holmes had to know about on the spot." Margriet, when talking about Internet use in the series, is a bit concerned though. She feels most fans and viewers forget that Holmes is a character who employs many methods to gain and order knowledge, such as indexes and telegrams. Thereby she shows that *Sherlock* is a dominant interpretation of the original that already showed Holmes as technologically savvy and modern.

The methods of obtaining knowledge in *Sherlock* differ from the original books, though (Hills, this volume). Roderick emphasizes that Holmes was a bit of a genius while Sherlock works differently. "Everything he knows is based on immediate knowledge and lab research and forensics." Iris describes that it has become more essential for Sherlock to combine facts in his deductions. "The art is not obtaining knowledge any more but bringing together disparate parts." Many interviewees emphasize that Sherlock selects information. Still, some, like Astrid, are concerned about what this entails for the Holmes formula. She states that the series features little actual deduction as such and that it bases itself on different types of knowledge too. The first episode, she tells, clearly shows Sherlock's deductive skills by bringing together facts; the second relies on finding codes while the third is linked by fast trials comparable to Agatha Christie's *The Big Four* (1927). Though the other interviewees think that *Sherlock* features a specific research method, Astrid discerns different styles that draw from a variety of crime series.

Other aspects of the Holmes formula still seem contemporary to the interviewees. Margriet is surprised by the ease with which some of the motives could be transferred to modern London. "They are still two guys living together in one apartment to be able to pay the rent, for instance." Margriet and several other interviewees mention the war with Afghanistan as being a one-to-one relation with the original texts that works especially well. Many interviewees mention certain references as being very clever like John's blog, Sherlock's "The Science of Deduction" site, and the use of nicotine patches. Iris and Marissa specifically mention the tie-in web sites as an interesting move by the BBC. These web sites are exemplary of transmedia storytelling (Jenkins 2006) that extends parts of a story to other media.

Some aspects of *Sherlock* lead to mixed interpretations, notably the titular character's occupation as a consulting detective. Astrid deems this a credible motive because freelancing is more plausible nowadays. She naturalizes this through other detective novels she reads that also feature private investigators. Roderick, however, is hindered in his viewing: "First, I find it less credible that in our present day the police would be so ignorant that they need to hire an external employee; and second, that they would accept him. I think that used to be more credible, when forensic science was not really a science yet. You can imagine that a genius, a savant, just shows up and tackles a case." The two readers' comments highlight a gap in naturalization, which can be explained because they both rely on different repertoires of detective fiction and ideas about labor in the past and today.

Though *Sherlock* is a modernization, some interviewees feel Victorian or historical motives still play a role in the setting and narrative. The evocation of, for instance, gothic themes is picked up by Roderick who also noticed this supernatural tension in Guy Ritchie's *Sherlock Holmes* (2009): "The good thing about these cases is that you believe something supernatural is happening, not the kind of *Ghostbusters'* ectoplastic but more in the sense that these events are not possible at all. The cab driver in the first episode for instance creates this air he can make people kill themselves." Though the supposed supernatural is a theme in, for instance, *The Hound of the Baskervilles*, Roderick is not familiar with the original texts. By comparing adaptations of *Sherlock Holmes*, he naturalizes the gothic motives in *Sherlock*. Although the interviewees mention *Sherlock*'s modernity as its most apparent feature, it becomes clear that many elements they consider to be modern (such as technology) or traditional (such as gothic) are naturalized as characteristic of *Sherlock Holmes* texts.

Heroes, Sidekicks, and Villains

Sherlock Holmes fandom has gone through a long history in which fans discussed the characters as if they were real. This kind of "ironic belief" is underlined in the audience studies of Sherlockians by Saler (2003). Fans have long since tried to make sense of the stories by reconstructing facts and creating character biographies. This character engagement is in line with Fludernik's experientiality, and it was also my lead when I asked fans to give their opinion of the characters. In this section I shall show how they interpreted Sherlock, John, and Moriarty.

First, what becomes apparent at the start of the interviews is that the characterization of Sherlock is often addressed through his accessories and hobbies rather than his personality features. For the broader public, the standard image of Holmes is indeed that of a slender man wearing a travel coat, cap, and smoking a pipe. Most interviewees start by referring to that image and describe how the coat is a great mediation of the travel cape. Others draw on details from the books. Sherlock plays the violin, is bored when he is off his cases, and shoots at the wall. Though Holmes originally depended on cocaine to alleviate boredom, some feel the implied drug use in *Sherlock* is a weak reworking of this motive. Iris compares it to the Guy Ritchie movie when Holmes is caught red-handed by Watson after using opium. Similarly, Margriet draws comparisons with *The Case of the Silk Stocking* (2004) in which he uses cocaine in the rest room. The interviewees feel that part of the character is lost in the translation since the drug-addiction has always been a vital element of other Holmes texts.

Sherlock's personality in the series, as well as in the books, evokes very different opinions. Iris thinks Sherlock makes a "very strong, charming figure" while Marissa calls him a "dandy." Margriet, though, perceives Sherlock as being too rude compared to the books. She thinks the original Holmes is an elegant, rational man who pays less attention to trivialities that do not fit in his world view. Marissa explicitly notes how BBC's Sherlock comes across as autistic through his social mistakes rather than purposely rude. She finds this is done quite cleverly. Indeed, the history of interpreting Holmes as autistic is a long one, albeit one that the interviewees seem less familiar with (Maher 1994).

The interviewees are quick to draw comparisons with other recent Holmes adaptations. Iris compares *Sherlock* to *House M.D.* and finds House "a much bigger bastard." Roderick thinks exactly the opposite. He sees BBC's Sherlock as annoying while he finds House charming: "He has a kind of natural authority." Those who allude to Robert Downey consider him to be scruffy like House but less mean and more eccentric. Marissa, though, thinks Downey echoes House a lot as "the type of grumpy older man, limp, badly shaven, that calls people off." She thinks this type of character has definitely put its stamp on Holmes, and she is glad *Sherlock* revolves less around a snarky character that enjoys outsmarting others.

Here, the appeal of Sherlock is often related to his age. Margriet finds this very true to the source text: "During the first case, they are not very old, so it makes sense." Iris and Shanna are very pleased with the youth of the characters and also think this helps to draw different audiences. Roderick naturalizes this differently. He argues that Sherlock's age affects the narrative and gives it a competitive edge: "It immediately changes Sherlock's dynamic, because the police get even more frustrated because he is young. If he is just a forty-five-year-old man, a genius, you assume he is right."

In their interpretations, the interviewees speak highly of John. Many of them stress they had few expectations of him when they tuned in for the series. Some explicitly evoke the popular image of Watson. Roderick describes: "Watson always seems a bit of a dumb, fat guy to me. Pretty incompetent too." Marissa, mainly drawing from *The Great Mouse Detective* (1986), stresses that aside from being the narrator, Watson often functions as comic relief. The interviewees praise John's skills in *Sherlock* that show him as a war veteran and doctor. "I used to always argue in favour of Watson to friends," Margriet tells me, "but they never bought it. Until now!" Many informants note that John functions as the everyday character one can identify with rather than a narrator or guide through whom Sherlock's thoughts are channelled. Both Iris and Astrid feel that John could have been even more "bad-ass" though, seeing as he is an ex-soldier. Meanwhile, Marissa naturalizes the war motif as trauma: "He is a sad character, someone who is at odds with himself."

Interviewees perceive the relation between Sherlock and John to be well portrayed in the series. Most interviewees highlight that they complement each other and three explicitly state Sherlock makes John's life less boring.

The intimate friendship with romantic aspects or *bromance* is often addressed. "It's friendship, but there are hints that there might be more," Shanna says. Marissa describes how they remind her of a married couple: "They have a household to run as well and make remarks about their groceries." As an outsider to fan communities, Astrid points out that she appreciates this homoerotic subtext in the longer, literary tradition of romantic interpretations of Sherlock and John. Notably Sanne, Shanna and Marissa are active readers of Sherlock/John slash fan fiction: written stories by fans in which characters are portrayed as romantically or sexually involved. They also explain elements of the text, such as the awkward restaurant scene from "A Study in Pink," in relation to this genre. Not all interviewees are equally positive about slash though. Iris likes reading about the characters as friends while slash fan fiction makes the general stories she would like to read harder to find. "Welcome to online fandom," she states sarcastically.

Some fans also consider Sherlock to be asexual (see Coppa, this volume). Both Iris and Margriet are well aware that entire online communities flourish around this theme and also refer to discussion threads. Iris though, thinks that in the end asexual fan fiction is still about romance. Indeed, such stories tend to portray Sherlock according to the standard slash formula in which the character explores his sexuality (Jenkins 1992, 206–219). Historically, the detective as asexual seems to be a much older trope related to the view of detectives as loners or priest like figures proclaiming rationality (McCracken 1998, 60). The use of such cultural imagery in *Sherlock* echoes these older discourses and can be seen in the reception of the fans as well, where the asexual genre has been well-received.

A last characterization I inquired about is that of *Sherlock*'s Moriarty. In fan communities, the character raises mixed opinions and the interviewees underline this as well. All interviewees stress that they find he comes across as creepy or insane. Some feel that this could have been carried a bit further while others find the character over the top. Magriet and Astrid mention that they were very excited to find out what Moriarty was like. Margriet describes: "I just did not know what to expect. I was prepared to see him as a woman, even." Others also stress their theories that Mycroft, or in the third episode, John, would be Moriarty. Notably Astrid notes a slight disappointment about the character and prefers Ritchie's version as being more true to the book: "He is a kind of puppeteer who pulls the strings but you hardly ever see him." What she likes about *Sherlock*'s Moriarty is that he is on an equal level with Sherlock as a consulting criminal: "They are literally opposites." Marissa emphasizes the line between Moriarty and Sherlock is thin though: "By blurring his morals and social features, Sherlock is portrayed as a freak that approaches criminality and the evil master mind."

Though Moriarty does not reflect the features he has in Conan Doyle's original, as a professor and criminal of status, most interviewees do not see this as a problem. They experience Moriarty's revamped character as fascinating and, sometimes, as more authentic. Particularly Marissa thinks that *Sherlock*'s Moriarty is what a criminal mastermind should be like, as opposed to Disney's version of Moriarty, an insane "monster" who loses his rationality. Insanity, though, is the same standard by which *Sherlock*'s Moriarty is measured. Most interviewees describe the villain's age and normal appearance as standing in contrast to his creepy personality. Particularly Astrid, Margriet, and Iris stress that Moriarty comes across as normal and young. Interestingly, all three naturalize this by speculating about his history and argue that his normal appearance is an advantage in the criminal circuit.

Here, experientiality, as behavior befitting a character, differs widely based on what texts and what popular types the fans relate to. Those unfamiliar with the books sometimes imagine Moriarty differently based on a few images they have come across. "I am not sure who the classic Moriarty is," Roderick says, "but he is probably eccentric, that type of old treasure collector who has become a villain." Fans naturalize Moriarty's role as antagonist in *Sherlock* differently. Marissa considers Moriarty a traditional mastermind, a credible villain who "keeps his calm when he hunts you down, knowing he is going to win." In contrast to this, Roderick argues Moriarty is nothing like the clichéd rational villains from *James Bond* that plot elaborate schemes. He compares Moriarty to *The Dark Knight*'s version of The Joker (2008) in a sense that both villains are chaotic and unpredictable. This classification of characters according to fictional tropes is a particular literary competence that the interviewees display and that they use to justify their interpretations. Some of these tropes, such as the standard villain and the atypical one, exclude each other and highlight how fans naturalize this content differently.

Knitting Detectives

During the interviews, I also asked fans to reflect upon *Sherlock*'s English qualities. They often compare the BBC production to the global media industry at large. For starters, the series is perceived as an essentially British production in terms of writing. Many interviewees mention that *Sherlock* reminds them of a movie, in contrast to American series that stick to a 40-minute formula but have longer seasons. Iris explains that this results in a different storytelling format with more focus on plot within episodes but which still comprises its arcs within seasons. Since Dutch television also features other European series and networks, some draw comparisons with content that is not Anglo-American or Dutch. Astrid compares *Sherlock* to *Tatort,* a German police series that also lasts one and a half hours but has a more specific format. "You can set your clock to when the body's found," she says.

In terms of writing, the interviewees distil different English elements from the text. Some mention the humorous undertones in *Sherlock* as specifically English. By relating *Being Human* and *Sherlock,* Marissa argues that BBC series focus better on smaller, everyday, domestic issues. Others draw comparisons in terms of casting and argue that British television is more prone to casting regular looking people that are not made up as overtly good looking as American actors. The authors, Steven Moffat and Mark Gattis, are also stressed in this discussion. Sanne and Iris think that the series has been written much like Moffat's (also BBC-produced) *Doctor Who* (2010–) episodes and compare *Sherlock* with the eleventh Doctor who appears to have some eccentricity in common with Sherlock.

As a detective series, the original English *Sherlock Holmes* books are considered by the Dutch interviewees as a hallmark of the genre that has influenced many other stories. *Sherlock,* as a later adaptation, is of course influenced by a wider tradition of detective and police series. Astrid, for instance, mentions that *Sherlock*'s third episode reminds her of Agatha Christie's *The Big Four* in which Poirot faces similar intellectual challenges as Sherlock. The interviewees often oppose *Sherlock*'s eccentric, younger titular character to the traditional English detective as depicted by characters as Morse and Miss Marple. The before-mentioned characters are considered to be textbook examples of English detectives, portrayed as older, single characters who indulge in leisure activities such as going to the pub or knitting. This is comparable to Thomas' research, which argued that fans understood *Inspector Morse* as an example of English culture because of, amongst others, the characterization of Morse as a bachelor in Oxford (2002, 31–58).

These traditional detectives often have two faces though. "Miss Marple for instance poses as a fluffy old lady, but she is anything but that," Margriet tells. Astrid alludes to Miss Marple as well as Patricia Wentworth's Miss Silver, a governess who, while knitting, cleverly distils knowledge from the witnesses. Roderick also mentions: "That is an entire genre in England, detective land. Older people that are knitting but meanwhile, they are fighting crime!" The methods that these traditional English detectives embody are juxtaposed with various *Sherlock Holmes* texts. While detectives like Miss Marple obtain knowledge by talking to people, Holmes relies on factual knowledge and forensics. Shanna notes that most detectives, including the American ones, appear to lean more on knowledge of people and finding out their dramatic life stories and motives. Others draw comparisons with American crime series that are more "official" or "bureaucratic" and "involve a lot of shooting" as opposed to *Sherlock*'s atmosphere. These series are considered to appeal less to the intelligence and creativity that Holmes stands for.

Though Dutch people see Holmes as a very English character, at the same time interviewees' remarks often imply that there are detectives that they consider to be even more English. Likewise, some interviewees imply that they consider Holmes to be a traditional English detective but Sherlock not so much so, even though he is described as a typical inhabitant of modern London. They claim that Sherlock fits in with a stream of newer detective series featuring eccentric detectives and cops. Marissa for instance, compares him to the brilliant but flawed Monk (*Monk* 2002–2009), who has many compulsive disorders reminiscent of Sherlock's obsessions and possible autism. However, interviewees like Margriet also stress that the original Holmes was already that character: an eccentric, middle-aged, and authentic detective. The qualities that are in *Sherlock* and its "new" portrayal of the detective were in the old novels all along.

Lastly, interviewees compare the more urban, modern *Sherlock* with other traditional detective series in terms of location. Other detectives seem to take place in remote, local communities. Iris, Astrid, and Roderick refer to the closed environments of Agatha Christie that feature vacation houses, islands, and trains as scenes of the crime with only a few suspects. "*Midsomer Murders*," Margriet, for instance, mentions, "is much more local and small. It often starts with local clubs of bird watchers or so in which a body is found." Margriet also implies how traditionally English she finds *Midsomer Murders* based on its idyllic country sceneries. She emphasizes its foreign qualities and attraction. *Sherlock*, then, she finds much more urban. When asked to draw comparisons with their own local culture, most interviewees argue *Sherlock* has little in common with Dutch police series. Some mention *Baantjer*, a detective show that takes place in Amsterdam and explores the city and its canalside houses. This reminds them of *Sherlock* as both series mediate local culture well.

As the interviewees implicitly notice, *color locale* is an important feature in most detective fiction (Reijnders 2009). The murder changes an ordinary landscape into an active place of imagination, a story that slowly reveals itself. Gattis and Moffat also show an awareness of the setting when they describe London as an extra character in *Unlocking Sherlock* (2010). Many interviewees mention that views of London in *Sherlock* stand out as realistic. Iris and Shanna find this a very different portrayal of London than in American series, which often showcase touristic hallmarks like the Big Ben in the background. The viewers have mixed interpretations of what constitutes authentic space. Though some draw comparisons with *Baantjer* because it shows the hallmarks of Amsterdam, others value *Sherlock* exactly because it does not do this.

Conclusion

I have shown that viewers actively connect the transmedia text of *Sherlock* with the original texts and legacy of Sherlock Holmes. As it turns out, the application of Jonathan Culler's and Fludernik's theories has been fruitful to understand fan interpretations of *Sherlock*. The framework has complemented Jenkins' notion of transmedia storytelling as a literary mechanism that evokes reader's activity. However, the ways in which fans interpret the texts are not necessarily the active viewing that Jenkins describes since he assumes viewers familiarize themselves with other versions of the text and rely more on fan communities in this process. In contrast, my interviewees show that viewers have a wide range of repertoires that guide them in their readings.

Though transmedial elements form cues for audiences, they often bridge these with other experiences and fiction. Aside from alluding to other versions of *Sherlock Holmes*, viewers rely on their own experiences, knowledge of popular culture and literature. Furthermore, though interpretive communities shape the viewers' interpretations of the material, shared community interpretations do not appear to conclusively determine an individual viewer's interpretation of *Sherlock*. The interviewees engage with fan communities in various degrees. Some only use them as a resource while other active users clearly reflect on what they observe there, especially in relation to "hot topics" of fan discussion.

Though the interpretations of Dutch fans are influenced by their culture, this is not as much the case as I initially had presumed. The popular culture of Dutch people, after all, largely consists out of Anglo-American television series. These texts are what the interviewees often allude to when they judge *Sherlock*'s quality, characters, and setting. Still, we have seen that fans articulate local interpretations of foreign content, for example relying on elements that they consider to be defining for English detective series, or elaborating on London as a scene of production. Even without the Victorian entourage, Sherlock is still understood as an iconic English character.

I am grateful to all the fans who helped make this article possible.

Works Cited

Ang, Ien. 1985 (1982). *Watching* Dallas: *Soap opera and the melodramatic imagination.* Trans. D. Couling. London: Methuen, 1985.

Culler, Jonathan. 1975. *Structuralist poetics: Structuralism, linguistics and the study of literature.* London: Routledge.

Den Boef, Hans. 2005. *Sherlockholmesering.* Leiden: Universiteitsbibliotheek.

Fish, Stanley. 1980. *Is there a text in this class? The authority of interpretive communities.* Cambridge: Harvard University Press.

Fludernik, Monika. 1996. *Towards a "natural" narratology.* London: Routledge.

Gillan, Jennifer. 2011. *Television and must-click TV.* London: Routledge, 2011.

Gray, Ann. 2003. *Research practice for cultural studies. ethnographic methods and lived cultures.* London: Sage.

Hermes, Joke. 2005. *Re-reading popular culture.* Malden, MA: Blackwell.

Iser, Wolfgang. 1974. *The implied reader.* Baltimore: Johns Hopkins University Press.

Jauss, Hans Robert. 1984. *Ästhetische Erfahrung and literarische Hermeneutik* 4th ed. Nördlingen: Suhrkamp.

Jenkins, Henry. 1992. *Textual poachers: Television fans and participatory culture.* London: Routledge.

_____. 2006. *Convergence culture: Where old and new media collide.* London: Routledge.

Long, Geoffrey. 2007. *Transmedia storytelling: Business, aesthetics and production at the Jim Henson company.* M.A. Thesis. cms.mit.edu.

Maher, A. Michael. 1994.Was Sherlock Holmes autistic? kspot.org.

McCracken, Scott. 1998. Detective fiction. In *Pulp: Reading popular fiction,* 75–99. Manchester: Manchester University Press.

Pugh, Sheena. 2005. *The democratic genre: Fan fiction in a literary context.* Bridgend: Seren.

Radway, Janice. 1987. *Reading the romance.* 2d ed. London: Verso.

Reijnders, Stijn. 2009. Watching the detectives: Inside the guilty landscapes of Inspector Morse, Baanttjer and Wallander. *European Journal of Communication* 24: 165–181.

Saler, Michael. 2003. "Clap if you believe in Sherlock Holmes": Mass culture and the re-enchantment of modernity. c. 1890–c. 1940. *The Historical Journal* 46: 599–622.

Thomas, Lynn. 2002. *Fans, feminism and "quality" media.* London: Routledge.

PART FIVE

Postmodern Sherlock

Sherlock and the
(Re)Invention of Modernity

BALAKA BASU

Abstract — *Sherlock* sells itself as a modern adaptation of Sherlock Holmes emi-
nently suitable for contemporary times. Using Fredric Jameson's theorization of
the postmodern, and Walter Benjamin's *The Arcades Project* as a framework, I
argue that unlike its textual progenitor, *Sherlock* consistently gazes back rather
than forward, projecting a carefully manufactured illusion of the modern "now,"
while actually producing a retrofuturistic narrative that constructs the present
only from the perspective of an imaginary, idealized past and is eventually incapable of clearly distinguishing between the two. Because it is invested both in
replicating the familiar affect of the original text and in being fashionably relevant,
the program exists in a state of belatedness, unable to interrogate its own ideology
fully and take part in a progressive, critical discourse that is truly contemporary.

Introduction

In the same year in which Sherlock Holmes returned to the small screen
in the BBC's *Sherlock* (2010–), he experienced another resurrection in print
within the pages of the pseudonymous Barry Grant's *The Strange Return of
Sherlock Holmes*. In this somewhat bizarre novel, the intrepid detective is flash-
frozen by an alpine avalanche (where else but in Switzerland?) in 1914, only
to be fortuitously discovered some ninety years later, by which time he can
be thawed with some combination of cryonics and stem cell research (where
else but at St. Bart's?) and left to resume a quiet life in the small Welsh book-
town of Hay-on-Wye. Here, he assumes a new identity as the eccentric Cedric
Coombs, but this disguise is easily penetrated by his new Watson (now called
Wilson), who finds his flat-mate's idiosyncratic avocations — violin-playing
and cocaine naturally among them — as well as his appearance to be somehow
familiar. This recognition doesn't seem due to any unusual perspicacity on
Wilson's part; the ubiquity of Sherlock Holmes in popular culture is so great

that almost any reader, or indeed, any alert media consumer in similar circumstance might conceivably do the same. Interestingly, despite its barefaced deployment of improbable sf (speculative or science fiction) tropes, *The Strange Return of Sherlock Holmes* is actually far less strange than *Sherlock*, which likewise purports to thrust Sherlock Holmes bodily into the postmodern "now," but actually places him in a pre-modern never-was, as removed from our own time as the 19th century itself, and twice as fictional. By collapsing the Victorian era into the 21st century, *Sherlock*'s setting becomes a fantastical backdrop upon which the narrative reinvents the wheel of modernity while seeming to believe it is doing so, not belatedly, but for the first time.

Sherlock's premise is simple: the program touts itself as a contemporary re-imagining that "blows away the fog of the Victorian era" as the "classic detective Sherlock Holmes enters the 21st century" (October 3, 2010; collider.com). Co-creator Steven Moffat claims that in this series, "everything that matters about Holmes and Watson is the same. Conan Doyle's original stories were never about frock coats and gas light; they're about brilliant detection, dreadful villains and blood-curdling crimes — and frankly, to hell with the crinoline" (March 3, 2010; www.bbc.co.uk). In other words, the program is meant to be not so much an adaptation as a temporal translation: keeping the heart of the story intact while discarding the "fog" of retrograde Victoriana, which Moffat and co-creator Mark Gatiss deem to be trivial ornamentation, irrelevant to the story and easily rendered into modern parlance. Indeed, the term *modern* is hard to escape in any conversation having to do with *Sherlock*; the whole point of the update is to dispense with everything old and ostensibly stodgy, and bring in all that is new and indisputably sexy — otherwise, it might as well have been set in the last decade of the 19th century, rather than at the beginning of the 21st. Vocabulary-wise, the substitutions are certainly ingenious. By some fortune, there is still a war in Afghanistan for John Watson to be wounded in, and instead of inheriting an engraved pocket watch from a brother Harry who died after taking to drink, he can use a similarly engraved mobile phone pressed upon him by an alcoholic sister of the same name. His memoirs transform into a blog, as do telegrams into text messages and monographs into web sites. Unfortunately, not all the crinoline is so easily thrown away.

Using a theoretical framework of postmodernism and modernity that relies upon the work of Fredric Jameson and Walter Benjamin, I want to demonstrate that *Sherlock* is *not* the modern adaptation of the Sherlock Holmes stories that it repeatedly claims to be. We are expected to believe in the program's modern character because of its lavish use of postmodern and contemporary technologies, but these merely obfuscate the ways in which *Sherlock* displays a retrofuturism that imagines the present solely in terms of the future of an outdated past. In other words, it projects the image of a postmodern visual aesthetic, which only superficially disguises its essentially conservative, pre-modern message. As a result of this commingling between past and present, the program fully endorses neither, and therefore is unable to comment on or even really acknowledge its own perspective, ideology, or genre. This means that it lacks the self-reflective awareness that ought to permeate a postmodernism relevant to a progressive cultural discourse. Finally, I will show how *Sherlock*'s updated interactions with the figure of the fan can function as metonymy for the way in which the program chooses to eschew the real issues of contemporary society and how, in doing so, it produces a reification of the retrograde and the nostalgic, which suggests that the past *is* actually the present.

Pomo or Faux-Mo? The Visual Aesthetic of Sherlock

Sherlock's London is a world where the intervening time between the Victorian era and the 21st century seems to have been collapsed, or indeed, has never taken place. The landscape is either glass-and-steel or Victorian — the purpose-built architecture of a post–World War II era and the second half of the 20th century simply do not exist. The "modern" glass-and-steel architecture that makes up the program's contemporary scenery is reminiscent of the structure and poetics of the arcade in Benjamin's *The Arcades Project,* that imaginatively forward-looking construction of the modern *in the nineteenth century.* In his section on mirrors, Benjamin locates the narcissism of modern identity in the profusion of liminal reflective surfaces that litter 19th century Paris, as well as, incidentally, *Sherlock*'s landscape.

> Egoistic — "that is what one becomes in Paris, where you can hardly take a step without catching sight of your dearly beloved self. Mirror after mirror! In cafés and restaurants, in shops and stores, in haircutting salons and literary salons, in baths and everywhere, 'every inch a mirror!'" [1999, 539].

In fact, for Benjamin, mirrors signify boundary destabilization; they expand, or at least deceptively *seem* to expand space into infinity, at once charting identity and reflecting merchandise into an endless series of desire. All lenses including the eye itself become ocular mirrors, meaning that any gaze is to be interpreted as a "perspective on infinity" (538) with its infinitely fractured succession of images, and this is amply exemplified by *Sherlock*'s cinematography and art design. So far, *Sherlock*'s mirrors literally illustrate the 'modern' reflective landscape envisioned by Benjamin. But has our conceptualization of the modern really remained unaltered since Benjamin's prehistory of the 20th century? Has time stood still since then? Perhaps so.

Frederic Jameson prophetically argues in "Progress Versus Utopia, or:

Can We Imagine the Future," that it often feels as if the 21st century no longer really has a modernity of its own to which it can look forward. He writes

> We can no longer entertain such visions of wonder-working, properly 'science-fictional' futures.... These visions are themselves now historical and dated — streamlined cities of the future on peeling murals — while our lived experience of our greatest metropolises is one of urban decay and blight. That particular Utopian future has in other words turned out to have been merely the future of one moment of what is now our own past ... [science fiction's] deepest vocation is over and over again to demonstrate and to dramatize our incapacity to imagine the future [Jameson 1982, 151].

In light of this thought, however, *Sherlock*'s 21st century seems almost like a reconstruction of the 19th century's version of the future, not the present in which we actually live. *Sherlock*'s neo–Victorian setting, like Benjamin's arcade, is outside of time; it "knows no history" and in it "events pass ... as always identical and always new"; its "most modern is ... 'the eternal return of the same'" (Benjamin 1999, 546). The subtle difference between the two, however, is that in Benjamin's work, the arcade's mirrors are seen to reflect future progress, but in *Sherlock*, the reflective surfaces literally display a wavering, blurred image of Sherlock Holmes that is not progressive, but regressive. His outline is not that of utopian futurity; it does not show what Marx calls the "anticipation and imaginative expression of a new world" (637); instead, it is the past, conservative and idealized — it even seems to be wearing a frock coat.

If we examine the flawlessly constructed costumes and cinematography of *Sherlock*, it becomes clear that the Victorian aesthetic is still very much with us. Disparaging comments from the creators on crinolines aside, the costumes are unmistakably designed to be evocative of 19th century clothes; Sherlock's ever present scarf works as a cross between an ascot and a cravat, and his coat, with its "pronounced collars and raised lapels" is, as noted by *The Independent*'s fashion commentators Paul Bignell and Rachel Shields, clearly a "modern re-working of ... Victorian designs" (August 8, 2010; www.independent.co.uk). As well, the wintry setting of the episodes allows for the layering of suit-jackets and coats, creating a formal Victorian silhouette for John as well, emphasized even more when the two protagonists are filmed, as they frequently are, such that they appear only as black shade-blocked figures in relief against a lighter background. These shots give the impression of a Victorian cameo in negative, while the color filter used often resembles that of daguerreotype photography. And when Sherlock is actually reflected in the program's numerous mirrored surfaces, the result is only to recall an older, Victorian Holmes.

Similarly, as we observe the cinematography of *Sherlock*'s second episode, "The Blind Banker," for example, we begin to notice that the London pictured here seems to have only black and white cars, the vast majority of which seem to feature the rounded, bulging lines that characterize traditionally English automobiles from some nostalgic, reified past. Through the glass windshields of the London black cabs in which Sherlock and John ride over and over again, we can observe how the color tint bleeds into sepia, and from there into black and white. As each frame dissolves into the next, through the cab's window an address on The Strand becomes visible, telling us subtly that we have not really stirred from the pages of the old print magazine in which this narrative was first nurtured. Only a few minutes later, another shot is framed, with reflections of the action dancing over large brass metal knobs, the reflected images flickering like the flame within a gas lamp's sphere.

However appealing and evocative the imagery, and pleasurable Benjamin's "eternal return of the same" may be, ideological progressives will find a problem with collapsing the Victorian period into our own in the unexamined, retrofuturistic way that *Sherlock* does so. It actually serves to ensure that history has no context and therefore both the past and the present become wholly fantastical, idealized constructs that have little to do with reality. In "Postmodernism and Consumer Society," Jameson suggests that the world of postmodern art has become pastiche, "a world in which stylistic innovation is no longer possible, all that is left is to imitate dead styles, to speak through the masks and with the voices of the styles in the imaginary museum" (1985, 115). Ironically, through its continual resurrection of the past in lieu of futurity, this kind of postmodernism provokes the loss of history itself, because it promulgates narratives, languages and aesthetics of the past as if they were current, rather than in their appropriate context. Jameson argues, for example, that the setting of *Body Heat* (1981), which recalls *The Postman Always Rings Twice* (1934), thoroughly undermines discussion of the contemporary, constructing the film as "a narrative set in some indefinable nostalgic past, an eternal '30s, say, beyond history" (116–118). He goes on to point out that the attempt to gain access to the past through fantasies about that past paradoxically makes certain that historical authenticity is essentially unattainable and that this destruction of time signifies the disturbing quality of the postmodern condition.

So far, *Sherlock*'s temporality-annihilating aesthetic seems to encapsulate both Jameson and Benjamin's conception of the postmodern completely. And indeed, practically every part of the program's visual composition seems designed to shout "postmodern." Consider the moment in the first episode of the series, "A Study in Pink" when Sherlock examines the murder victim's wedding ring and the words "dirty/clean" appear across the screen with the curve of the ring as divider: this seems to be a literal illustration of a poststructuralist binary and is just one example in a veritable sea of such moments. In fact, regardless of its actual content, the floating text that appears superimposed on the screen to communicate both unspoken thoughts and other unvoiced text is a continual feature of the show, and further emphasizes a postmodern union of word and picture. As well, throughout the series, figures repeatedly come to life to illustrate Sherlock's explanations — as in the third episode, "The Great Game," when a black ghost appears to represent Sherlock's account of the assassin known as the Golem — demonstrating that this is a world which consistently draws attention to the embodiment of its own stylistic mechanics, and therefore its own artifice.

Even the most basic device of film, the frame, is similarly embodied, as the screen is repeatedly divided into segments, often by distinct lines such as a yellow police line or the outline of a car's windshield. Each of these segments frequently runs its own reel, displaying the ongoing scene from several angles often separated by perspective and time, and theoretically at least, fracturing the closed cohesion of the screen into postmodern multiplicity (Deleuze 1993, 173–80). The resulting collage of image-layers makes us feel that Sherlock and John might have simply been pasted into the narrative's plane and might not really be there at all.

What is missing from *Sherlock*'s postmodernism, however, is the vast panoply of uncontrolled signs, verging on information overload, that reject hierarchy or what Jameson defines as schizophrenia: "an experience of isolated, disconnected, discontinuous material signifiers which fail to link up into a coherent sequence" (1985, 119). For Jameson, the postmodern is noisily achronological, and its lack of order is what condemns us to the perpetual present. Thus, *Sherlock*'s careful construction — its perfectly chosen backdrops and design elements; Sherlock's reliance on the normative, totalizing laws that permit him to make his deductions without error — actually works against its postmodernism. Sherlock's thought processes, as illustrated on our screens, purport to be unordered, but are still subject to the anti-pluralistic idea that only one interpretation fits the facts. The presentation of information flow is deceptively overwhelming, but only seemingly disunified; in reality, it is so streamlined and ordered that it includes almost no cultural "white noise" that might work against the reactionary hierarchies that its cautiously selected elements subscribe to, whether unconsciously or not. As we shall see, the result is to illustrate, with a visual aesthetic that only *appears* postmodern, content that is anything but.

The Future Is Then; the Past Is Now: Sherlock and the Modern Misdirection

Even a cursory examination of the novels and short stories shows that Holmes was designed by Conan Doyle to be of the scientific vanguard, looking forward to the future. Moffat and Gatiss's Sherlock, despite his contemporary trappings and much vaunted similarity to his predecessor, is clearly meant to be nothing of the kind. *A Study in Scarlet* introduces us to a 19th century Holmes who performs revolutionary experiments in forensic science such as "beating the subjects in the dissecting-rooms with a stick ... to verify how far bruises may be produced after death" (19). Though "A Study in Pink" presents us with an ostensibly identical scene, where a 21st century Sherlock is depicted beating a cadaver with a riding crop and saying to the pathologist, Molly, "I need to know what bruises form in the next twenty minutes, a man's alibi depends on it," the two situations carry entirely different valences. In the first case, Holmes is actually experimenting; in the second, Sherlock is merely investigating a question, the answer to which is already well established by contemporary forensic medicine. Sherlock's actions are obviously not scientifically motivated; instead their intent seems to be purely masturbatory, whether for the character himself, who clearly gains some fetishistic entertainment in taunting Molly with sado-masochistic paraphernalia, or for the audience-members who have read Conan Doyle and are thus provided with a pleasurable *frisson* of nostalgia from the scene's familiarity. Thus, the experiment, which denotes Holmes's scientific progression in the novel, here demonstrates Sherlock's gaze backwards.

This nostalgic perspective is carried thematically throughout the series. "The Blind Banker," which takes its inspiration from "The Adventure of the Dancing Men," revolves around the decryption of yellow spray-painted symbols in which messages of mysterious provenance are encoded. As soon as we first encounter the symbols of the code, Sherlock informs John that today — presumably unlike in the 19th century — the "world's run on codes and ciphers ... from the million-pound security system at the bank to the PIN machine you took exception to. Cryptography inhabits our every waking moment." Luckily, however, he can tell that this particular code is "an ancient device" that can't be unraveled by "modern code-breaking devices." It becomes clear that the mysteries that Sherlock and John are going to solve can't really be modern ones; in order for Sherlock's methods to work (and for the adventure to produce the affect of recognition), the universe must provide problems with "ancient" solutions instead.

This reification of the past is further underscored by other, frankly racist elements of "The Blind Banker": in its first few minutes, we see Sherlock battling a mysterious, turbaned Arabic antagonist who is inexplicably armed with a scimitar. Leaving aside for the moment the thoroughly outdated and offensive stereotypes that overwhelm this particular episode — which also features practically every Yellow Peril Orientalist trope imaginable — is it rational to expect an Arabic antagonist of today to be armed with a sword instead of the equally offensive but more *au courant* bomb? But in fact, the sword may signal the program's privileging of archaism; despite its reliance on text messages, mobile phones and other modern technologies, it is possible to read *Sherlock* as having an essentially conservative ideology — a natural byproduct, perhaps, of its nostalgic desires.

Indeed, with its emphasis on clear resolutions, the fixing of identity and guilt, and the elevation of order, the genre of the detective story itself is a naturally conservative one that does not tend toward postmodern figurations of ambiguity, instability, fluidity and multiplicity. In order to update the universe in a way that would make it more relevant to contemporary discourse, these elements would have to be problematized and complicated. *Sherlock* seems as if it is doing so, with its nods towards intertextual postmodern pastiche, but doesn't actually follow through in a substantive way. For instance, though Sherlock's position as hero is called into question by the police force on numerous occasions throughout the series, the narrative never seriously demands that we question his alignment or worry about whether he will throw in his lot with the villains. If he did, he wouldn't be Sherlock Holmes, and Moffat and Gatiss are thoroughly invested in making sure that he *is* Sherlock Holmes or at least a reasonable facsimile thereof. No real uncertainty as to outcome or character seems possible, and without this narrative instability, it's hard to recognize *Sherlock* as a representative of anything but a belated modernism. Wherever or whenever *Sherlock* takes place, it doesn't seem to be now.

But how could it? "Now" is in some sense a product of the immense popularity of the Sherlock Holmes mysteries. Like the best of hard science fiction, such as that of Conan Doyle's beloved Jules Verne, the original stories imagined and anticipated the future, and in some ways, helped to construct it. As Ronald Thomas states in his book, *Detective Fiction and the Rise of Forensic Science*, authors like Conan Doyle

> often reflected and popularized contemporary scientific theories of law enforcement, the detective stories they wrote also sometimes anticipated actual procedures in scientific police practice by offering fantasies of social control and knowledge before the actual technology to achieve either was available. At times, these texts seemed to call those technologies into being. It became commonplace for early criminologists to attribute inspiration for their theories to the methods of Sherlock Holmes or an Auguste Dupin. In developing what he called "a new police science" which focused on the examination of microscopic particles on the criminal body, for example, the pioneering French forensic scientist Edmond Locard went so far as to instruct his colleagues and students "to read over such stories as 'A Study in Scarlet' and 'The Sign of the Four'" in order to understand the basis of the principles he was recommending [1999, 4–5].

It's easy, then, to read the detective story and its most famous representative, Sherlock Holmes, as implicated in the very fabric of modern culture; the genre itself seems to be wound deeply into our conception of science and philosophy, our sense of truth and order in the universe, and our ability to know them. Therefore when *Sherlock* is ostensibly set in a universe in which there has never yet been a Sherlock Holmes, the alternate universe created by his removal from literary history ought to be — and is, in my opinion — immediately recognizable as a fantastical one. It's not just that the tube station at Baker Street, currently papered wall to wall with images of a fellow with a pipe and deerstalker hat, would look completely different, but that many of the seminal texts that regularly inform our popular discourse like *Star Trek*, *Batman*, and *CSI* would have an entirely different form if they existed at all, and thus so would our cultural landscape.

Moffat and Gatiss tacitly claim that their *Sherlock* retains everything essential about Conan Doyle's universe, that it takes place "today," and that this "today" exists in a time-line in which there has never before been a Sherlock Holmes. Unfortunately, all three claims cannot be true. *Sherlock's* creators want to rely on the myth of Holmes to produce affect on the part of the audience, while simultaneously asserting that their text stands alone, and that the myth we are familiar with never actually happened. Having to believe all of these things at once strains credulity as well as the narrative's integral continuity and while this threefold suspension of disbelief may produce a sense of delight on the part of *Sherlock's* audience, it comes at the price of being officially evicted from the story. Though this version of Sherlock Holmes could not exist without the Holmes fandom, the fandom itself is negated and preempted, ironically, by creators who are themselves fans.

Sherlock is not the first of Moffat's temporal translations; the mostly brilliant *Jekyll* (2007) also took a foundational Victorian text and moved it into the present. Unlike *Sherlock*, however, *Jekyll* does not suggest that it exists in a universe absent Robert Louis Stevenson and *The Strange Case of Dr. Jekyll and Mr. Hyde;* though it retells the narrative, it doesn't overwrite it. In fact, the existence of the classic narrative is indispensable to the new one, and as a result, despite the essentially supernatural nature of the story, there is no suggestion that the time-line in which *Jekyll* takes place is not our own. Conversely, *Sherlock's* timeline cannot be the same as ours, and this means that though it might not seem so at first glance, and contrary to its advertising, *Sherlock's* modern is not ours either.

Instead, *Sherlock's* "now" is not located in time, but in aesthetics. It manifests the 19th century without being *in* the 19th century and thus has no real obligation or allegiance to historical accuracy; it is neo–Victorian in every sense of the word as it resembles, revives, and is reminiscent of the period. Jameson, as I have discussed earlier, seems to suggest that all such retrofuturistic texts are postmodern, because any such text would express the condition of the perpetual present, and the death of history and futurity in one fell swoop. I have argued that *Sherlock*, though retrofuturistic in aesthetic, is not postmodern in content because its careful construction does not display the uncontrolled and schizophrenic atemporality that might conceivably reject cultural hegemony. I want to suggest as well, more optimistically, that although I believe *Sherlock* does not quite succeed in doing so, it is entirely possible for a retrofuturistic text to remain relevant if it actually interrogates the issues of the present, albeit in a pseudohistorical setting. While it may remove history from its own context, it need not unmoor the present as well.

Writing on the 19th century roots of steampunk, a subgenre that is also often neo–Victorian, scholar Jess Nevins suggests that the locus of such retro-futuristic writing is often found in the Victorian period because, more than other historical time-frames, this period resembles and models our own, and thus can be deployed more easily to comment on our own circumstances than those set in other time frames. He writes that the Victorian era is

> extremely useful for ideological stories on subjects such as feminism, imperialism, class issues, and religion, as well as for commentary on contemporary issues such as serial murderers and overseas wars ... without the authorial straining of allegorical novels set in previous historical eras [Nevins 2008, 8].

Thus, though I find *Sherlock* particularly conservative, it is not solely or even mainly due to its retrofuturism. It is because while the substitutions employed by *Sherlock* are made possible by the way our period mirrors the Victorian era (such as the fact that there's still a war in Afghanistan), the writers do not uti-lize this mirroring to comment on the valence of the present, merely congrat-ulating themselves on having escaped the oppressive yoke of Victorian mores, while simultaneously demonstrating that they haven't actually done so. Sher-lock's misogyny (as evidenced by the way he humiliates the pathologist Molly, who has a crush on him) and classism (as evidenced by his conversation with the murderer in Minsk, during "The Great Game," where he seems more con-cerned by his potential client's class as demonstrated by his diction and gram-mar than by his situation), are taken directly from Conan Doyle's 19th century and deposited whole into this contemporary retelling, but *Sherlock* presents these elements without comment, just as it presents the offensive Orientalist tropes in "The Blind Banker."

In many ways, *Sherlock*'s neo-liberal philosophy seems very much the same as its source material. As a consulting detective, Sherlock's practice is a triumph of the free market and the private sector; he performs all tasks better than the public servants who are employed by the State. Even public trans-portation is for other people; Sherlock rides in taxis. In fact, the individual comes out on top of any conflict with a collective community that takes place here. This is a Britain that may well have never experienced the welfare state or the social revolutions of the 20th century; it is only imaginable as a Victorian dream of the future. Just as one would expect, therefore, in this universe, all problems still have rational solutions based on the sorting of information, all of which is tangible; indeed, totalizing explanations of all history, science, and culture are not only possible, but essential. Sherlock's deductions rely on them, as well as upon the myths of social and cultural unities, the invariable distinctions of class hierarchies, universal ethnic as well as national values, and a master narrative of technological progression. The idea of contingent truths and pluralized disunity does not seem to inform the program at all. Ideologically speaking, *Sherlock* seems to depict disturbing normative hierarchies unabashedly and without interrogation. It wants, apparently, to retain the comfortable traditionalism of Conan Doyle's world, combined with what it perceives as the streamlined sexiness of ours. As a result, it cannot afford to recognize or reflect on the regressiveness of either, for fear of sacrificing the myth of clarity in favor of the contemporary reality of mutually contradictory truths.

In his meditation on postmodernism, *Postmodernist Culture*, Steven Connor writes that

> self-reflection is, if anything, more significant than the reflection upon, or description of contemporary culture which seemed to be offered in postmodernist critical theory. Postmodernism finds its object neither wholly in the cultural sphere, nor wholly in the critical-institutional sphere, but in some tensely renegotiated space between the two [1997, 7].

By implicitly claiming that their program takes place not in this Victorian/21st century mash up, but in a "now" where we are apparently post-homophobic, post-racial, post-nationalist, post-misogynist and so on, it seems like *Sherlock* wants the trappings of postmodernism without being willing to do any of its self-reflective cultural work; it does exactly nothing to reject the dominant paradigm.

In "A Study in Pink," for instance, the question of whether Sherlock and John are queer (as has frequently been wondered about Holmes and Watson over the years) is raised explicitly. Everyone around the two men seems to assume that they are, including Sherlock's brother, their landlady, and various strangers. Finally, in a restaurant, they have a conversation about the matter, but only in order to dismiss the possibility. In interviews, when asked about this exchange, the producers explain that the characters are not actually queer, and certainly not for each other. Moffat remarks,

> It's just that thing of two blokes hanging around together living together — in this nice modern world it leads to people saying, "Oh, are they a couple?" And that's nice. I thought how the world has changed, there is no disapproval. How much more civilized the world has become [July 25, 2010; www.digitalspy.com].

But has it really become more civilized? In some ways, we could read the

Victorian text, which never alludes to sexual orientation explicitly, as *more* open to queer possibilities because there a reader could imagine that such possibilities remained unvoiced only because of the constraints of the period. Here, where the text can refer to the subject forthrightly, we might interpret the dismissal of queerness as "homosexual panic": the writers know that when two men live together these days, questions about sexual orientation will be raised and they must explicitly deny the possibility. I would argue that this is only the illusion of postmodernity; when we talk about queerness openly, but it is never really on the table as a feasible alternative, how far have we truly come?

For instance, when Sherlock is deducing the situation of Watson's sibling from the handed-down mobile, he (unlike Holmes in an analogous circumstance during *The Sign of Four*) actually gets one part of it wrong: he does not account for the possibility that Harry may be a lesbian sister. Their ability to deduce people's situations correctly from the minutest detail is evidence that both Sherlock and Holmes live in a world of social conformity; the fact that Sherlock is unsuccessful here might argue that *Sherlock*'s world isn't as normative as the Victorian era, although Sherlock himself may be. But Harry is invisible; much like the conversation between Sherlock and John, queerness is gestured at, but never actually present on screen. It is a choice that can't be followed through, any more than it could in a pre-modern world. Queer readings may exist, but they remain unauthorized, exerting no greater force on the text than they ever have.

The teasing of queer possibility on *Sherlock*—complete with lack of follow-through—does not end with Sherlock and John, however. Sherlock Holmes's nemesis Moriarty makes his appearance on the program complete with an assumption of queerness that also contributes to the totalizing discourse that infuses the program. Although queerness in a myriad of forms (for example, homosociality taken an extra subversive step, polysexuality, multiple identities) is often a marker of the postmodern, Moffat and Gatiss use its presence as a tactic to close off subversive readings and keep tight control of the narrative, while seeming to do the opposite; queerness here is tied to specifically controlled signs that only permit one interpretation and this determinate language is used by Moriarty to communicate with Sherlock. Moriarty's "gay" underwear, for instance, is a morpheme with only a single possible definition. Like the other gestures towards queerness I mention, it is only the image of a doorway, not the door itself.

Sherlock's Fan: Moriarty and the Portrayal of Fandom

Of course, sometimes fans choose to cut their own entrances into the narrative, regardless of the authors' intent. Fandom and its choices, in fact, have been tied to the story of Sherlock Holmes practically since its inception: the readership of Conan Doyle's mysteries — and therefore of Watson's memoirs — was probably its first example. Holmes's death in "The Final Problem" at the hands of Professor Moriarty caused distraught readers to wear black armbands in unprecedented mourning for a fictional character; the outcry was so severe that in 1903, the reluctant Conan Doyle was forced to bring Holmes back to life with "The Adventure of the Empty House," demonstrating for perhaps the first time, the power that readers can exert over a narrative in which they are invested. Sherlockians in particular can be very invested in their ownership of the narrative, as they play The Great Game, where Holmes and Watson are assumed to have really lived, and Conan Doyle to be no more than their literary agent. The ludic potentials of such fannish activity and its postmodern toppling of authorial dictatorship are fairly well established, and have been so for some time (Tobin 2006, 83).

When we think of such subversive fan work (and play) today, however, we're usually thinking about reading ostensibly straight narratives with a queer lens and more specifically slash fiction, which can be defined, according to critic Henry Jenkins, as "one of the most pervasive and distinctive genres of fan writing [positing] a romantic and sexual relationship between same-sex characters drawn from film, television, comic books, or popular fiction" (2006, 61). Fan writing in general, and perhaps slash in particular, is a postmodern project: it challenges the domination of the author over the text with an overwhelming plurality of signs, readings and potentially subversive queer interpretations. With dissemination over the Internet, it also utilizes the instant technologies that seem to be emblematic of postmodernism in the popular imagination. Opening the door on queer possibilities only to close it, as I have suggested *Sherlock* can be read as doing, seems like a rejection of this phenomenon, but fan writing is not so easily silenced, and there is still an immense body of it based on the program. However, it's interesting that although Holmes and Watson continue to live a rich and varied extra-canonical life (of which *Sherlock* itself is only one example), the narrative of this supposedly postmodern program includes a portrayal of fandom, which seems quite condemnatory.

In "The Great Game" we discover that Watson's blog and Sherlock's web site have attracted a new reader: Moriarty. Described by Sherlock as "a fan," he follows the detective on the Internet just as a contemporary fan would. However, though he uses social networking tools to create an in-universe narrative, he is doing so in order to lure Sherlock and John toward their confrontation with him. Thus, in one stroke, the fannish reader has been conflated with the villain of the piece; instead of saving Sherlock Holmes and bringing him back to life, his reader/fan is trying to kill or defeat him. Through this device, the reader's power over the narrative has been rendered malign and, undoubtedly, impotent — since it is clear that Moriarty's scheme is not going to work in the end. Elsewhere in this volume, Ellen Burton Harrington makes a beautifully nuanced argument that also reads Moriarty — a proactive rather than reactive figure — as a fan who constructs the plot; she concludes that his resonance with the show's creators/plotters, themselves fan writers, playfully celebrates fan writing itself. However, Moriarty's malevolence and the show-runners' resistance to fan readings that are not their own make it hard for me to read him as a celebratory authorial representation. I think Moffat and Gatiss reposition Moriarty as a fan in order to take the professional author's side against fandom, in an argument that was definitively lost in 1903 no less!

This impression of authorial control, which undercuts and chokes off alternative readings with its universalizing discourse, does not lend itself to a postmodern authorial model of plurality. It does, however, mirror all the other ways in which the show-runners gesture towards multiplicity while simultaneously asserting their own "one true narrative." Just as *Sherlock*'s universe seems to long for a simpler future-of-the-past, where every problem has a single solution, the program's interaction with its fandom seems to demonstrate a nostalgic yearning for a past in which the author could act as benevolent despot, determining by fiat how the text was to be read and completed in the mind of the reader.

It's ironic that the potential democratization of the narrative has been subverted in this adaptation of the very text that first inspired the fannish impulse. But this should come as no surprise; it's like all the other dazzlingly flashy postmodern gestures and theoretical challenges to the dominant paradigm in *Sherlock*'s narrative. While the program constantly points to its contemporary exterior, it's all smoke and mirrors endlessly obscuring and reflecting a vision of the past in order to make us think it's the present.

Works Cited

Benjamin, Walter. 1999. *The arcades project,* ed. Rolf Tiederman. Cambridge: Harvard University Press.

Connor, Steven. 1997. *Postmodernist culture.* Oxford: Blackwell.

Deleuze, Gilles. 1993. Cinema and space: The frame. In *The Deleuze reader,* ed. Constantin V. Boundas, 173–179. New York: Columbia University Press.

Jameson, Fredric. 1982. Progress versus utopia, or: Can we imagine the future? *Science Fiction Studies,* 9: 147–158.

_____. 1985. Postmodernism and consumer society. In *Postmodern Culture,* ed. Hal Foster, 111–125. London: Pluto Press.

Jenkins, Henry. 2006. *Fans, bloggers and gamers: Exploring participatory culture.* New York: New York University Press.

Nevins, Jess. 2008. The 19th century roots of steampunk. In *Steampunk,* ed. Ann and Jeff Vandermeer, 3–12. San Francisco: Tachyon.

Thomas, Roland. 1999. *Detective fiction and the rise of forensic science.* Cambridge: Cambridge University Press.

Tobin, Vera. 2006. Ways of reading Sherlock Holmes: the entrenchment of discourse blends. *Language and Literature* 15(1): 73–90.

Sherlock as Cyborg

Bridging Mind and Body

FRANCESCA COPPA

Abstract — A postmodern man-machine, Benedict Cumberbatch's Sherlock is popular with fan fiction writers because he evokes the figure of the cyborg: the binary-straddling hybrid of machine and organism that Donna Haraway describes as a site of progressive possibility. While people have been writing new stories about Sherlock Holmes almost since his inception, the fan fiction writers of media fandom, a community historically comprised predominantly of women, have a specific history of rewriting mass media texts so as to integrate somatic experiences into the narrative. As a character who claims his body is just for transport, the famously cerebral Sherlock offers fans a distinctive (though not unique) invitation to imagine how he might express his sexuality within a relationship; in this respect, Sherlock is just the most recent of a long line of beloved "aliens," of which *Star Trek's* Mr. Spock was arguably the first. A distinctive subgroup of *Sherlock* fan fiction stories argue that Cumberbatch's Sherlock embodies one of many complex forms of asexual sexuality, the articulation of which challenges the limited categorization of sexuality as either gay or straight. These stories show the continued power of the cyborg, and of fan fiction, to blur mind-body boundaries and overcome either/or thinking.

Introduction: Sherlock as Cyborg

Sherlock Holmes came into the world a transmedia figure, instantly and iconically characterized by a deerstalker hat and Inverness cape that originate, not in Sir Arthur Conan Doyle's stories, but in Sidney Paget's contemporary paratextual drawings. These clothes gave Holmes his distinctive physical silhouette, and Paget's visualization of Holmes is at least partly responsible for the ease and rapidity with which Holmes transcended text and moved into the medium of performance.

Theatrical and filmic adaptations of Holmes are, by necessity, more focused on Sherlock's body than are Conan Doyle's short stories, which tend to emphasize Holmes's abstract mental processes and deductive prowess. In fact, Holmes's body in Conan Doyle's fiction is by turns invisible, polymorphic, or problematical, there to be repressed or overlooked, both within the stories and by the reader. Holmes's body is subject to his will: disciplined by drugs, it is also infinitely mutable, capable of any disguise, even appearing to change height. But Holmes's body functions differently on stage and screen, and more recent incarnations — featuring heartthrobs such as Rupert Everett, James D'Arcy, and Robert Downey Jr.— have focused as much, if not more attention on Holmes the physical man as Holmes the mind.

This tendency has perhaps reached its apogee with Benedict Cumberbatch's Holmes in the BBC's recent miniseries, *Sherlock*. Cumberbatch's portrayal of Holmes as a tall, artistically dressed young man clutching a Blackberry is an almost perfect synthesis of man and machine. One the one hand, he is a highly Romantic figure, almost Byronic with his flowing black hair, long coat, and trailing scarf; on the other, he first appears to us in the cold and disembodied form of a text message: a personality of pixels. Both Sherlock himself and the show's omniscient perspective seem to see him more as a technology than as a person; Sherlock refers to his brain as a "hard drive" (in Conan Doyle's stories, Holmes conceptualizes his mental storage space more physically as an "attic"), and the *mise en scene* visualizes Sherlock's thought processes in a manner more suited to explicating the workings of a search engine than those of the little gray cells of the brain.

In fact, both *Sherlock,* the show, and Sherlock, the character, repeatedly swoop between embodied and disembodied positions, hybridizing three-dimensional space and cyberspace. This Sherlock, who self-identifies as a sociopath, likely because he so nakedly prefers technology to people, seems to have both a biological and synecdochal relationship to his PDA. He has a Blackberry for a hand and appears to see London — depicted from above in a hyperreal series of shots that make the city seem like a child's toy — with the eyes of nothing so natural or organic as a bird, but rather with the satellite's eye view of something more akin to Google Earth.

As a result, we have a Sherlock Holmes who is denoted both by a highly iconic physical body rushing around London and by a disembodied cognitive self which hurtles across the web in search of links and information. Cumberbatch captures Holmes's physicality as delineated in canon — his rapid transitions between languor and energy, for instance — and invents for Holmes the kind of ecstatic, far-away stare that solves the actor's eternal problem of how to visually depict cognitive inspiration, but which here looks like nothing so much as "processing mode."

This Sherlock is, in Donna Haraway's terms, a cyborg, which is to say, not a robot or a machine but "a hybrid of machine and organism" (1991, 149) which Haraway argues is a site of "transgressed boundaries, potent fusions, and dangerous possibilities which progressive people might explore as one part of needed political work" (1991, 154). Part of that work is to intervene in "the tradition of racist, male-dominant capitalism; the tradition of progress; the tradition of the appropriation of nature as resource for the productions of culture" (1991, 150), which arguably extends as far back as Aristotle, but took its modern form and force during the late Victorian era, or the original age of Sherlock Holmes.

While Conan Doyle's Holmes employs Victorian technologies — he rushes for trains, sends cablegrams, and makes strategic use of mass media forms like the classified ad and the agony column — these are the industrial tools of an outwardly-directed, colonialist "tradition of progress," not the cybernetic tools which *Sherlock* uses to hybridize the embodied self. Conan Doyle's Holmes engages — and disengages — with the tools of his age, while Sherlock's technologies are so much a part of him as to have changed his relationship to the normal: the difference between smoking a pipe and wearing a patch. If, as Ellen Burton Harrington claims, Conan Doyle glorifies the man of science in ways that "consolidate a normative national identity" (2007, 365), *Sherlock* presents a far more disruptive persona. Haraway argues not only that the cyborg represents the change from "an organic, industrial society to a polymorphous, information system" (1991, 161) but also that it embodies both radical politics and revolutionary potential, particularly for women and other sexual minorities.

This is not at all the same as saying that the paradigmatically rational Holmes might be ideally realized as a supercrunching computer (see McAleer 1994), or that he has a personality well suited to cyberspace. Such ideas are neither new nor revolutionary; Heinlein among others named a fictional computer HOLMES, and the UK police run an actual database called the "Home Office Large Major Enquiry System." In her 1997 essay "It's Always 1985: Sherlock Holmes in Cyberspace," Roberta Pearson talks about the ways in which Holmes fans use the Internet to obsessively gather and trade information about their hero, and elsewhere in this volume, Matt Hills argues that the BBC's *Sherlock* is constructed so as to "ideologically and narratively" validate the obsessive epistemological practices of this kind of online fan. But these creations and arguments imply a schema in which the signifier "Holmes" stands for a series of rational intellectual processes that would attain perfection only when set *apart* from the body; or, to put in another way, they still seem invested in a classical framework that reaches (as Haraway warned it would) back to Greece: to a platonic ideal of abstraction, a perfection only obtainable at the expense of *transcending* the body.

I want to make the opposite argument: that, as cyborg rather than a computer, the BCC's new Sherlock is a machine/human hybrid whose cerebral processes are not confined to the cerebrum; his brain is in his clapping hands, in nicotine-enhanced blood, in his Blackberry, in the nearest cell phone tower: he is streaming across the network. This Sherlock knows he has a body and struggles with it; on the one hand claiming that his body is mere "transport"; on the other, describing a particular case as a "three-patch" problem, meaning that he requires three nicotine patches' worth of stimulants to solve it. This Sherlock is not just a figure of science, but of science fiction, and his blurring of organic/mechanical and mind/body boundaries calls other important boundaries into question: as Haraway notes, the cyborg puts "dichotomies of public and private, nature and culture, men and women, primitive and civilized" (1991, 163) into ideological question. The collapse of those binaries can be seen as marking an end of the white, male, Western, industrial narrative which was in full swing when Conan Doyle published his stories; today, Sherlock Holmes is an easily-fetishized cyborg whose sexuality, morality, and even sanity are questioned within the text.

This version of Sherlock has consequently, and not at all incidentally, been embraced by female fans — in particular, the predominantly female community of media fans studied in ethnographies from Camille Bacon Smith's *Enterprising Women* to Henry Jenkins' *Textual Poachers* and more recently described in works like Karen Hellekson and Kristina Busse's *Fan Fiction and Fan Cultures in the Age of the Internet*. While people have been writing new stories about Sherlock Holmes almost since his inception, the traditions of media fandom are analogous to, but distinct from, the history of literary pastiche; moreover, the fan fiction community has a strikingly different composition, featuring women of all sexual orientations and significant numbers of gay men and transmen. The popularity of Cumberbatch's Sherlock with the media fan fiction community is not simply a matter of his sexual attractiveness (Robert Downey Jr. is a fan favorite, but his Holmes has not inspired the same level of devotion) or even slashability, that is, openness to a queer reading (Holmes and Watson have always been paradigmatically slashable.) Rather, I would argue that it is the emphatic performance of a mind-body struggle that attracts female media fans — and always has. I have previously argued that famous fan avatars like *Star Trek*'s Mr. Spock — a character as famous for his pointy ears and alien physiology as for his logical brain — have to some extent served as stand-ins for the intellectual and often scientifically-minded women who identify as science-fiction fans (and who know all too well what it's like to have parts of your anatomy be the subject of public commentary); I have also argued that fan fiction is a genre that appeals to women because of its essentially transmedia quality: fan fiction is a mélange of textual, visual, and performative genres. fan fiction turns television into text, and allows female fanwriters to direct a corpus of familiar, iconic bodies — Captain Kirk, Buffy Summers, Lex Luthor — in scripts of their own devising (Coppa 2006). By writing about television and film characters, fan fiction writers assert the primacy of bodies even as they engage in creative activities that embody "the life of the mind."

The Lie of the Mind

However the detective story has historically been about the *lie* of the mind; that is, the assertion of intellectual superiority through a false pseudo-scientific performance. The modern literary detective emerges out of a Victorian male sense of science and rationality that was more pose than reality (and that has led, in its contemporary incarnations, to the impossible and unrealistic deductions of police procedurals like *CSI*). Both of the genre's two most significant innovators — Edgar Allan Poe and Conan Doyle — created private investigators that, true to the spirit of their age, were defined by their allegiance to ratiocination and the new, popular interest in science. Poe's seminal "The Murder in the Rue Morgue" begins with a treatise defining and celebrating analytical thought, and his detective, Auguste Dupin, has such keen powers of observation as to appear psychic. Sherlock Holmes, who was supposedly inspired by the diagnostic physician Joseph Bell, is similarly presented as someone whose insights result from meticulous observation and a disciplined deductive process: in short, both Poe and Conan Doyle suggest that any man with sufficient brains — properly trained and motivated — could come to their conclusions; any failure is your own. As Watson remarks in "A Scandal In Bohemia," "When I hear you give your reasons ... the thing always appears to me to be so ridiculously simple that I could easily do it myself, though at each successive instance of your reasoning I am baffled until you explain your process," to which Holmes famously responds, "You see, but you do not observe" (I:10).

But the detective story isn't science; in fact, in its absolute un-reproducibility of result, it is *anti*-science. Despite the attempt by "golden age" mystery writers to codify rules of fair play — that is, to give the reader "all the clues needed to enable him to anticipate the solution by the exercise of his logic and common sense" (Crispin 1962, 7) — a reader can't actually *solve* a mystery novel; she can only *guess*. The job of the mystery writer is to stage a *performance* of fairness, something that lets readers believe that they could have figured it out if only they'd been as smart as the detective. But this game is, by definition, rigged. A detective's explanation of his chain of reasoning is not a demonstration of scientific process or even mental agility: it is a magic trick that leaves its audience *oohing* and *ahhing* in amazement.

As a teacher, I am particularly sensitive to the falseness of this perform-ance, the essential lie of it, because for all of detective fiction's endless expli-cation of method, nobody — within or outside of the story — ever actually learns anything, and of course they can't. Sherlock Holmes may be able glance at Watson's boots and immediately conclude he's been to a Turkish bath, but it's not a genuinely reasoned conclusion (which is of course why detective stories are so open to parody; Holmes can glance at Watson's boots and con-clude that he's been to a square dancing festival; a sheep-shearing contest; the moon.) Nonetheless, from Poe onwards, fictional detectives have lectured their companions — and often a story's entire cast of suspects expressly assembled for the purpose, not to mention the reader — with the ostensibly educational purpose of training their weak, undisciplined minds.

It's only when women come to the forefront of mystery fiction that the detective's elaborate ratiocinations begin to be seen as false. Ironically, it is the genre's famous *female* authors — Agatha Christie, Ngaio Marsh, Dorothy Sayers, etc. — whose work is typically criticized for being overly cerebral. Once defined by the brilliant mental processes of its male Victorian detectives, the mystery genre as helmed by women in the 1920s and 1930s was criticized as artificial; bloodless; lacking physical (and explicitly masculine and sexual) vitality; that is, of not being embodied *enough*. In his famous essay "The Sim-ple Art of Murder," Raymond Chandler critiques detective fiction for being both intellectual and effeminate: a radical switch of conventional binaries that mark the mind as male and the body as female. Chandler gives Conan Doyle and Sherlock Holmes an almost dismissive free pass: "Conan Doyle made mistakes which completely invalidated some of his stories, but he was a pio-neer, and Sherlock Holmes after all is mostly an attitude and a few dozen lines of unforgettable dialogue" (Chandler 1950, 5). Nevertheless, he com-plains that detective fiction is too cut off from embodied realities, which results in a distorted and false picture of the world:

> The master of rare knowledge is living psychologically in the age of the hoop skirt. If you know all you should know about ceramics and Egyptian needlework, you don't know anything at all about the police. If you know that platinum won't melt under about 2800 degrees F. by itself, but will melt at the glance of a pair of deep blue eyes when put close to a bar of lead, then you don't know how men make love in the twentieth century [Chandler 1950, 4].

Here, detective writers are explicitly feminized and disembodied; Chan-dler's references to hoop skirts, ceramics, and needlework depict these authors as effeminate and spinsterish ("the flustered old ladies of both sexes [or no sex]," as Chandler puts it) as well as lacking any understanding of "real" violence or "real" sex (as "real" American men presumably do) (Chandler 1950, 16). Chandler is, of course, advocating for his own kind of detective fiction, the hard-boiled American crime novel that came out of so-called "pulp" fiction, was made popular by Dashiell Hammett, and itself went trans-media through film noir.

The hard-boiled crime story is certainly, as Chandler suggests, a more embodied form (revealingly, Chandler refers to Hammett's writing as "meaty" while traditional detective characters are mere "cardboard"). And the emphasis on the body, on the carnality of sex and violence, is part of why these stories translate so well to cinema and other media (including, most recently, video games such as *L.A. Noire* [2011]). The hard-boiled crime story is perhaps even more successful in performance than on paper, but in all its forms it has been a male fantasy of hypermasculine P.I.'s and slinky *femme fatales*. A mere glance at the covers of pulp novels will provide enough scantily clad, impossibly long-legged vixens to sustain a charge of first-degree misogyny, or at least reveal an extremely sexist cultural fantasy, though recent work by Gregory Forter, paralleling Carol Clover's groundbreaking work on the horror movie, has argued that hard-boiled crime is not simply a masculinist fantasy but a masochistic one: a male fantasy of relinquishing power and becoming a vulnerable, beaten, and life-threatened body (see *Detective Mysteries*, whose cover depicts a powerful and a vulnerable man almost as two sides of the same coin, or perhaps in a homoerotic embrace).

But where does this leave the woman reader, setting aside for now the notion that she might engage with the male masochistic or homoerotic fantasy? With whom is a smart, physical, modern woman to identify? One line of Sherlock Holmes's literary descendants, the pre-dominantly female writers who perfected the ingeniously constructed puzzles of the Golden Age, have been criticized as sexless old biddies; another line, the male writers whose private eyes walk the mean streets of— not of Victorian London, but those of San Francisco or New York — are interested in the body but seem to see women only as malevolent or threatening sexual objects; that is, if they're not the story's murdered victims. Miss Marple or Veronica Lake: these are not ideal points of identification. With so many women in mainstream detective fiction reduced to frigid minds or objectified bodies, the importance of the figure of the cyborg, who signifies bothness and otherness, becomes clear.

The Truth of the Body

The BBC's *Sherlock* makes apparent the lie of the mind from the very first episode, at least to anyone familiar with Sir Arthur Conan Doyle's stories.

In "A Study in Pink," Sherlock discovers a dead woman whose last act was to carve RACHE into the floor with her fingernails. A policeman, lounging in the doorway behind him, suggests that the woman was German, and that "Rache" is German for revenge, whereupon Sherlock says, "Thank you for your input," and slams the door in his face. Sherlock's solution is that the woman was in the process of writing the name Rachel — "No other word it can be." — but in Conan Doyle's *A Study in Scarlet*, the roles are reversed: it is the plodding policeman who says, "You mark my words, when this case comes to be cleared up you will find that a woman named Rachel has something to do with it," and Holmes who deduces the actual solution: "'Rache' is the German for 'revenge'; so don't lose your time looking for Miss Rachel."

What we get instead of the demonstration of a fake scientific process is Cumberbatch performing the rush he gets from the rapid-fire (and machine-aided) processing of information: what appears to be a surge of almost orgasmic joy. This Sherlock Holmes doesn't appear to believe that everyone can do what he can do, even if they take the infinite pains that genius requires; instead, he makes disparaging remarks like "Dear God, what must it be like in your funny little brains; it must be so boring" (ASiP), suggesting that he himself is not simply different from them in *method*, but in *kind*: in *species*. This is Sherlock the cyborg, lying on a sofa with his Blackberry in his hand and three nicotine patches on his arm, boosting his brainpower through both circuitry and chemistry. Holmes's "three pipe problem," a measure of time ("I beg that you won't speak to me for fifty minutes"), has been replaced by Sherlock's three patch problem: a measure of chemical intensity in the bloodstream. "Breathing is boooooring," Sherlock intones, sounding like no one so much as Marvin the Paranoid Android from the *Hitchhiker's Guide to the Galaxy* ("Here I am, brain the size of a planet..."), but this Sherlock is too organic and too excitable to be a robot, or even a Nexus 6 replicant. He takes too much physical pleasure — laughing, clapping, gasping, running down stairs — in the cerebral work of creating patterns out of information, even as he sees his body as secondary.

But the real drama of *Sherlock* turns on the question of whether or not Sherlock the cyborg, under John Watson's influence, will be able develop the moral emotional responses (the "heart," so to speak; the *felt* experience) he needs to be a true hero. For, despite all the pseudo-deductive dithering about whether the dead woman has scrawled "Rache" or "Rachel" in "A Study in Pink," Sherlock fails the plot's key test of knowledge: when it is revealed that Rachel was the woman's still-born daughter, Sherlock blithely says to a shocked room: "That was ages ago: why would she still be upset?" In spite of — or perhaps because of — his souped-up brains and wired-up body, Sherlock, like Mr. Spock before him, produces a range of startlingly alien (non)emotional responses. To evoke Chandler's critique, the greatest mind in the world here seems not to understand grief, or loss, or — implicitly — love: but in *Sherlock* that inability is thematized and problematized in the show itself.

I have written before about how female fans both identify with and desire Mr. Spock as a figure representing hybridity (Coppa 2008, [3.12]): human and alien, male and female, heterosexual and homosexual, reason and emotion, control and desire. Similarly, *Sherlock*, by putting all these binaries on the table — man and machine, intellect and desire, public and private, nature and culture, primitive and civilized, sane and crazy, straight and gay — but not quite managing to put them together in a way that looks normal (or, to flip that, by giving them to us in a form that evokes the alien), attracts a female and queer mediafannish audience that is looking to renegotiate and integrate these binaries in new ways for themselves. As a man-machine who gets physical pleasure from doing cerebral work, the cyborg Sherlock is already undoing the kinds of false binaries that fans are interested in reimagining through creating fan fiction and other transformative works.

In her recent blog post, "sex, and slash scenes," longtime fan Shoshanna explains that slash, a genre of fan fiction which is not only homoerotic but also tends to be sexually explicit, was important to her because it tore down the false barrier between sex and the rest of human experience: "[I]t was the first literature I ever saw that integrated people's (characters') sex lives with their lives outside of bed" (Shoshanna April 5, 2011; www.dreamwidth.org). She notes that in most genres of fiction, "people maybe had sex, but the narrative never showed exactly how they carried themselves, how they interacted with their partners," while in pornography "the characters had no regular lives; they pretty much just had sex." And then there was slash fiction:

> Slash was the *only* genre of literature I had ever found that followed the characters into bed and back out of it; that investigated and demonstrated how the people they were outside of bed were connected to the people they were in bed; that modeled how to be with someone in everyday life, go to bed with them, and then wake up next to them and continue everyday life with them. In slash, "everyday life" wasn't differentiated from "sex life." Who people were outside of bed and during the day critically, obviously, *demonstrably* influenced how they behaved in bed with each other, and vice versa.... The two parts of life weren't disjunct; indeed, they were crucially connected, mutually influential, even indivisible. In fact, that indivisibility was often *the whole point.*

"Indivisible," "connected," "mutually influential": Shoshanna's post is all about erasing false narrative boundaries between "the two parts of life," everyday life and sex life. In most fan fiction, "everyday life" correlates with a character's work life (starship captain, Hogwarts student, Time Lord, consulting detective) while "sex life" encompasses a broad range of romantic relationships and erotic complications. In identifying slash as that rare literature that connects who we are in bed with who we are outside of it, Shoshanna explicitly critiques mainstream storytelling for giving short shrift to important areas of human experience. Shoshanna's focus is obviously on sex and sexuality, but I would add that mainstream storytelling tends to ignore large areas of embodied experience: characters in television and film rarely stop to eat, shower, fulfill caregiving obligations, or even go to the bathroom, though fan fiction is obsessed with all these things. In other words, Shoshanna sees mainstream media narratives as providing a view of reality as narrow and stunted in its way as pornography is commonly thought to be; in fact, because fan fiction always supplements a larger narrative (Coppa 2006; Derecho 2006), even the most pornographic or otherwise apparently contextless fan story is always already in context, for example, the context of *Star Trek*, *Harry Potter*, or *Doctor Who*.

Because of this supplemental quality, fan fiction corrects this narrow worldview, and not only erotic fan fiction like slash. All fan fiction, to the extent to which is fleshes out (pun intended) parts of a universe that haven't yet been seen or tells stories that haven't been told, is interested in expanding the depiction of experience in that universe; moreover, fan fiction is as likely to focus on precisely those small practical details that comprise a character's daily life — food on the Enterprise, entertainment options on Atlantis, bathrooms on the TARDIS — as on their extraordinary heroic adventures; or more accurately, it is likely to connect the practical details of life *to* those extraordinary adventures the way that slash connects the self in and out of bed. So in fan fiction we have a literature that unifies not only "everyday life" and "sex life," but the heroic and the domestic, the professional and the pornographic. It is a literature written by (and for) the sexual mind and the intellectual body.

A Case in Point: Asexual Sexuality

In the fandom for the BBC's *Sherlock,* fans are not only writing slash stories that extend Sherlock and John's partnership from the consulting room into the bedroom, thereby erasing mainstream distinctions between their work life, their domestic arrangement, and their sexual selves, but also creating artworks that complicate the very binary of gay/straight. A substantial subcategory of fanworks created about *Sherlock* give Sherlock an asexual (or *ace*) sexual identity, defined by the Asexual Visibility and Education Network as "a person who does not experience sexual attraction" (asexuality.org). Asexuality advocates argue that asexuality is wrongly seen as a phase, problem, or disorder when it is a sexual identity as rich and nuanced as any other. Asexuals may define themselves as romantically inclined or aromantic; they may be gay, straight or other; and in practice, may be found in any kind of relationship, sexual or otherwise. They may even have a strong sex drive, but that drive may not be other-directed.

The character of Sherlock Holmes has long been adopted as a symbol by the asexual community, appearing alongside such figures as Ozymandias from Alan Moore's *The Watchmen*, The Professor from *Gilligan's Island*, and the classic-era Doctors Who in lists of fictional asexuals at sites like TV Tropes, the AVENwiki, and Fanlore. But the *Sherlock* BBC series coincides with a renewed wave of interest in queer sexualities beyond gay, lesbian, and bisexual, and within which the acronym LGBTQ (Lesbian, Gay, Bisexual, Transgender, Queer/Questioning) is in the process of being supplanted by the longer QUILTBAG (Queer/Questioning, Undecided, Intersex, Lesbian, Trans, Bisexual, Asexual, Gay). So it is both a matter of this version of Holmes being particularly open to a modern asexual interpretation and that an asexual-interested audience in fandom has emerged, self-defined and articulate about its interest, to create works about Sherlock. Cumberbatch himself, for example, has noted that he thinks Sherlock is "asexual, rather than gay or bisexual" (Tim Oglethorpe, "Sherlock's Got Sexy," July 23, 2010; www.dailymail.co.uk), though his idea of asexuality does not accord with those of activists.

In their various blog posts and manifestos, fans have not only argued for Sherlock's asexuality, but have made fine distinctions about how and in what context he experiences his asexuality. In "Sherlock Holmes: Poster Boy for the Aven," Saucery argues that Sherlock is a romantic asexual; that is, "he is equally uninterested in men and women — sexually, that is — but there is one person and one person alone that interests him emotionally, and that is John Watson, the man with whom he is, given all the canonical evidence, in love" (Saucery August 17, 2010; LiveJournal). Another fan, writing as scienceofdeduction, cites this post in her "Ace Manifesto" posted to asexual-fandom before counter arguing that Sherlock may in fact be an aromantic asexual:

> Interestingly, not a lot has been written about Sherlock possibly being an aromantic asexual, possibly because of how incredibly possessive he tends to be about John. Case in point: Sherlock effectively cock-blocks John on his date...
> However ... Sherlock never demonstrates any overtly romantic undertones toward John in any way, and it would appear that John has no romantic feelings to reciprocate. This is definitely room to explore, for obviously these two men have a very complicated relationship together [scienceofdeduction October 24, 2010; www.livejournal.com].

Sherlock fan fiction has explored a variety of asexual characterizations (including gray–A, hyposexual, demisexual, semisexual, and others) with great specificity. In fact, in a recent blog post at asexual_fandom, Melannen outlined "50 caring consensual sexual situations for at least one ace character," using the nondescript character-marker names, "Alex" and "Bailey" (April 26, 2011; www.dreamwidth.org). Her 50 scenarios include:

> 6. Alex sleeps around a lot because pretending to be sexual is a survival strategy. When Alex starts sleeping with Bailey, Bailey slowly realizes that something is wrong, and together they figure out another way to be together.
> 25. Alex and Bailey start dating and agree to try sex. Alex surprises both of them by actually liking it, and has to struggle with how to reconcile being sexually active and liking it with an asexual identity.
> 38. Alex is a virgin, but wants to try sex with another person just once, just to see what it's like, so asks Bailey, and Bailey tries to show Alex how it can be good. The result isn't a life-changing experience for either of them, but it's a treasured memory for both.

These scenarios are a lot more nuanced than conventional representations of sexual desire, action, or orientation (which are routinely given short-shrift anyway). Melannen's plots articulate something subtler than *either* gay or straight, *either* wanting sex or not, and they require characters not only to pay close attention to their own minds and bodies and those of their partners, but also to be willing to revise their expectations and understanding of themselves based on experience. Bailey "slowly realizes that something is wrong" over the course of the story, or Alex "has to struggle" with how to reconcile his sense of self with his lived experience. This, I would argue, is more of a demonstration of a reproducible scientific process than is the literary detective's performance of deduction. It also stages the close observation and out-of-the-box thinking that characterizes great detective work: or, to put it another way, in matters of sexuality as well as murder, whatever remains once you have eliminated the impossible must be the truth.

In fact, in *Sherlock* fan fiction, sexuality is the primary mystery that needs investigating, and any ostensible "case" is just an opportunity for a sexy performance by Sherlock. For example, in Kantayra's "The Elephant in the Room," we are given a glimpse of Sherlock working on a case that we otherwise hear absolutely nothing about:

> "Westcott," Sherlock mumbled under his breath. "Westcott, Westcott ... Ah! Harold." He snatched up two strips of paper and pressed them together neatly, side by side. "But why did he arrange the fireworks? Oh. Oh!" Sherlock jerked to his feet with the burst of frenetic energy that accompanied all his revelations [Kantayra 2011; archiveofourown.org].

Sherlock's muttered thoughts might, in another story, be a parody of deduction, but here, they're sincere and important as a marker of what makes Sherlock attractive to John (who responds to this performance by checking out Sherlock's ass.) You might think that this would lead to a sexual relationship, but no: the story concludes with John, not turning gay for Sherlock, but turning into a romantic asexual for him. John concludes that in his love relationship with Sherlock, the detective cases *are* the sex:

> It wasn't like sex at all, and yet — somehow — it was. The jolt of adrenaline when a new case first arose, the long build-up as they investigated, and finally the climax when Sherlock's mind inevitably conquered the most perplexing mysteries.... They had even, John thought with some amusement, had themselves a rather pleasant morning-after today [Kantayra 2011; archiveofourown.org].

While asexual stories are currently popular in *Sherlock* fandom, they are not by any means the norm in fan fiction broadly speaking; however, I do believe they are emblematic of the female media fan's desire to blur boundaries and unite binaries. Fans have always been interested in thinking through conflicts like those between mind and body, work and romance, friendship and sex, desire and lived experience, and have invented genres like slash, emo-porn, and smarm to parse them out. In this cultural moment, asexuality is one of the ways in which fans are redrawing the sexual map. From that perspective, we can see these stories as just a specific manifestation of a larger trend, and Sherlock as just a particular incarnation of fannish cyborg: the most recent in a line of fannish BSOs (Beloved Sex Objects) that includes *Star Trek: The Next Generation*'s Data, *The X-Files'* Fox Mulder, and *Stargate Atlantis'* John Sheppard. At the same time, this Sherlock seems to be a particularly generative representation; as I noted earlier, other recent portrayals of Holmes have not triggered this outpouring of fan response, nor have they been taken up by the asexual community to this degree. So while asexuality may be a newly-assertive sexual identity currently embraced by fans, it is also fair to say that something special about Sherlock has put him at the center of something new in fan culture.

That being said, there are resonances in *Sherlock* fan fiction that go back to the very foundations of modern media fandom. Gene Roddenberry, who supported *Star Trek* fans in general and Kirk/Spock slashers in particular, formally acknowledged the gay reading of their relationship with a footnote in the novelization of the first *Star Trek* movie, but explained — or, more oddly, had Captain Kirk himself explain, in first person — that as human and alien, he and Spock wouldn't be sexually compatible:

> As for myself, although I have no moral or other objections to physical love in any of its many Earthly, alien, and mixed forms, I have always found my best gratification in that creature *woman*. Also, I would dislike being thought of as so foolish that I would select a love partner who came into sexual heat only once every seven years [Roddenberry 22].

In other words, Kirk argues that he doesn't have any moral or intellectual objection to homosexuality, it's just that he and Spock have mismatched sexual drives. While Kirk's acceptance of homosexuality is advanced for 1979 (if not for 2271, when the story takes place), his explanation still puts an obstacle in the way of the most famous romance in media fandom: their minds may meld, but their bodies keep them apart. Thirty years later, *Sherlock* fans would overcome that particular iteration of the mind-body problem by writing stories in which another tall alien genius and his canonical life partner come to sexual terms, demonstrating a continuing interest in the "transgressed boundaries, potent fusions, and dangerous possibilities" the cyborg represents.

Works Cited

Chandler, Raymond. 1950. The simple art of murder: An essay. In *The simple art of murder.* New York: Vintage Books.

Clover, Carol. 1993. *Men, women, and chainsaws: Gender in the modern horror film.* Princeton: Princeton University Press.

Coppa, Francesca. 2006. Writing bodies in space: Media fan fiction as theatrical performance. In *Fan fiction and fan communities in the age of the Internet,* ed. Karen Hellekson and Kristina Busse, 225–44. Jefferson, N.C.: McFarland.

_____. 2008. Women, *Star Trek,* and the early development of fannish vidding. *Transformative Works and Cultures,* no. 1. *journal.transformativeworks.org.*

Crispin, Edmund. 1962. Foreword. *Beware of the trains.* New York: Walker.

Derecho, Abigail. 2006. Archontic literature: A definition, a history, and several theories of fan fiction." In *Fan fiction and fan communities in the age of the Internet,* ed. Karen Hellekson and Kristina Busse, 61–78. Jefferson, NC: McFarland.

Detection Club. 1979. *The floating Admiral.* Upper Saddle River, N.J.: Gregg Press.

Forter, Gregory. 2000. *Murdering masculinities: Fantasies of gender and violence in the American crime novel.* New York: New York University Press.

Haraway, Donna. 1991. A cyborg manifesto: Science, technology, and socialist-feminism in the late twentieth century. In *Simians, cyborgs and women: The reinvention of nature,* 149–81. New York: Routledge.

Harrington, Ellen Burton. 2007. Nation, identity, and the fascination with forensic science in Sherlock Holmes and *CSI. International Journal of Cultural Studies,* 10:365–382.

McAleer, Michael. 1994. Sherlock Holmes and the search for truth: A diagnostic tale. *Journal of Economic Surveys* 8(4): 317–370.

Pearson, Roberta. 1997. "It's always 1985": Sherlock Holmes in cyberspace. In *Trash aesthetics: Popular culture and its audience,* ed. Deborah Cartmell, Heidi Kaye, Imelda Whelehan, and I.Q. Hunter, 143–161. London. Pluto Press.

Roddenberry, Gene. 1979. *Star Trek: The Motion Picture.* New York: Pocket Books.

Conclusion

Transmedia Sherlock and Beyond

Kristina Busse and Louisa Ellen Stein

London Burning

As we finish this collection in early August 2011, we are surrounded by reports of violent riots all over London and other British urban centers. Reading *Sherlock* and the arguments in this collection against contemporary politics and media coverage suggests more contrast than comparison. Images of baseball bats and lawless collectives are a far cry from the *Sherlock* series cliffhanger. Moriarty's poolside bomb serves as the latest incarnation of his individual (and as Ellen Burton Harrington argues, even personal) brand of terror, where in contrast the images of rioting in London are bound up in discourses of political and generational unrest. And yet the images of violence at the heart of Great Britain reassert the need for political and ideological readings of the show to not only accompany but inform the literary, historical, televisual, theoretical, and aesthetic interpretations we have offered. Indeed, as Basu suggests, the overly aestheticized images that make *Sherlock* so stand out themselves hold political and ideological weight, infusing London's hypermodernity with nostalgia, and thereby creating a very particular vision of the city, a vision that couldn't be farther from the omnipresent representations of rioting London youth.

When looking at *Sherlock*'s London and the city we see ravaged on TV at the moment, we can't help but note how the show's imaginary landscape covers over the social, political, and economic realities of a country torn by immigration and multicultural conflicts and ravaged nationwide unemployment. Considering the social capital of Sherlock Holmes in general and BBC productions in particular, the disparity raises the question as to what "imagined community," as Benedict Anderson describes it, the new *Sherlock* creates, what Great Britain it represents and evokes. Most urban crime shows of the past decade set in London feature prominently poverty and joblessness, squalor and racial violence, council estate housing and institutional bureaucracy: *The Fixer* (2008–09), *Whitechapel* (2009–10), *Thorne* (2010), and *Luther* (2010–), to name only a few recent ones, depict a world that is congruent with the images we have seen in the past week. Whereas these shows visualize London as mostly urban and gritty, *Sherlock* in its stead creates a tension both in *what* and *how* the city is represented. *Sherlock* moves away from depicting industrial and poorer areas, in its place often showing London as a careful meeting of stately old city homes and the glass and chrome monuments of transnational postcapitalist corporations. While the series showcases a variety of public and private spaces, the overall image — as exemplified in the city skyline of the opening trailer — seems to create a virtual advertisement for the new post-industrial London.

The opening skyline also illustrates how the show succeeds in presenting a more glossified and aestheticized version of even the more mundane aspects of the city. In so doing, *Sherlock* doesn't merely overlook or ignore the realities of this multicultural metropolitan center but instead showcases the entirety of the city as if all aspects were part of this larger, shinier vision of London. The social anxiety that pervades the entire show, then, is the internal contradiction of economic uncertainty and limitations on the part of John (and, to some degree, Sherlock) at the same time as both go everywhere by taxi, rather than bus or tube (and indeed, as Balaka Basu argues, there are joint visual and ideological reasons for that choice, recalling the clearly Victorian era Holmes-associated hansom cabs). The internal tension and ambiguity of the show's relationship to socio-economic issues is clearly illustrated in Sherlock and John's home at 221B Baker Street itself: the fact that both adult males need to share housing could be read as a socio-economic commentary on life in contemporary London, but this establishing plot development is necessary to align the series with Conan Doyle canon, and rather than making way for investigation of economic realities, at most allows for some passing humor. Likewise, the apartment itself looks run-down, which could again raise economic concerns for viewers, but the sets include various objects that quite clearly invite viewers to recall Victorian aesthetics, such as the wallpaper and the oil paintings. Any less than wealthy elements characterizing Sherlock and John's lives are thus rendered charming, homey, and nostalgic. Drawing on viewers' love for Holmes' Victorian era, the show exhibits moments of realism yet gilds any sense of realism with a veneer composed of part historical nostalgia, part ultramodern glitz.

This tension between nostalgia and modernization forms a contradiction investigated by many of the essays in this collection. Matt Hills in particular comments on the way the show is caught between heretical fidelity and transformative creativity, between adhering to Conan Doyle's canon and updating not just details like the pocket watch, but also overall ideological concerns. This tension creates moments of brilliant modernization, such as the cell phone replacing the pocket watch, but also generates more problematic mergings of old and new. "The Blind Banker" gets taken to task by Anne Kustritz and Melanie E. S. Kohnen among others for its more or less wholesale adaptation of the Orientalist stereotypes, and is possibly one of the least successful aspects of Moffat and Gatiss's re-envisioning of Sherlock for the 21st century. Or rather, one could argue, it is the series' tendency toward heretical fidelity and its use of historical tropes that may allow the show to present an ideology far less radical than that suggested by its surrounding narrative of modernizing, updating, and blowing out cobwebs. Basu, in fact, suggests that in negotiating between Conan Doyle's 19th century heritage and the series' contemporary spin, *Sherlock* fails to fully confront and acknowledge the often reactionary ideology it has inherited alongside its Victorian aesthetics.

Neoliberal Sherlock

Not unlike the heritage film of the 1980s (which incidentally often is read as an aesthetic handmaiden to Thatcherite reactionary politics), *Sherlock* flirts with a neoliberal ideology of self-reliance and individual duty, all the while overlooking problematic socio-economic realities. In situating Sherlock, the character, as the clear hero of the show, the series may highlight his antisocial tendencies but it never truly questions them: his brilliant and enterprising mind, which can merely pity normal humans ("It must be so boring"), solves all the crimes the Metropolitan police force cannot. Such a genius solitary mind fit perfectly into Conan Doyle's time and into Thatcher's 1980s' project of recalling those olden glory days and trying to return to individual enterprising minds. Many recent urban crime shows incorporate the archetype of the original independent genius, but cast their maverick heroes as bound by bureaucratic restraints and socio-political pressures: in *Luther* and *The Fixer*, the heroes indeed move outside the system for justice to be carried out; likewise, the U.S. drama *The Wire* (2002–08) brilliantly showcases the paralyzing effects of bureaucracy across all forms of societal infrastructures, leaving its protagonists helpless and frustrated. In contrast to these characters' constant frustrations with the system, *Sherlock* returns us to the genial individual who is smarter and better than everyone else and, and who, rather than being wholly restrained by the system, can often employ the system to work for him — thus proving his superiority and the seeming superiority of the outsider individual over the bureaucratic system.

This particular role of the outsider who uses but isn't fully part of the system is an appealing attribute for a main character as identificatory figure. Online fans often look toward fandom for representations alternative to the white young middle class cis straight able-bodied males who continue to populate heroic positions in contemporary film and television. Many fans cathect Sherlock's potentially non-neurotypical status and uncertain sexuality, but at the same time they question the race and gender dynamics in the show, critiquing the mostly passive and subservient women and the absent or heavily othered people of color. Thus, like Basu's essay, which connects Sherlock, the individual, to larger ideological subtexts, in a work of fan "meta," fan theorist magnetic_pole questions the very characterization of Sherlock himself in an essay entitled "Neoliberal Holmes, or, Everything I Know About Modern Life I Learned from Sherlock" (LiveJournal, Oct 10, 2010). What does it mean, she asks, if a show celebrates a character like Sherlock, and what political ideologies underlie such a universe? Prefacing her essay with "Every age gets the Holmes it deserves," she offers blunt declarative statements that reveal the full rational force of Sherlock's characterization: "All problems have solutions. / All solutions are rational. / Everything that is rational can be comprehended, analyzed, and discarded. / By you. / You know everything worth knowing. / You are the master of the universe."

By taking seriously Sherlock's un-, if not antisocial brilliance and intelligence, magnetic_pole suggests that the show valorizes an individualist view where structures such as the police force are incapable and ignorant while independent and individual brilliance always succeeds. Rather than offering contemporary social commentary alongside its depiction of technological progress, *Sherlock* barely gives lip service to the large social changes that have taken place in the past century. Instead, we see the success of a global late capitalist economy whose accompanying neoliberal social and cultural values find an easy match with Conan Doyle's Orientalist plots. "The Blind Banker," in particular, contrasts the world of finance, numbers and modern office spaces and skyline views of the city, with the world of Oriental crime, ancient cyphers and non–English speaking old women in cluttered shops. Sherlock's intellect cuts through these contrasting worlds, but it is his disinterest in both that ultimately presents the clearest view of "our" age. "The Blind Banker" reveals and, to a degree, even celebrates a version of Sherlock Holmes who is so removed from everyday life that he doesn't care about economic and social disparities. Perhaps even more problematically, the episode offers an essentialized depiction of social disparities dependent on dangerous Orientalist tropes. Thus *Sherlock* gives us the Sherlock Holmes we may indeed deserve at a time when conservatives are making disinterest policy, as the government challenges many of the long-established social structures of the welfare state.

Sherlock offers a celebration of the postmodern that barely conceals a nostalgia for the certainties of the past: tools and aesthetics may be updated, but underneath there remains a desire for a universe in which one strong individual can outsmart dozens of professionals, where raw intelligence supersedes compassion, and where everyone fulfills their role by remaining in his or her proper place. The opening credits in particular evoke this image with their aestheticized view of London and Sherlock's magnifying glass all but studying the ant-like humans below on London's city streets. Like Mycroft, who runs a government that clearly is far less democratic than we'd like to believe, his brother uses the same hereditary gifts to solve problems of life and death — except, to Sherlock they remain merely intellectual challenges. And yet, the show complicates Sherlock's seemingly simplistic view of the world around him through the course of the first series: whereas before meeting John he only ever *uses* the network (and the people who are part of it), he learn to appreciate its reciprocity over the course of show, beginning to recognize his place within the network. *Sherlock* thus leaves us with a more complex (and possibly more idealistic) millennial ideology that slowly gains prominence throughout the series and takes center stage in the final scene of "The Great Game."

Millennial Sherlock

When Sherlock encounters Moriarty in the swimming pool at the end of "The Great Game," viewers suddenly must rearrange the entire season and its meaning retroactively: Moriarty has orchestrated all the crimes; he has, as Harrington discusses, become the plotting author of the entire show. More importantly, though, Sherlock himself gets rewritten in those last moments, moving away from the individualist brilliant loner who needs no one — intellectually or emotionally — and toward being part of a networked intelligence and emotional community. At the beginning of "A Study in Pink," John is little more than an amazed audience, but by the end of the episode Mycroft already realizes that the two together are a force to be reckoned with. When Mycroft intones "Sherlock Holmes and John Watson," at the very conclusion of "A Study in Pink," he in a way transcends the diegesis to address us, the audience, directly (and indeed this extradiegetic weight is enhanced by Gattis's double role as series creator and actor playing Mycroft). Thus the series suggests that a core part of its project and its pleasures lie in its purposeful depiction of Sherlock and John coming together and being stronger as a result of their inevitable alliance. This trajectory is set in motion in "A Study in Pink," and by the end of "The Great Game," John's importance for Sherlock is clear to everyone, including Sherlock himself.

The conclusion of "The Great Game" depicts Sherlock as a networked hero of the millennial generation, finding strength in his social network as much if not more than in his individualized expertise and brilliance. Programming featuring and directed at the millennial generation often depicts young people not only mastering the world through digital technology but also finding strength in the social collectives that can be understood as a result of digital, social-networking technologies. Thus, *Sherlock* reinvisions the figure of Sherlock Holmes as an evolving archetype familiar from other popular online fandoms such as *Buffy the Vampire Slayer, Veronica Mars,* and, not coincidentally, *Doctor Who.* Such a networked and collective sense of millennial interdependence, where heroes must struggle to understand and welcome their need for networks of support, stands in clear opposition to the neoliberal individualist Sherlock we have just discussed. We would argue that *Sherlock* capitalizes not only on the duality of these two takes on Sherlock, but that *Sherlock* exploits the very *tension* between the two visions of Sherlock, between the notion of Sherlock as brilliant iconic loner, set above and set apart, and Sherlock as networked, millennial hero.

This reinforced duality drives fan creativity, and, moreover, has shaped this collection in many ways. Indeed, one of the key questions left hanging in the season one cliffhanger is whether Sherlock's newfound emotional interdependence will be his downfall or his success. One certainly has the sense, given the celebratory modernization at work in *Sherlock,* that the answer can only be success. And yet we would argue that it is crucial that the first season ends with this question unresolved, the cliffhanger asking us, as viewers, to negotiate between the old and new ideologically framed takes on Sherlock Holmes. Thus both fan authorship and our acafan critical authorship enter into the conversation around *Sherlock* in a purposefully ambiguous, if ideologically pregnant, terrain. This ambiguity is both a challenge and a boon for this collection; our multiple authors offer multiple interpretations, following at times contradictory but co-existing threads within the series itself.

We have written this collection in the break between season one and season two, just as fans have created many a story, artwork, and fan vid, exploring the questions raised by the series cliffhanger, which left Sherlock, Moriarty, and John in a frozen tableau with the bomb ready to go off for an entire year. This provocative cliffhanger has engendered interpretive analyses, post-series fan fiction, and other intellectual creative responses that try to resolve this moment, and indeed one could argue that the cliffhanger motivated this collection as well. And as if a year's wait for canonical resolution weren't enough, an even longer delay was just announced that pushes Series Two even further into the future. Whereas we knew that our contributors could not possibly address the events of Series Two, we as editors had hoped to at least acknowledge the additions three more episodes would bring. Any media scholar who works on current productions has to face the problem of writing within an unfinished canon, where any argument could easily be undermined or utterly belied in an upcoming episode. Showrunner Joss Whedon, whose *Buffy the Vampire Slayer* spawned countless academic essays, collections, and even its own academic journal, became so infamous for overturning expectations that the term *Jossed* was coined to describe the experience of a fan fiction or a theory completely being contradicted by future canon. In the case of *Sherlock*, however, we are luckily a bit safer: as Moffat and Gatiss write with and against the original Conan Doyle stories and a century of collective fan readings, they can only veer so far from the original characterizations without losing the one thing that makes the show so appealing, namely the intertextuality with Sherlock Holmes canon, adaptations, and transformations. And even more so, we see the in process moment as an opportunity to explore what meanings and questions *Sherlock* has left purposefully in motion, unresolved in the televisual text, and resolved many times over in the ongoing processes of fan (and academic) creativity.

The conclusion of the first series, with its terrorizing cliffhanger, returns us yet again to the cultural and political moment in which we contemplate the collection and the show's ideological context. All forms of terrorism and violence are difficult to analyze and leads to myriad, often value-laden interpretations. At this moment, the British media and its politicians alike are trying to make sense of the reports of rioting youth, all too often dismissing them as only criminals without trying to understand motivations or reasons. In contrast however, *Sherlock*'s narrative creates the opposite misreading, as we are invited to speculate that Moriarty is politically motivated or has an underlying purpose when, in fact, he seems mostly motivated by personal feelings of competition and pride, ennui and boredom. Indeed, the false lead of the Bruce Partington plans, which Sherlock mistakenly believes to be Moriarty's motivation, serves as a Hitchcockian McGuffin, thus rendering political motivations as red herring. However, as Harrington suggests, in all cases we need to consider the crucial relationship between the personal and the political; a more abstract reading of Moriarty's bombing terror throughout London must address the way the entire series has ultimately been scripted by his possibly mad genius mind. In so doing, Moriarty's individual authorship, which seems to be based mostly on his whim, ultimately creates an urban terror that threatens the London populace, and thus can only be read as public if not overtly political by its victims.

Fandom and Agency

How one reads the role of Moriarty may indeed depend on where one places agency within the show and beyond. Matt Hills opens the collection by arguing that Moffat and Gatiss's heretical fidelity to Conan Doyle ultimately creates a hierarchy where their fannish transformations delineate all permissible interpretations, valorizing them as authors at the expense of (other) fans. Looking at *Sherlock*'s production discourses and the official transmedia texts, we can clearly recognize this valorization of official authorship that seems to subsume the possibilities of fan authorship, and yet when we end with Francesca Coppa's reading, Moffat and Gatiss's *Sherlock* has suddenly been transformed into this multiplicity of potential fan creativity, made all the more powerful because of its long history of fan engagement and the openness of the series' cliffhanger conclusion. Coppa's focus on the fan (and the aggressively transformative one at that) allows her to approach the very constrained media text Hills describes and focus on the moments that fans use, on the very powerful if selective processes of fan interpretation as authorship.

As Harrington points out, Moriarty may very well have been intended as a critical (even murderously criminal) metaphor for the fans who take media texts and interpret and rewrite them in their own desires and images. But in the hands of fans, Moriarty as fan-metaphor becomes everything from the hero of the story to a central figure of agency. Indeed, the fanvid that we discussed in opening this collection, "Whole New Way," posits Moriarty as the fan stand-in who encompasses and channels fan aggressive investment in Sherlock Holmes from his very first creation. Although the vid's title is "Whole New Way," by bringing together active and aggressive fan investment in Sherlock Holmes across history and adaptations, Mr. E. Sundance's vid suggests that Sherlock Holmes fans have always actively pursued the figure of Sherlock Holmes, wanting to know more and have more and create more. In this vid, *Sherlock*'s Moriarty becomes the synthesizing figure of agency that unites generations of Sherlock Holmes fans in the active and at times aggressive processes of engagement and authorship.

Not all *Sherlock* or Sherlock Holmes fans may find their cathartic mirror in this re-envisioned Moriarty, but in the end, this vid speaks to a larger continuity; the continuity of the active agencies of fan engagement with Sherlock Holmes canon, new and old. For at the end of the day there's limited canon (whether it be Conan Doyle or Moffat/Gattis) but a zillion works of fandom, and always in the process of becoming a zillion and one. It is this ongoing process of transmedia multiplicity, born out of the relationship between canon and fan engagement, that we hope to have captured and conveyed in this collection. And indeed, as *Sherlock and Transmedia Fandom* is fueled by the energy of scholars who are also fans of Sherlock Holmes (and vice versa), we hope that this collection also contributes to the very transmedia multiplicity of fan spirit that it studies.

About the Contributors

Balaka Basu is a doctoral candidate in English literature at the Graduate Center, City University of New York, and a lifelong fan of Sherlock Holmes. She has published and presented articles on British literature, science fiction television, and fan studies in multiple venues, and she is coediting a forthcoming essay collection, *Brave New Teenagers: Young Adult Dystopian Fiction*. Her dissertation examines why certain fictional universes have inspired and provoked continuation by successive authors.

Kristina Busse holds a doctoral degree in English from Tulane University. She is co-founder and editor of the online peer-reviewed academic journal *Transformative Works and Culture* and coeditor of *Fan Fiction and Fan Communities in the Age of the Internet* (McFarland 2007). Her work on media fandom and fan communities has appeared in numerous journals and anthologies.

Francesca Coppa is an associate professor of English and codirector of film studies at Muhlenberg College, where she teaches courses in dramatic literature, performance studies, and mass media storytelling. She is a founding member of the fan advocacy group Organization for Transformative Works, and her recent publications on fan culture, performance studies, and fan vidding have appeared in various books and journals, including *Cinema Journal, Camera Obscura,* and *Transformative Works and Cultures.*

Elizabeth Jane Evans is a lecturer in film and television studies at the University of Nottingham. Her research focuses on cinema and television audiences, narrative and technology. She is the author of *Transmedia Television: Audiences, New Media and Daily Life* (Routledge 2011), and her work has appeared in *Media, Culture and Society,* and *Participations.*

Lyndsay Faye is author of several published Sherlockian tales, including the acclaimed pastiche "The Case of Colonel Warburton's Madness," and the novel *Dust and Shadow: An Account of the Ripper Killings by Dr. John H Watson* (Simon & Schuster 2009). She is a member of the Adventuresses of Sherlock Holmes and the Baker Street Irregulars.

Ellen Burton Harrington is an associate professor of English at the University of South Alabama. She has published on 19th-century sensation and detective fiction and the influence of these genres and criminal anthropology on the work of Joseph Conrad. She is the editor of a collection of essays on women's short fiction, *Scribbling Women and the Short Story Form* (Peter Lang 2008).

CB Harvey is a principal lecturer in the Department of Culture, Writing and Performance at London South Bank University and a member of the International Association of Media Tie-In Writers. He has written tie-ins for the *Doctor Who* and *Highlander* spinoff ranges produced by the British company Big Finish. He works on storytelling, especially in the video game medium, and is the author of *Grand Theft Auto: Motion-Emotion* (Ludologica 2005).

Matt Hills is a reader in media and cultural studies at Cardiff School of Journalism, Media and Cultural Studies. His research interests focus on cult media and fan cultures, situated more generally in terms of cultural studies work on audiences. He is the author of *Fan Cultures* (Routledge 2002), *The Pleasures of Horror* (Continuum 2005), and *How to Do Things with Cultural Theory* (Hodder-Arnold 2005).

Melanie E. S. Kohnen is a postdoctoral fellow at the Geogia Institute of Technology. Her research focuses on representations of queer sexuality and race in American media and has been published in various journals. She is writing a book titled *Queer Representation, Visibility, and Race in American Film and Television*.

Anne Kustritz is a visiting assistant professor of television studies at the University of Amsterdam. Her research focuses on fan communities and the politics of representation, particularly with regard to sexuality, gender, and systems of pathology. Her work has appeared in *The Journal of American Culture* and *Refractory*.

Nicolle Lamerichs is a Ph.D. candidate at Maastricht University. Her research on intermediality and fan practices combines a literary approach with ethnography conducted online as well as offline. It focuses on costume play, role-playing games, and fan discussions to provide new insights in our current participatory culture.

Roberta Pearson is a professor of film and television studies at the Institute of Film and Television Studies, University of Nottingham. A long-standing Sherlockian, she is author of two seminal essays on Sherlock Holmes fan culture. She also has published and edited numerous books and articles in television studies and fan studies.

Ashley D. Polasek is a Ph.D. candidate at De Montfort University. Her research focuses on textual and contextual issues surrounding adaptations of Sherlock Holmes; she has presented papers on the subject at several conferences, including the 2011 Association of Adaptation Studies Conference in Istanbul. Her article "Sherlockian Simulacra: Adaptation and the Postmodern Construction of Reality" is forthcoming in the peer-reviewed journal *Literature/Film Quarterly*.

Paul Rixon is a principal lecturer in media and culture at Roehampton University. He has published in a number of areas, including the rise of the information city, new media coverage on the Iraq war, American television on British screens, and the role of British television critics.

Ariana Scott-Zechlin is an undergraduate student at the University of Puget Sound, where she studies English with emphases in creative writing and Victorian literature.

Louisa Ellen Stein is an assistant professor at Middlebury College. Her work focuses on transmedia authorship, gender, and generation in media culture. She is coeditor of the collection *Teen Television* (McFarland 2008), a Futures of Entertainment fellow, and book review editor for *Transformative Works and Culture*. She is writing a book,

Millennial Media, which explores the construction of the millennial generation across media.

Tom Steward is a lecturer in television studies, film studies, and history. His Ph.D. dissertation in television studies from the University of Warwick focuses on "Authorship, Creativity and Personalization in U.S. Television Drama." He has published essays on television studies in collections and journals.

Index